INTRODUCTION TO
WISCONSIN INDIANS

Prehistory
to Statehood

INTRODUCTION TO WISCONSIN INDIANS

Prehistory to Statehood

Carol I. Mason

University of Wisconsin, Fox Valley

Sheffield Publishing Company

Salem, Wisconsin

For information about this book, write or call:
Sheffield Publishing Company
P.O. Box 359
Salem, Wisconsin 53168
(414) 843-2281

Cover photo: Bag with Woven Quillwork *Neville Public Museum* (854/461)

Copyright © 1988 by Carol I. Mason

ISBN 0-88133-308-5

7 6

Printed in the United States of America

Preface

Introduction to Wisconsin Indians: Prehistory to Statehood is not intended as the last word on the Indian people of Wisconsin. It is rather a *first* word for students and for anyone else interested in understanding something of Wisconsin life in the thousands of years before 1848. Readers will find it a place to start and a means of obtaining a general introduction to an enormous, varied, and complex subject matter. I hope that its straightforward presentation will be easy to follow and relatively painless to read. References in the text have been deliberately kept to a bare minimum, and they are mainly sources that are available in good university or public libraries. Readers are urged to look them up and do more on their own. This book is meant to be a good horse, but it must be ridden further or it will have failed in its intent to be a jumping-off place for greater learning.

A word about organization might be helpful. I am very interested in the ways people managed to live on the resources of the land in earlier times, and the organization of this book reflects this concern. Thus flora, fauna, biotic zones and climate loom very large in the text, and how people earned their living is a matter of great importance. Wisconsin has the peculiar attribute of being divided between an area where people were unable to plant and grow their own food and one where growing crops could yield pretty reasonable returns. In Indian life, then, the contrasting lifeways are between horticulture on the one hand and hunting-gathering-fishing on the other. As far as examples are concerned, I have stressed the Chippewa as an example of the latter and the Winnebago as an example of the former. The choice of these two groups rested more on the matter of availability of sources for the one and the unique historical position of the other: there are many references for Chippewa, and the Winnebago constitute the only fully horticultural people known to be resident in Wisconsin from the earliest historic periods.

This book, like all work in Wisconsin studies, rests heavily on the shoulders of the intellectual giants of the past. Archaeologists, historians, diarists, ethnographers: all of them are part of the fabric of knowledge, and I am grateful for every one of them. If I have mangled their thoughts or failed to do justice to their contributions and insights, I am sorry; but at least I have pointed out the way for others to be more exacting.

A large number of today's scholars have given generously of their expertise so that books like this might be written. I am grateful to them all and hope they will be charitable should I have run roughshod over favorite interpretations. I am particularly grateful to several scholars who read most of the manuscripts *en utero*: Dr. James A. Clifton, Dr. Alice B. Kehoe, Dr. Nancy O. Lurie, and Dr. Ronald J. Mason. Their criticisms and suggestions were enormously helpful, and their generous gift of their time is much appreciated.

Many individuals and institutions have aided and abetted the writing of this book. The University of Wisconsin Center System provided me with a semester of sabbatical leave in 1984, and the University of Wisconsin - Fox Valley Library was of great help in locating sources. The University of Wisconsin System American Ethnic Studies Coordinating Committee provided a grant to support preparation of maps. The Neville Public Museum generously allowed me access to its ethnographic collections and provided photographs of artifacts I wished to use as illustrations; the museum's cooperation and scholarly hospitality are greatly appreciated. Dr. David Overstreet, Great Lakes Archaeological Research, Inc., gave me permission to use material written for him in another context. The State Historical Society and especially Dr. Joan Freeman, State Archeologist, kindly provided photographs of artifacts. Dr. Nancy O. Lurie gave permission for the reproduction of maps from her book *Wisconsin Indians*, and Dr. Charles Cleland allowed the reproduction of his classy drawing of a gill net. Maps were prepared by Win Thrall, Lawrence University, with her usual skill. The Lawrence University Computer Center was of endless and long-suffering assistance in giving me time and space on the university computer. The Department of Anthropology, Lawrence University, has been a major support; as always, I am grateful for house room, library privileges, and the stimulating collegial atmosphere. And finally, several generations of University of Wisconsin - Fox Valley students gave me advice on what they wanted to know about Wisconsin Indians and--more importantly--how best to persuade them to learn what they really ought to know.

C.I.M.

CONTENTS

Part I: Introduction

Part II: Wisconsin Indian Life

Part I: Introduction

CHAPTER 1
Wisconsin Land and People

Indians were the first human beings to live in the land that later became Wisconsin. It is more or less common knowledge that Indians were here in the "old days": everyone knows they lived somewhere in the forests and out on the prairies long before the time of European settlement. What they thought as Europeans began to live on land they once considered their own is not generally known nor do many descendants of those Europeans think about the uncomfortable truth that Indians were displaced and dispossessed to make way for others. Indians have been pushed aside and their role in history diminished. They are certainly acknowledged as having some role in Wisconsin's past; they even regularly appear in courthouse murals showing the discovery of Wisconsin by Europeans; they are the background figures behind the explorers, missionaries, and French voyageurs. Indians have come to play a minor role in someone else's history, stage props in a time that is past and gone.

In recent years, Indian pressure for old treaty rights and modern Indian political activism have made them more visible in everyday life in Wisconsin (for example, see Spindler and Spindler 1971). They no longer fit the comfortable picture of "vanishing Americans," people of a time that is no more. Who they are, who they were, and what makes them different as a group from other Americans are as important a part of the Wisconsin story as the same facts about any of the other major ethnic groups in the modern population. Because Indians had no written records to tell about their past, what is known about them often depends on indirect evidence. Information on Indian life comes from a combination of archaeological, ethnohistorical, and ethnographic research; and their story is far more complex than the footnotes they often get at the beginning of Wisconsin history.

The first reasonable question to ask when beginning to learn about Wisconsin Indian life concerns which Indian groups are known to have lived within the state at one time or another: who are Wisconsin Indians? Those that have been documented in historic records include Winnebago, Potawatomi, Menomini, Stockbridge-Munsee, Santee Dakota, Huron, Ioway, Chippewa (Ojibwa), Petun, Kickapoo, Sauk, Miami, Fox, Illinois, Mascouten, Oneida, Ottawa, and Brothertown. This formidable list is complicated by the fact that some of them have been called by more than one name. The names Indians called themselves were often not the names later recorded by Europeans, further causing problems in identification. Names might have been given to them by their neighbors or by the Europeans who first met them, and frequently these names changed their spelling through the years, causing more confusion in identifying them in written accounts. A case in point is "Issati," another name for Mdewakanton, one of the eastern divisions of the Dakota; over time Issati came to be written as "Santee" and the people called the Santee Dakota. These same people were also called Santee Sioux, Eastern Dakota, Sioux, or Nadiousioux (Landes 1968b).

Only a few from this extensive list were in Wisconsin at the time of European contact. Figuring out where the others originally came from and how they arrived is no mean task (see Chapter 3). A best estimate of the original native groups present at contact includes only Winnebago, Menomini, and Santee Dakota. A reasonable case can be made for some of the people who later became Chippewa using northern Wisconsin for hunting from time to time in prehistory and during the contact period, and perhaps Illinois or Ioway occasionally moved north to hunt in southern Wisconsin before Europeans arrived. For Huron, Petun, and Ottawa, historic records clearly show that they moved into Wisconsin or through it in the seventeenth century (Blair 1971). Potawatomi, Sauk, Fox, Mascouten, and Miami also came from somewhere else, and various groups of them stayed on as long term residents (Trigger 1978). Oneida, Stockbridge-Munsee, and Brothertown acquired lands in Wisconsin early in the nineteenth century and moved in during relatively recent times.

Wisconsin Indian languages

Keeping the long list of Indian groups in mind may be easier if they are put into their appropriate language families. Language can be a means to understanding relationships and similarities among cultures that otherwise may seem distinct. With only a few exceptions, all the people who lived in Wisconsin or came to live there spoke languages belonging to either the Algonquian or Siouan families, two of the major language stocks of North America (Kehoe 1981). Siouan languages were found mainly in the Midwest, in the Mississippi Valley, and in adjacent areas. Algonquian languages were spoken over much of Northeastern North America when Europeans first arrived. Algonquian was very important in Wisconsin, particularly during the seventeenth and eighteenth centuries when most Indian groups were Algonquian speakers. As a modern reminder of that time, Wisconsin place names with an Indian connection are mainly Algonquian in origin: Outagamie, Manitowoc, Milwaukee, Waukesha, Oshkosh, and even Wisconsin itself. Very few names of Siouan origin have survived.

Wisconsin speakers of Algonquian languages formed part of the Central Algonquian group, which includes Southern Ojibwa, Menomini, Potawatomi, Sauk-Fox-Kickapoo, and Miami-Illinois (Goddard 1978). All five of these languages have many features in common: similar structures, sounds, and rhythms. They are not like fingers on a hand, though, all equally distant from one another. Some of them are more closely related to each other than they are to other members of the group. Southern Ojibwa and Menomini, for example, are much more like each other than either is like Miami-Illinois; and Potawatomi has more in common with Sauk-Fox-Kickapoo than it does with Miami-Illinois.

This classification of Wisconsin languages helps to clarify relationships among the speakers since closeness of language ties says something about past history. People who live next to each other tend to sound more alike than different, and when they move apart, separation can correlate with changes in language. The speakers of Potawatomi, for example, once lived close to Southern Ojibwa speakers, and as expected, they shared many language traits with them at that time. When the Potawatomi relocated nearer to Fox villages, language changes moved in the direction of Fox-Sauk-Kickapoo. Later separation of different communities of Potawatomi speakers have produced a number of recent dialects that reflect the scattering of settlements in modern times.

Siouan, the other major linguistic stock in Wisconsin, was a geographically widespread language in the middle of the North American continent. In the Wisconsin part of its distribution, three different Siouan languages were spoken: Dakota, Winnebago, and the Ioway dialect of Chiwere

(Chafe 1973). Dakota proper, the language spoken by the Santee Dakota, was first recorded in the seventeenth century, and a pioneering dictionary was even prepared at that time (Hennepin 1966). Winnebago is less well known from a historical point of view. Not many language texts were actually written down in Winnebago until the early nineteenth century, even though Europeans had come into Winnebago territory on a more or less permanent basis as early as 1672. Jean Nicolet himself had actually met with Winnebago even earlier. The third Siouan language, Chiwere, is represented by the Ioway, who lived in Wisconsin for only short periods of time. Winnebago and Chiwere are closer to each other than either one is to Dakota, and people who speak Winnebago can usually easily understand Ioway. Some linguists actually classify Winnebago and Ioway together and call them both "Chiwere." 'This linguistic closeness has some interesting implications for Wisconsin prehistory (see Chapter 2).

When the last of the major Indian immigrant groups came to Wisconsin, the third major language stock, Iroquoian, permanently joined the native Algonquian and Siouan speakers. The first Iroquoian speakers were very early, a few Hurons and Petuns in the seventeenth century, but they did not remain long. The largest group of Iroquoian speakers was the Oneida, who came in the nineteenth. Historically, Iroquoian languages are "at home" in the farming communities of Ontario and New York, and their presence in Wisconsin represents a real break in ancient settlement patterns (Trigger 1978). The Huron and Petun in the seventeenth century were very few in number, but Oneida speakers of the nineteenth century came in larger groups, and they are an important part of modern Indian life.

An interesting linguistic problem is the question of how the different Indian groups of Wisconsin communicated with each other and with strangers who came among them. People who originally spoke Winnebago, for example, could not easily understand Menomini speakers, and even people who spoke the closely related Central Algonquian languages could not always understand each other. In other parts of the world, pidgin or even sign languages might have developed. What happened in Wisconsin was that one language came to be the common means of communication, a kind of "lingua franca" or common tongue understood everywhere. In the beginning of historic times, Huron served as the powerful common language across the lakes country, probably because of

Huron control of trade. For years, the Huron language let Indians and later Frenchmen communicate with people as far away as Lake Superior. The French quickly understood that they had to know Huron, and young men were sent to live with Indians in order to learn the languages and serve as interpreters (Thwaites 1906).

Huron was later replaced as a common tongue by Southern Ojibwa, and speakers of that language, the Ottawa in particular, became universal interpreters across the lakes country. In the eighteenth century, the British trader John Long wrote that Southern Ojibwa, in addition to being the language most often used in trade with Europeans, was the language people spoke in council throughout the Great Lakes, no matter what their native languages happened to be (Quaife 1922). Even the Menomini, somewhat isolated on the western lakes, used Southern Ojibwa to communicate with strangers (Hoffman 1986). In the nineteenth century, it was still important, the "court language among all the tribes" (Kinzie 1975: 63), including the Siouan-speaking Winnebago. In villages of the historic period, when different people lived together in joint communities, Southern Ojibwa must have been especially useful as Mascoutens lived with Miamis, Sauks with Kickapoos, and even Winnebagos with Algonquian-speaking neighbors. Many Indians also learned French or English as they came to know speakers of those languages and found it useful to be able to speak to them in their own tongues.

Physical Setting

What Indians did in Wisconsin begins with a grasp of the land as they saw and experienced it. The physical setting for the state created in 1848, is not well-marked or clearly defined as a natural area. It does not have distinctive physical features or any special group of native plants and animals that might set it apart from its neighbors. Wisconsin, like every other state, is the outcome of recent history, the result of political events whose major focus was, for the most part, somewhere else. Those who drew up the boundaries and created governments were in the thick of political give and take (Smith 1973), not concerned with natural areas or physiographic provinces. For an understanding of Indian life of both past and present, Wisconsin has to be treated as part of a larger region that includes the Upper Peninsula of Michigan and parts of the neighboring states of Illinois, Iowa, and Minnesota (Dice

Map of Wisconsin with counties.

Map of the Upper Great Lakes.

1943). All of this region in recent times had similar plants and animals, a similar climate, and similar opportunities for native peoples. Wisconsin as part of it has to be set off in terms of a locally peculiar landscape.

Wisconsin waterways

On a map, Wisconsin's most impressive local features are lakes and the waterways that connect them. For Indians, lakes and rivers were useful places where fresh water could be obtained, fish caught, and wild rice gathered. They also served the less obvious functions of moving people about and forming boundary lines between human groups. As part of the transportation system, waterways were, until the coming of horses, the chief means of travel, either by boat or along the banks or shores on foot. Waterways guided people in certain directions just by being where they were: water routes went in one direction or another and people followed them. The waterways were also dividing lines between one group's territory and another's, and they must have been prominent features in the mental maps that people had of the land.

The most important bodies of water are the two Great Lakes, the sweet inland seas of Superior and Michigan. Lake Superior to the north is one of the largest fresh water lakes in the world, so large as to astonish early French explorers even after they had already seen Lake Huron to the east (Adams 1961). The long Lake Superior shoreline has many different kinds of features; it includes sandy beaches, rocky headlands, and even small mountains. Along the shores, many rivers give travelers a means to move from the lake far into the interior. Indian settlers were attracted there because of resources such as fish and the copper deposits of Isle Royale and the Keeweenaw Peninsula. Fur rich lands could be reached from Lake Superior, and the country around the lake became very important in the days of the fur trade. Lake Michigan was an equally powerful presence in the landscape, stretching directly north and south with tongues of rivers all along its western shore. It was a barrier to free movement from the east because it was too broad to cross, but it was a means of movement north and south as people found its shoreline to be a natural highway.

Lake Michigan and Lake Superior were in a position to guide movements of people from the east. When they came along the northern route, along the shores of Lake

Huron to the Straits of Mackinac, people were funneled through the angle formed by the two lakes. Then they could enter the land beyond or follow the lake shores, south along Lake Michigan or west along Lake Superior. For people coming up into Wisconsin from the south, the shoreline of Lake Michigan made a direct route straight north, but Lake Superior blocked a free flow of traffic between Wisconsin and the north country in Canada.

Lake Winnebago is west of Lake Michigan in eastern Wisconsin. It is truly a giant lake in its own right, but it is so dwarfed by its massive neighbors that it looks rather small on modern maps. Lake Winnebago played an enormous role in Indian life in prehistory and historic times. It was always a natural larder, producing many different kinds of food for people with the right tools and the proper skills. It is a biologically rich body of water with abundant microscopic plant life that supports many kinds of freshwater fish. A skilled fisherman might expect anything from small fry such as perch and channel catfish to drum and giant sturgeon. In addition to what is in the water, birds are attracted to the lake surfaces and surrounding marshes; even today many shore birds depend on it for food and nest around it or its smaller neighbors, Lakes Poygan, Butte des Morts, and Winneconne. In the recent past, the descriptions of water birds that lived or stopped near Lake Winnebago during spring or fall migrations seem unbelievable; travelers reported such great numbers of them coming and going that they seem surely to have exaggerated (Kinzie 1976). In former times, Lake Winnebago was also rich in wild rice in many places along the shore; people came to settle there partly for the sake of the wild rice (Hoffman 1896). The lake was also a source for the freshwater clams whose shells are common enough in archaeological sites there to produce large middens in some places at its north end (McKern 1945). As a source for fish, clams, birds, wild rice, and many other animal and plant foods, Lake Winnebago was important in the settlement patterns of Indian societies for thousands of years.

In addition to all these larger lakes, many others, large and small, were important to Indian life. Some of the larger ones include Lake Koshkonong, Lake Geneva, and the four lakes in and around what is now the city of Madison. Many smaller lakes are scattered over other parts of the state, especially in the north, and their importance depended on local circumstances. The lake country of north central Wisconsin contains thousands of little lakes in the watersheds of Lake Superior and the Mississippi

River, many of which have had unique Indian occupations in the past (Salzer 1974). All the lakes were important as resources for human beings, whether for providing food or being used as a means of travel over ice in winter or by canoe in summer; all lakes were important centers around which the lives of native peoples moved in cycles dominated by the seasons.

One lake was linked to another by rivers, those indispensable and useful water highways. Before horses, rivers everywhere were the roads of the past. They were the way people moved camps and villages as the seasons changed; they served as trade routes; and they were used by people going to war. Whatever needed to be done by moving people from here to there and back again was done on rivers or along their banks. There were many useful river roads in Wisconsin, but the major waterways were the Fox-Wisconsin system, crossing the state from east to west, and the Mississippi River in the west. Over the centuries, these two routes were followed by so many travelers going through Wisconsin that the other river routes are hardly mentioned, at least not in historic records.

The Fox-Wisconsin route started at the foot of Green Bay, but the people who used it often began their journeys as far away as the Ottawa Valley or beyond the St. Lawrence River in distant Quebec. From there a traveler would paddle his canoe along the northern shore of Lake Huron through the Straits of Mackinac and then along Lake Michigan to the Garden Peninsula. The islands crossing the mouth of Green Bay--Summer, Little Summer, St. Martin's, Rock, Washington, Detroit, Plum--became stepping stones down to the dangerous Porte des Morts passage. People made this "Grand Traverse" with usually only one break in the middle, often on Rock or Washington Island. Once the stormy Porte des Morts Strait was crossed, travelers entered the safe waters of the eastern shore of Green Bay. Sight of the end of the Bay and the narrowing waters of the Lower Fox River must have been a relief to more than one traveler bound from the east to the Mississippi. After leaving Green Bay, the route went up the Fox through the rapids--called "chutes" by early French travelers along the same route--and led into Lake Winnebago. From there it went through the smaller western lakes (Butte des Morts, Winneconne, and Poygan) into the Upper Fox. Lake Poygan was an important intersection on these river roads since the Wolf River met the lake there, letting people move from the Fox into the Wolf or vice versa, depending on the direction they were traveling.

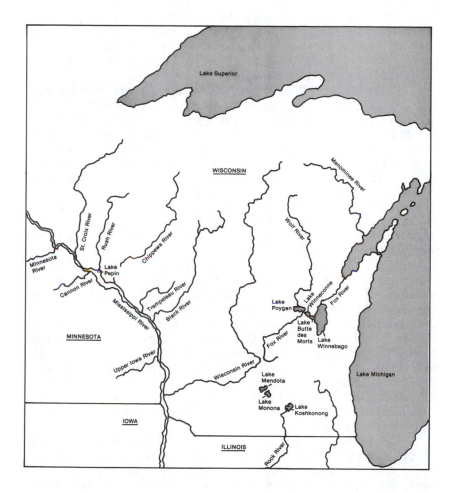

Map of Wisconsin lakes and rivers.

The Upper Fox River wound westward in a graceful coil; and at its westernmost curve, it came close enough to the bend of the Wisconsin River for people to portage across. Moving from one river into the other was not a matter of lifting one's canoe out of the water here and then putting it down there. The portage was swampy in places, confusing because of hard-to-follow channels, and often choked with wild rice. It was very difficult to cross, and even those who used it often sometimes made mistakes. A false start might set a journey back for hours or even days (see Father Marquette's experience in Thwaites 1896-1901: lix). One of the important nineteenth century events at the portage was when a road was built across it, and Indian canoes could be hauled by oxcart from one river to the other (Kinzie 1976).

Once on the Wisconsin, the route to the Mississippi was straightforward, mile after westward mile. When travelers reached it, they could go south toward the Gulf of Mexico or north to the Mississippi's headwaters. To the north, Lake Superior was within reach over one of several well-traveled routes: up the St. Croix from the Mississippi to the southern shore of the lake via a short portage and the Brule River. Another route was the Chippewa River as it went from the Mississippi just below Lake Pepin north towards Lake Superior. To the west, people could move toward Mille Lacs Lake through the lake country or go directly north on the Rum River.

The Mississippi was also a thoroughfare east and west. It opened up western Wisconsin by means of a number of rivers intersecting it ladderlike above the Wisconsin River: Black, Trempealeau, Chippewa, Rush, St. Croix. On the western side of the Mississippi, other rivers helped people move from the western lands to the "Great River" itself and from there into the heartland of Wisconsin. Some of these--especially the Upper Iowa, Cannon, and Minnesota Rivers--became temporary boundaries for Indian land claims at times during the historic period while all of them remained as important water highways east and west.

Other waterways are the Rock River and the Fox River in Illinois. The Rock River connects the area around Lake Koshkonong with the Mississippi; tendrils of the Rock act as a widespread network, including streams with the modern names of Crawfish and Bark. One branch of the Rock River even reaches north to Horicon Marsh, almost to Lake Winnebago. The Illinois country was within reach from Wisconsin along the other Fox River, which is a part of the Illinois River and should not be confused with the northeastern Fox, draining into Green Bay. The other Fox wanders into southern Wisconsin through a country rich in lakes and is a natural water route south to the Illinois River and eventually to the Mississippi itself.

Along the northern shoulder of Lake Michigan, one major river and many small ones allow free movement into the interior west of the lake. From the ends of some of these rivers, it is actually only a short distance north and overland to Lake Superior from Lake Michigan, but none of them is long enough to reach from one Great Lake to the other. They go far enough inland, though, to let people move more or less as they pleased in the land between the lakes. The largest of the rivers is the Menominee, which separates into smaller streams as it goes inland to the northwest. Most of these little streams end in tiny lakes.

Events of the Pleistocene

Wisconsin as a modern land crossed by rivers and covered with lakes came to be what it is after many thousands of years of physical changes. Most of these changes came about because of what happened in the Pleistocene, the Ice Age of North America (Fitting 1970). No one saw the earliest glaciers covering parts of Wisconsin, but Indians were there to see the last of them. The land that all recent Indians lived in was an end product of long years of glacial action.

The main thing that glaciers did was to change the physical shape of the land. They were enormous sheets of ice, thousands of feet thick and very heavy. As they slowly moved, they planed and scoured Wisconsin, grinding down old parts of the landscape and destroying whatever was in their path: any dramatic relief or sharp contrasts across the countryside were flattened to almost nothing. The glaciers left behind a gently rolling landscape with no mountains and scarcely any real hills. Much of it would be monotonous without the features left behind by the ice. Earth and rock were deposited at the ends or along the sides of glaciers by the weight and force of the ice as it advanced and then retreated, leaving behind the complex systems of low hills referred to as moraines (Wright and Frey 1965).

Glaciers did other things to the land: they carried away what was on the surface of the ground, reworked it, and put it back again as layers of what is called "drift." Glacial drift can be many things--large boulders, sheets of gravel, pebbles, and even sand--and each glacier worked over what it found in its path, often the drift of other, earlier times. A large part of southwestern Wisconsin was not covered by glacial ice, and this "Driftless Area" looks quite different from other parts of the state. It still has unusually shaped hills and fantastic rock formations, remnants of a past that was not swept away by glaciers.

As the ice melted, it accumulated great puddles of cold water along its edges: the glacial lakes. These lakes changed patterns of water drainage by forcing melt water into new channels; there was too much water for old drainage patterns to carry. Some of these new channels later shifted, but many of them remain as Wisconsin's modern river beds. Glacial Lake Duluth, for example, was a cold lake at the western end of the ice that stood over much of the Lake Superior basin thousands of years ago, getting larger and larger as the glacier melted (Hough 1963). It finally drained into the Mississippi over what was to become known as the St. Croix channel many years later. The Dells area of the Wisconsin River was cut by water draining from another ponded glacial lake, and the Rock River was moved westward by water derived from glaciers. The interior of Wisconsin was drained by rivers that carried water into the Mississippi, glacial run-off channels that often have ancient deltas of glacial gravel at their mouths.

Among the glacial lakes that survived into modern times are both Lake Michigan and Lake Superior. Originally puddles at the edges of glaciers, these Great Lakes are true children of the Ice Age. To early Indian settlers in Wisconsin, they were a permanent part of the world, as solid and enduring as they are to recent people, but their modern shorelines are not very old. They took shape over several thousand years and only after many risings and lowerings of lake levels. The earliest of these changes began about 11,000 years ago when there were two glacial lakes: Lake Algonquin in the Michigan basin and Lake Duluth in the Superior basin (Hough 1963). Both of these lakes stood at much higher elevations than modern Lake Michigan or Superior, and they covered much more land. Later, Lake Algonquin spread and became a huge lake, sprawling over the basins of Lakes Michigan and Superior both, as well as the basin of modern Lake Huron.

By about 7,500 years ago, Lake Algonquin had drained away to very low levels, leaving a much shrunken lake where Lake Superior is now and a very small lake in the Michigan basin. Following this low period (called the

Chippewa-Stanley low water stage), the lakes began to rise
again to levels higher than they are today but not as high
as they were in the days of Lake Algonquin. At least two
major high water levels were reached and held in the years
between Lake Algonquin and modern lake levels: Nipissing
around 2,000 B.C. and Algoma about a thousand years later
(R. Mason 1981). The only signs of these higher water
levels today are extinct beaches sometimes visible in places
back from the modern shore. Some very dramatic ones can
be seen along Lake Superior (Martin 1982) and in Door
County, were a few of them rise to nearly 22 feet above
modern lake level on Washington Island. There are many
areas along the shores of the modern lakes where these
ancient beaches stand today, ghosts of lakes that used to
be.

**Physical background for Wisconsin
biotic zones**

The Ice Age affected more than the shape of the
land and the creation of lakes: it directly influenced how
people managed to live in Wisconsin. As far as humans are
concerned, the important resources of the land were the
plants and the animals that lived on the plants. Both kinds
of resources are distributed in what are called biotic
provinces or life zones (Curtis 1959; Cleland 1966; H.H.T.
Jackson 1961). Each zone is a large area of land with its
own special combination of plants and animals dependent
upon a specific climate and specific soil conditions. In
general one biotic zone can be separated from another on
the basis of its overall nature, and one plant or one kind
of animal is not enough to characterize it: biotic zones are
made up of complexes of traits. In Wisconsin the zones
changed boundaries over time, providing people with different resources in different places, depending on the time
period involved.

As the last ice sheet melted, the plants and animals
that had lived in less harsh southern climates extended
northward as the land slowly warmed up. The retreating
glacier opened up areas that had been covered by ice for
thousands of years, and plants could grow there again. As
the ice melted away, however, it continued to chill the
neighboring landscape, and plants and animals of a more
cold tolerant kind still lived there. By between 16,000 and
14,000 B.C. spruce forests grew south of the glacier,
perhaps with small stretches of tundra along its margins
(H. Wright 1983). What the land looked like then is a

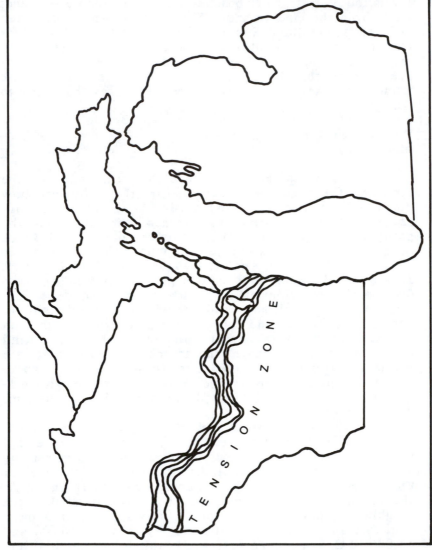

Map of major biotic zones (see text).

TENSION ZONE

matter of debate. Probably it was an open parkland with stands of stunted spruce trees and stretches of moss or lichen-covered ground. It certainly did not look like the modern Wisconsin landscape.

By 12,000 B.C., whatever tundra had been there was gone, and spruce forests spread into the state; between then and about 10,000 B.C., the melting of the ice continued and more changes occurred as the land warmed up. By 9,000 B.C., fewer and fewer spruce trees grew in southern Wisconsin, and the spruce began to be replaced by oak and pine (Ogden 1977). It took thousands of years, but by 6,000 B.C., a forest of oak, hickory, and hemlock covered Wisconsin and the edges of the ice were far away to the north. By 4,000 B.C., all the ice was gone, even from the north country, and a mixed deciduous forest was the major tree cover in Wisconsin. By 1500 B.C., the familiar modern climate with its modern vegetation was the rule; and from that point onward, Indians had to deal with recent biotic communities (Martin 1932).

The recent vegetation and animal life depends on modern conditions. Wisconsin is today far enough north that really intense heat is not usually a problem, at least not for long, and far enough south that it escapes severe cold. It has a temperate climate blessed with four separate seasons: spring, summer, fall, and winter. The Great Lakes themselves influence climate through what is called the "lake effect." The surfaces of the lakes absorb heat from the sun in the summer, and in the winter this heat is radiated, warming up the temperatures along the shores. Through the lake effect, temperatures in a zone along the shores can be 10 or 15 degrees higher than inland winter temperatures. In some cases the temperature differences can be even greater. In summer the lake shores are often cooler than inland, of less importance to survival, perhaps, but a source of human comfort nonetheless.

Temperature differences from north to south obviously play an important role in determining what plants can grow in Wisconsin. This was especially important in prehistory when domestic plants appeared for the first time and people began to rely on farming (see Chapter 4). Many domesticated plants originally came from the south, and they could be successfully grown only where temperatures were within their limits. The differences between northern Wisconsin, where the mean annual temperature is 39°F. or under, and the south, where 48°F. is the average, are not very great, but it is enough to seriously affect where food crops could grow. In places where the temperature stayed around freezing for a longer time in the spring or began to freeze earlier in the fall, the frost free season could be less than 120 days. A crop such as corn would be difficult to raise under these conditions; to actually depend on it would be impossible (Yarnell 1964). Temperature, frost, and growing seasons were important not only to domestic plants such as corn but also to wild plants as well. Trees, shrubs, and ground cover varied with the same climatic factors, and Indians learned to use them or not, depending on the circumstances.

Abundant rainfall is still another characteristic of Wisconsin's biotic zones. Dependable rain year after year means that streams do not usually dry up in the summer and people are certain of a permanent everyday supply of water. Indian farmers could usually count on the rain provided by nature; they were not irrigation farmers or builders of water control systems. The other side of the coin is the water that comes in winter as snow. Accumulating amounts on the ground changed the way people lived and where they could live in comfort. Snow directly affects life in many ways--from tracking game to the not so simple business of moving around in it or on it. Rain and snow were both important in everyday Indian life.

One other factor affects plant cover and is at the root--so to speak--of plant distribution, and that is the character of the soil. Much of Wisconsin is covered by soils that are derived from the drift materials originally left behind by glaciers. Some soils were laid down by water: they were carried by running water or deposited as layers in the still depths of glacial lakes. When the lakes drained, the water-deposited soils were left on the land and then reclaimed by plants. However, most Wisconsin soils are what are called "podzols," post-glacial soils that have developed as a result of many centuries of forests growing on them (Hole 1976). Stretches of podzolic soil are fertile, but they were hard for Indians to cultivate because of the trees that grew on them. If Indians had a cleared area, it was likely to be used over and over again as a place for villages simply because it was cleared and open. Besides podzols, Wisconsin has prairie soils, found to the south and east. They have a higher organic content than the podzols, but they were hard for Indians to cultivate with simple tools. Prairie soils, even though they were open, remained, along with peaty and boggy areas, as hunting lands rather than farmland. In the far northern part of Wisconsin, soils are mostly very shallow and rest on the bedrock of the great Canadian Shield; very little organic material has built up there, and the potential for farming is certainly not as great as it is in the south. Even today the northern part of Wisconsin is not counted as a prime agricultural area.

Modern biotic zones

Temperature, rainfall, and soils are the background for defining the modern biotic zones of Wisconsin (Curtis 1959), the ones that later prehistoric and historic Indians had to deal with. In the north is the Canadian Zone, where the plant cover is predominantly conifers and mixed hardwoods. Specifically, the trees are likely to be white spruce, balsam fir, sugar maple, basswood, white pine, or hemlock. Underfoot, the ground covers include bearberry and twinflower. South of the Canadian Zone, the Carolinian province has oaks, hickories, and black maple-- trees that are often called "prairie forest border" species. Between these two zones is an area of overlap where some Carolinian plant species reach their northern limits and some kinds of Canadian plants reach their farthest southern points. This area of overlap is sometimes called the "Transition" or "Tension" Zone. These three--Carolinian, Canadian, and Transition--are the major biotic zones of Wisconsin, but there are some others. In a few places mixed forest and prairie occur, forming another important plant community. Prairie, appearing as large open areas, includes a number of plants that grow nowhere else: bluestem, needlegrass, purple prairie clover, and many others. So many of the native prairie plants have been pushed out that few places remain today where prairie exists undisturbed; few modern people in Wisconsin have ever seen prairie in bloom. The trees of the mixed forest and prairie areas are oak, hickory, elm, cottonwood, maple, basswood, and beech.

Each of the biotic zones has its own typical set of mammals (H.H.T. Jackson 1961). For the Canadian Zone, for example, the usual animals are porcupine, moose, woodland caribou, wolverine, and lynx. The characteristic Carolinian species are raccoon, opossum, gray fox, white-tailed deer, and striped skunk. The Transition Zone had the greatest number of different species since, like plants, the ranges of both northern and southern animals overlapped there.

The overlapping plant and animal distributions of the Transition Zone were important to Indians because of the "edge effect" (Cleland 1966). Transitional "edges" between major biotic zones are places where some plants and some animals do better than they can in the zones on either side. Many more animals are able to live there because of greater food sources. More and different kinds of plants mean more and different food supplies for the animals that eat the plants and the animals that eat the plant eaters. People who came to hunt or gather plants found the Transition Zone attractive because of the relative abundance of animals and edible plants there. Studying what happens in the Transition Zone has produced some of the most interesting attempts to understand Indian life in Wisconsin: the richness of the resources there, and competition for them are a potent combination (see, for example, Hickerson 1970).

The biotic zones are basic intellectual tools for understanding Indian life in Wisconsin; they are first causes and foundations for everything else. Each had a special character as a place for Indians to live, and each laid down special parameters that governed human life. The Canadian Zone had a particularly narrow range of what was possible. It was unsuitable for extensive farming because the growing season was too short, and the solitary habits of most large game animals and the scanty supply of edible plants made it a less than optimal foraging place. However, the Canadian Zone in Wisconsin had one feature that transcended the expectable life of hunters and gatherers there. Things were made much more complex by the presence of very rich fishing grounds. Fishing was a vitally important part of economic life, helping broad spectrum hunting and gathering produce very large returns at specific times of the year. In Wisconsin's Canadian Zone, hunting and gathering need not have been a predictably meager existence when the Great Lakes fisheries could be depended upon for food. In the Carolinian and mixed prairie zones, longer growing seasons meant that people could garden, raising their own food, once the plants and technology for growing them were available. They did not grow all of their food, though; hunting and gathering were important parts of economic life for farmers, too. The Transitional Zone was perhaps the most fruitful part of Wisconsin for Indians: many things could be done there very well. Hunting, fishing, collecting wild plants, and gardening all delivered in their proper seasons.

From north to south through the major biotic zones, Wisconsin Indian societies can be grouped according to the lifeways they were able to follow in those zones. The range is not great; it runs from hunters and gatherers to farmers who were also hunters and gatherers. The northern Canadian Zone was home to the strictly hunting and gathering people: Santee Dakota, Chippewa, and Menomini. South of it, the Carolinian Zone contained all the rest of the Indians, gardeners whose commitment to growing crops was sustained and persistent even though they spent time as hunters, gatherers, and fishermen as well. The dividing line between these two basic types is not a sharp break but a gradual gradation from one into the other just as the biotic zones grade one into another. All the farming people hunted game and gathered wild foods when they could, and the hunters and gatherers would plant corn if and when a good year or the lake effect let them do so.

Human effects on the land

Indian populations were generally rather low, and deliberate attempts to change the environment were rare. In spite of this, some very impressive alterations were made in the plant cover, using simple techniques that everyone knew. A case in point is the use of fire to change the face of the local earth. Fire seems to have been widely used for this purpose all over North America. For example, very early historic records from the East Coast include many references to repeated burning off of the land by Indians (Day 1959). In Wisconsin, a good part of the vegetation looks as if it, too, had been subjected to fire over a long period (Curtis 1959). The evidence is not so much historic records as it is the nature of the forests themselves: terminal hardwoods of the type encouraged by repeated exposure to fire. Other features--including prairies, certain kinds of grasslands, openings in oak forests, meadows, and shrub areas--also appear to have been caused by firing the land again and again. In the opinion of experts, lightning is not the only or even the main reason for fire in the woods; Indians were setting fires themselves.

Why Indians would burn the vegetation cannot always be figured out, but some factors were more important than others. Accidental setting of fires must have occasionally happened as campfires escaped control or were left to burn on their own after people went somewhere else. Other fires may have been set in order to help in hunting by driving game. Fires may have been set to create conditions attractive to grazing animals by burning off the old plants and encouraging fresh green ones to spread. Any fire left to itself might burn large areas, stopping only when reaching a natural barrier, a lake or a river. In the days before lumbering left so much kindling on the ground, there was less understory to burn. Very widespread fires such as the Peshtigo Fire of 1871 were unlikely in spite of free use of fire by Indians. The most important effect of burning by Indians was probably in helping to maintain prairie areas. Prairies need regular burning for seeds to germinate, and at least part of the decline in Wisconsin's prairieland is because regular firing no longer occurs (Curtis 1959).

Other Indian practices that affected the environment included hunting, fishing, and methods of gardening. When the fur trade became part of Indian life, some animals were hunted out of their former ranges and became locally extinct. With all the movements of people in the historic period, hunting pressure on certain large animals became so great that some of them became completely extinct in Wisconsin (Kay 1979). Farming techniques also had an effect on the land. Such things as clearing and introducing new plants into areas where they had not been before were bound to affect the land. Even the plant cover changed around villages where people disturbed the soil and improved conditions for weeds to grow. Human waste, garbage, and debris from butchering animals all helped to change the soil and eventually the plants that lived on it. However, large scale environmental changes such as those caused by heavy commercial lumbering or modern agriculture were unlikely to have taken place.

Summary

Many different Indian groups lived in what is now Wisconsin. Some of them were here when Europeans came to the New World and many others came afterwards looking for new places to settle. They found a land rich in lakes and rivers and with many different natural resources. It was divided north and south by temperatures and soils, length of growing season, and vegetation. It offered different possibilities, given where people were able to live and what tools they brought with them. They often had to change as the resources changed, whether that came about through their own actions, the effects of climate, or competition with other societies. In terms of Indian life over the long run, all of these factors were important.

CHAPTER 2
Prehistoric Prelude: Archaeology

Most of what happened in Wisconsin Indian life took place in prehistory and must be studied through archaeology. The basic principle of archaeology is very simple: in order to know about a past for which there are no written records, the physical remains of the past must be studied in an orderly way. This often consists of looking at the land to find out where people settled or excavating ancient sites to learn how they lived. The kinds of information that archaeologists look for include how old things are, how cultures have changed, and how societies used the resources of the land around them.

Archaeological research in Wisconsin began during the days of the Moundbuilder debate in the nineteenth century. This debate concerned the earthen mounds found in the United States east of the Mississippi and who had built them. Wisconsin became important in the discussion because of the many kinds of mounds found inside its borders, especially the famous effigy mounds. Some of those taking part in the debate were convinced that Indians had nothing to do with mounds. They were supported by Indians who denied knowledge of a time when their own ancestors had built mounds.

If Indians had not built the mounds, who had? A Moundbuilder race was thought to have developed a complex culture in North America and then mysteriously vanished. The vacant lands they left behind them were then claimed by American Indians (Silverberg 1978). The popularity of the Moundbuilder idea may be partly explained by a love of the mysterious, but an important idea running through it was a feeling that Indians were too degraded or "savage" to have been responsible for the moundbuilding cultures. In Wisconsin, archaeological work clearly showed that the builders of mounds were Indians (Lapham 1855). Both skeletons and artifacts buried in the mounds belonged to Indians, and there has been no serious challenge to this conclusion ever since. The prehistory of Wisconsin was taken back from the mysterious ancient Moundbuilders and restored to Indians, whose past was at that time equally mysterious but at least was their own.

The appeal of having non-Indians appear in the Indian past has not died away, however, at least not in some circles. Even today there are many ideas explaining away Indian prehistory by proposing that someone else taught them how to live in complex societies and make elaborate artifacts. A few of these stories have been around for a long time: wandering Norsemen in prehistoric Minnesota and Wisconsin, for example. The most unusual is the proposal that people from outer space came to the earth and taught Indians how to live. No evidence supports any of these ideas, and present information indicates that for better or for worse, Indians made their own mistakes and had their own triumphs without interference from elsewhere.

Paleo-Indian Hunters and Gatherers

The history of Wisconsin Indian life starts in Alaska with Ice Age people, called Paleo-Indians, moving into the New World to become its first discoverers. They came to America on foot across a broad land area that came out of the ocean when sea levels lowered during the Pleistocene. This now-vanished continent is called Beringia. The earliest Indians did not realize what they had discovered nor could they move immediately and directly south into the American continent. In fact, they may have been confined by ice barriers to Beringia and only slowly made their way through ice-free corridors down into North America (Fitting 1970, R. Mason 1981, Stoltman 1978).

By about 11,000 years ago, some Paleo-Indians were able to enter land in Wisconsin that was newly freed from glacial ice. In places, this land included a narrow band of low latitude tundra. Tundra means "frozen ground" and the few kinds of plants growing on it. In Wisconsin, evidence for tundra consists of frost-heaved soil in deposits of the right age as well as the bones of small tundra animals. The plants included lichens and mosses in an open parkland with spruce shrubs in sheltered places. Where the ground was not permanently frozen, boreal forest trees could spread over large areas.

As far as people were concerned, the tundra was a landscape with many possibilities. For one thing, animal life was plentiful near the glacier as it slowly retreated. At that time, North America was home for many large animals (Martin 1967). More than a hundred species had adult body weights of over 100 pounds: mammoth, mastodon, giant moose-deer, horse, camel, ground sloth, peccary, giant beaver, tapir, antelope, caribou, and musk-ox. Some of these, especially the herd animals such as caribou and musk-ox, and perhaps mastodon and mammoth as well, lived on the tundra and in the forest edge behind it. When Paleo-Indians were living in Wisconsin, typical tundra mammals--musk-ox, barren grounds caribou, and mammoth--were gradually replaced by a group of animals that included mastodon, giant moose-deer, bison, and giant ground sloth as well as mammoth and caribou (Ogden 1977). Evidence for many of these animals is rare in Wisconsin, probably because fossils were destroyed by the movements back and forth of the glaciers. In southern Wisconsin, bones have been found from mammoth, mastodon, giant beaver, musk-ox, extinct forms of bison, peccary, and caribou (West and Dallman 1980). Given all these animals, a hunting way of life could be a good one.

Information about Paleo-Indians has come from two sources, places where they lived and studies of some of their artifacts found on the surface of the ground. Most of the first Paleo-Indian sites to be excavated were mammoth kills in western North America. As more sites were excavated, Paleo-Indian traces were found all over North America and in Central and South America as well. The Paleo-Indian people, widespread and successful, were the American Indian pioneers. Their most famous artifact is the Clovis fluted point, named after the Clovis site in New Mexico. Clovis points do not look like the familiar triangular stone tips used on arrows; they are shaped like lance-heads with parallel sides; the bases and the little basal side ears were often ground smooth as though the maker wanted only the business end of the point to be sharp. On one or both faces, a broad channel flake was removed, leaving a long flake scar or "flute" down the point, parallel to the edges. The special appearance of these points makes it easy for them to be spotted in collections and the Paleo-Indians followed even where Paleo-Indian sites have not yet been found.

Reconstructing the lives of Paleo-Indians in Wisconsin begins with the fact that they were hunters and gatherers who relied on only a few resources rather than a broad range of plants and animals. Because the plants growing south of the glacier did not include many that people could eat, they had to live on animal food much of the time. Paleo-Indians hunted large animals when they could find them, but fell back on other things when they could not (R. Mason 1981). Life involved moving around, and Paleo-Indians seem to have been tent nomads, going easily from one place to another. Little is known of their social or intellectual life, although by comparison with living hunting peoples, much may be guessed. Their societies were probably small, perhaps bands of around 25 people, but in good years these little bands might join together in larger groups established by marriage or common descent. In harder times, groups might just as easily break into small hunting parties. Not much else is known about them. In appearance, they most likely dressed in skin clothing that was tailored to the body, decorated with fur, and designed to help them live and work in a climate that was often very cold. One hard fact known about Paleo-Indians is that they were very particular about the raw material they used to make their tools. Sometimes a special kind of stone appears in sites hundreds of miles from its place of origin, indicating either trade from one group to another, or people traveling many miles to reach it. In some parts of North America, Paleo-Indians returned again and again to certain quarry sites even when local materials were more easily available.

Paleo-Indian chronology

Since Paleo-Indians were the first people in Wisconsin, a fair question to ask is when did they arrive? The answer depends on understanding local glacial geology (R. Mason 1981). During the last major glacial advances, there was a time when, except for the Driftless Area, Wisconsin was covered with ice and no one could move in. As this ice began to melt, its smaller advances and retreats were the factors that determined when people could expand farther north. The glacial sequence allows three possible times when people could move north. The earliest is during the Port Huron advance between 11,000 and 10,000 B.C. At that time, only half the state was covered by ice. South of the Port Huron ice, people might have come into Wisconsin, following the animals they hunted. The second period is the Two Creekan Interstadial between 10,000 and 9,000 B.C. when the ice retreated again and much more land was open. Two Creeks, named for the geological type location near the town of Two Creeks in eastern Wisconsin, is an important base line for dating events of Paleo-Indian times. A forest covering much of Wisconsin at that time was drowned by standing water. The remains of this forest lie underground and can be seen along the shore of Lake Michigan near Two Creeks or in other places where digging for building goes deep enough. Because the Two Creeks forest bed is wood, it is perfect for radiocarbon dating. Many tests of Two Creeks wood have produced consistent results of around 10,000

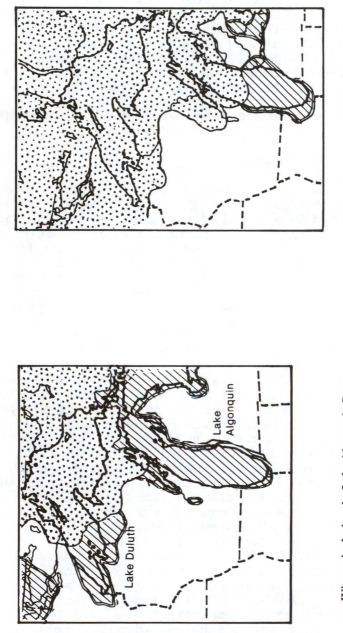

Wisconsin during the Lake Algonquin Stage.

Wisconsin during the Port Huron period.

years ago. The third geological period is the Two Rivers (formerly Valders) ice advance between 9,800 and 9,500 B.C. Two Rivers represents a thinner, more rapid movement that once again covered parts of the state with ice. For Paleo-Indians, part of the state was open during the Port Huron advance, and during the Two Creekan Interstadial. When the Two Rivers ice advanced, people would have been pushed out again, but after Two Rivers, the way was permanently free of ice and clear for settlement (Green, Stoltman, and Kehoe 1986).

Archaeological evidence

So far, no human traces are known in Wisconsin from the time of the Port Huron advance, and none is dated during the Two Creekan Interstadial. The Two Rivers advance is another matter entirely. Across Wisconsin, finds of Clovis fluted points have followed a line matching the end of the Two Rivers ice or the melt-water lakes that followed it. Clovis points are not usually found north of that line, suggesting that Paleo-Indian hunters lived in Wisconsin at the same time as the ice and the melt-water lakes (Martin 1967).

Most of the information about Wisconsin Paleo-Indians has come from studies of fluted points (Stoltman and Workman 1969). Many of them were picked up by farmers in their fields or acquired by collectors. As long as the place where they were found is known, each one is a valuable bit of information on the coming and going of the Paleo-Indians. Generally, fluted points occur in many sizes, shapes, and styles of fluting. The raw materials from which they were made often tell of contacts far beyond Wisconsin. Some of them are of beautiful Knife River chalcedony from North Dakota and others are of dark gray Indiana hornstone or blue-gray Upper Mercer flint from Ohio. A very important local source in Wisconsin is a place called Silver Mound in Jackson county. Silver Mound is a surface deposit of an excellent grade of pseudo-quartzite (technically known as "Hixton silicified sandstone") that was a favorite of many early Indian craftsmen. Fine grained and beautiful, it was the material people chose for spearpoints and other tools over several thousand years (Porter 1961).

What animals Paleo-Indians were hunting in Wisconsin is not known for sure. The only data directly bearing on this matter come from the Holcombe site near Detroit, Michigan (Fitting 1970). Holcombe was originally on a corridor of tundra that stretched through spruce

Paleo-Indian Points: Clovis (left), Scottsbluff (right) *Lawrence University*, and the *Neville Public Museum.*

forest beginning to grow on land recently freed from ice. The Indians at Holcombe were a small group who lived there for a time, made their tools on the spot, and then moved on. Their fluted points are of a type now known as Holcombe points; they are small, perhaps because the right stone was scarce and people had to rework broken points rather than throw them away. What is most interesting is that among the bits and pieces of stone at the site were fragments of the bones of barren grounds caribou. These animals are no longer found in Michigan or Wisconsin, although they are not an extinct species. During the end of the Pleistocene, they lived in the north and Paleo-Indians evidently hunted them. The people who lived at Holcombe, or their close relatives, spread into Wisconsin, too, since Holcombe fluted points have been found there. If barren grounds caribou were among their prey in Michigan, they may have hunted them in Wisconsin as well.

The Boaz mastodon

Another animal often believed to have been hunted by Paleo-Indians is the American mastodon. Numbers of these large elephant-like animals have been found in North America in areas where Paleo-Indians lived. Until recently, however, not a single one had been proved to have been killed by human beings. Most mastodon remains were found by accident--soil erosion or in construction-- and no one has had the chance to look for archaeological evidence with the bones. An exception to this record is the Kimmswick site in Missouri, where mastodon remains were actually found with the tools used to kill them (Graham et al. 1981).

In Wisconsin, there is one known mastodon kill site, and how archaeologists recognized it as a true Paleo-Indian site is in the best tradition of archaeological detective work (Palmer and Stoltman 1976). The mastodon remains were found in 1897 by four boys near the town of Boaz in southwestern Wisconsin. The bones were given to the University of Wisconsin where the reconstructed Boaz mastodon is an impressive exhibit in the Geology Museum. Recently, a fluted point of Hixton pseudo-quartzite was found in the University collections with a label saying that it belonged with the Boaz mastodon. Further checking with the surviving original discoverers showed that they had found the Clovis fluted point near the mastodon's ribs. This gives Wisconsin the distinction of having one of the few associations of human beings and mastodons during the Pleistocene. There must be others still in the ground that have not yet been found.

Plano peoples: Late Paleo-Indians

Wisconsin's earliest Indians were not local people in the sense of being unmistakably local in origin. They were part of a widespread culture, Paleo-Indian hunters, whose artifacts and sites are found across the continent. As the Pleistocene world ended, however, movements were already under way that would bring about more localized Indian life. This birth of more regional cultures was in part caused by climate change on the heels of the retreating glaciers. Once the glaciers were gone for good, Wisconsin was freed of ice, but the unity of the glacial environment that stretched across North America was gone, too. The patchwork of forest edge-tundra that had been for a brief time an excellent hunting land for Paleo-Indians, moved north. What happened to the Paleo-Indians is an unsolved problem. Did they move north with the forest they knew well, becoming eventually the ancestors of modern tundra and boreal forest people? Or did they change their ways of doing things and remain in Wisconsin to become part of something else? The "something else" is what is called the Plano culture, also called "Late Paleo-Indian" or "Early Archaic." It is different, not so much in tools and weapons as in the means used to survive in a land that itself had become different.

As Wisconsin moved more toward modern climate, boreal forest was everywhere for a brief time. Boreal forests are not good places for hunting and gathering: boreal forest trees do not produce nuts, the animals that live in them are solitary and scarce, and food resources as a whole are not plentiful. Fewer people can be supported in the boreal forest than on a low latitude tundra-forest edge, in spite of severe conditions there.

However, Wisconsin had something that was to become more and more important: lakes and waterways that joined them. They were rich in fish; and maybe this was when Wisconsin Indians began to fish in earnest. Positive evidence has not been found so far even though fish as a resource may look obvious in hindsight. Much of Plano culture seems to be lake or water oriented, but lake shores might have been attractive for something other than fishing. Maybe the shores were useful for walking along or as places to get away from blackflies. Perhaps near the shores, the plant and animal life of former times lingered the longest and the old ways could still be followed.

One real effect of the concentration on lake shores was a breakup in the uniformity of the earlier Paleo-Indian cultures. When Paleo-Indians followed herds of caribou or other animals across more open ground, they moved freely over distances. What they left behind them is very much alike, whether it is from New England, Ontario, Wisconsin or Minnesota. Keeping closer to the lakes seems to have led to greater local interest, smaller home ranges, and greater differentiation among groups (Fitting 1970).

Archaeological evidence for Plano people

What is known about the Plano people comes from studies of their tools and a few archaeological sites. Plano spearpoints are often seen in collections picked up from plowed fields, and they are a step away from the older fluted point traditions. A common form is called "Scottsbluff," a parallel-sided spearpoint with a squared base and the beginning of a stem. The workmanship on these tools is often excellent, sometimes with beautiful parallel flaking right across the width of the blade. The workmanship is all the more impressive when the points are made of hard-to-work Hixton pseudo-quartzite, a material that Plano people preferred. Like fluted points, Plano points are carefully ground all around the base and along parts of the edges, probably to prevent the binding from being cut by the sharp stone. When Plano points are found with animal bones in western North America, the animals are most likely to be now-extinct forms of bison. What animals the people hunted in Wisconsin is unknown. Whatever they were, Wisconsin Plano people hunted them using kinds of tools that had become a distinctive local variety, different from similar points found elsewhere (R. Mason 1963).

Two archaeological sites, Renier and Pope, give a little information on the lives of Plano people. The Renier site (Mason and Irwin 1960) is north of Green Bay on a beach ridge left by Lake Algonquin. It consisted of a small area of scattered broken tools, a few scraps of charcoal and fire-cracked rock, and a tiny handful of burned bone, all mixed into the top of a sand dune. Study of these things showed that the dune was a cremation site where the remains of a very young man had been put on a stone-lined pit and burned along with a number of Plano spearpoints. Afterwards the spot was abandoned, and what was left gradually scattered into the sand. Cremation as a custom was also found at the Pope site in Waupaca County, where a similar burial took place (Ritzenthaler 1972).

As time passed, Plano people moved north, responding to changes that are not yet understood. Their traces are found in the north central lakes country where they lived on tiny lakes, moving from lake to lake in small bands (Salzer 1974). Perhaps they were hunting woodland caribou that moved north with the boreal forest and finally became too scarce to support them. A sort of decline set in, at least as far as Plano tools were concerned. The beautifully made Hixton pseudo-quartzite tools were gradually replaced by more crudely made points of local stone. Perhaps trade contacts with Silver Mound were broken or people could no longer travel there to get their raw materials. The drifting north of the last of the Paleo-Indian cultures happened at the same time as the development of new ways of life across Canada. Perhaps the descendants of the Plano culture live far north of what is now Wisconsin. It may also be true that some of them stayed put and were a part of what was becoming a more complicated story.

Archaic Lifeways

Part of the reason for new ways of doing things lies in changes in the climate. The world was now beyond Pleistocene times, and the chilling effects of the glaciers no longer influenced temperatures. Wisconsin was in what is called the "Atlantic Interval," when modern conditions were on their way. The changes in plants that began south of Wisconsin extended northward as temperatures warmed up. The most important of these changes was the replacement of boreal forests by conifer-hardwoods and plants of the prairie-forest border. In terms of the biotic provinces, it meant that the Canadian Zone persisted in the north and the Carolinian and Transition Zones spread into the south.

Green leafy trees and new kinds of plants meant an opening of opportunities in the forests for people, a lifeway called "Archaic" (Stoltman 1978). The resources of the Carolinian and Transition areas included not only nuts and tree sap but also many animals that lived on plants. Nuts and low-hanging branches and shrubs were attractive to deer and small game. With both fish and birds added to these resources, the forests became a place, if not of abundance, then of sufficiency for those who knew it well. The first Archaic people in the east lived far south of Wisconsin. They invented and adapted techniques for dealing with forest resources, and as deciduous forests spread into Wisconsin, these people moved with them.

Archaic Ground Stone: grooved axes (top right), bannerstones (lower right), grinding stone and celt (ungrooved axe) (left) *Lawrence University*

Archaic tools and weapons

Most of the things that have survived from Archaic times are made of stone. Among these are the familiar projectile points for hunting, but they have changed: new types replaced the older Clovis or Plano styles. The new points are often plain, functional rather than decorative, and with an overall sturdy appearance. Less care was taken to make them beautiful, and they come in many shapes and sizes. The common shape is triangular with notched or stemmed bases to aid in hafting. This change in style may have had a functional reason: a shift from heavy, hand-held spears by Paleo-Indians to lighter darts thrown by Archaic people using a spearthrower. However, nobody really knows.

Ground stone tools also appear in Archaic sites. They are even more interesting than the chipped stone points because they represent something new (R. Mason 1981). Ground stone tools often look as if they required a long hard job of painstakingly pecking out and then grinding down hard stone. However, grinding the right kind of stone with sand, water, and another stone is no more difficult than knitting a sweater: stitch after stitch produces a whole, just as patient rubbing creates an axe. Handwork only seems amazing in retrospect to those who have lost the knack. Archaic people made many ground stone tools over several thousand years, and a lot of them have been picked up in plowed fields by farmers or artifact collectors. Ground stone tools were an important addition to the tool kit as people came to deal with the forest. Ground stone axes were the means to handle wood and what can be made from trees. They served for chopping wood, preparing logs for dugouts, stripping bark, sharpening stakes, grinding nuts, and whatever else needed to be done by people who lived in the forest and on its resources (Quimby 1960).

Generally practical and useful, ground stone tools also include some that are harder to classify: bannerstones and birdstones. Bannerstones are tablet-shaped, rectangular, square, or shaped like a butterfly. All finished examples have a hole drilled through the short axis, presumably for mounting on a handle. Birdstones look like little birds, sometimes with popping eyes and erect tails (Quimby 1960). The stone for both was chosen with an eye for the way it looked: gray or beautifully banded slates or colorful granites. No one knows what these things were used for, whether they were parts of other tools or kinds of ornaments. They are among the prehistoric artifacts that are judged in modern times as works of art and displayed in art museums (Coe 1977).

Archaic peoples left behind other tools and weapons. They used bone for awls, fishhooks, harpoons and needles; shell for spoons and hooks. Their fishing equipment, tools for mat and basketweaving, and needles for preparing clothing are all evidence of a varied way of life. In addition, Archaic Indians were the earliest Americans to discover how to use copper, which was widely available in Wisconsin (Ritzenthaler 1957). The copper deposits of Isle Royale and the Keewenaw Peninsula could be mined with simple techniques, and float copper, pieces of relatively pure copper found on the surface of the ground, was common in many places. This use of copper is one of the earliest attempts to use metal anywhere in the world, but it never led to a true metal industry. For one thing, copper, while it was sometimes heated, was never melted, cast, or reduced from ores. It was cold-hammered and annealed in a stone age treatment of metal. Tools of many kinds could be made using this simple process. The question of whether or not copper tools were any better than stone or bone tools has not been answered. Copper was used extensively during the Archaic, but afterwards it was never of any importance for heavy tool making. Brass and iron in historic times caused the death of the stone age, not copper in the Archaic.

Wisconsin Archaic complexes

The earliest Archaic people in Wisconsin were apparently few in number since not many of their sites have been found. Some rare evidence was found in the bottom levels of rockshelters in southern Wisconsin (Wittry 1959), where simple hunters and gatherers had lived on many kinds of food--shellfish, birds, deer, beaver. Other sites include places where people stopped to make stone tools or to gather stone from glacial gravels or from deposits in cliffs. Some of these sites spread over acres and contain thick layers of densely packed chert flakes and only an occasional point or scraper to identify the workmen.

Archaic people lived in the forest and used its resources. They did not live in large villages, but instead made small camps in the forest or in caves or rockshelters while making their rounds. They seem to have used many kinds of foods without depending too much on any one thing except in its season. No one knows when they began to live in Wisconsin, but some of their sites date to around 6,000 B.C. As time passed, Archaic populations grew larger, and life became more complex. Between about 3,000 B.C. and perhaps 500 B.C., a "good life" based upon hunting and gathering was possible, a time period called Late Archaic. The Late Archaic Indians of Wisconsin are known as "Old Copper," in honor of their use of copper as a raw material. European settlers were puzzled by Old Copper artifacts. As land was cleared, more and more of the ancient copper tools and weapons were found, and the quantity of them lost or abandoned is amazing. Collections in Wisconsin museums contain only a small fraction of what was picked up, and these in turn are only a sample of the tools once in use. Their appearance in plowed fields made local people think that ancient Norsemen or other Europeans had once wandered around in prehistoric North America. There is no question now, however, that Old Copper represents Indian culture of great age and growing complexity.

Old Copper artifacts are found over a large area, but Wisconsin is at the center of their distribution. Many are hunting weapons, spearpoints of different kinds and shapes. The most common is the socketed spearpoint, a usually small point (about 5 inches in length) with a tapering triangular blade. Other kinds of copper spearpoints have different forms--spearpoints with long rat tails for inserting into shafts, others with serrated bases, and some that look as if they were shaped after older stone point styles. Copper spuds were heavy woodworking tools that were slipped on antler handles, and other copper tools included gaffs, probably used to land sturgeon. Celts, narrow axe-like tools, were made in sizes from miniature to gigantic. Awls, knives, crescent knives and sometimes even bannerstones were made of copper. People wore beads of copper, often so heavy as to make the neck ache to look at them, as well as simple bracelets, several for each arm. Sometimes necklaces had clasps of beautiful, red-gold copper. Today all the Old Copper tools and ornaments are corroded from long exposure to air and water. They have a dark, greenish coating that makes them look as old as they really are (Mason and Mason 1967).

Only a few Old Copper sites have been found in Wisconsin: cemeteries discovered by accident. The Old Copper cemetery at the Reigh site near Lake Butte des Morts (Ritzenthaler 1957) is a good example. It was found as the result of sand and gravel operations and was a salvage excavation. At least 75 people of both sexes and all ages were buried at Reigh, some as primary burials and some as cremations. Many things were placed in the graves with the dead: copper projectile points, crescent knives,

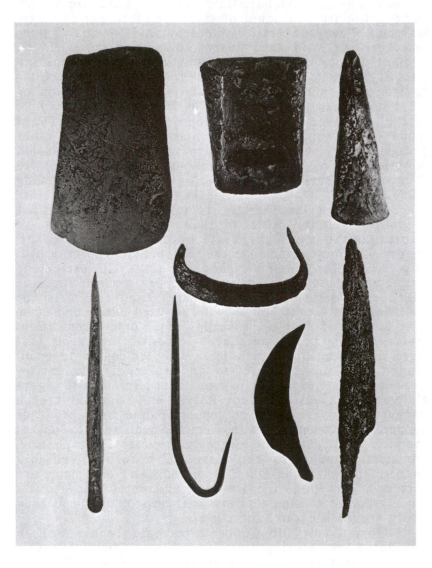

Old Copper: axes (top); crescent knife (center); knife, hook, awl *Lawrence University*

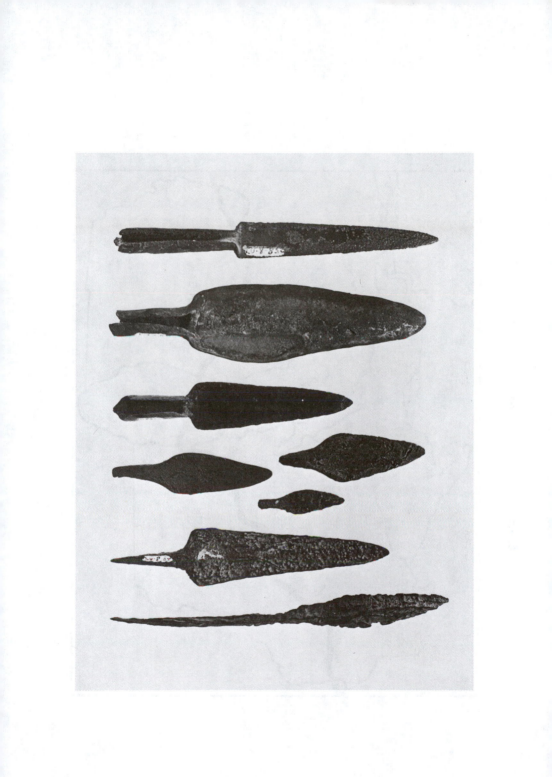

Old Copper: spearpoints *Lawrence University*

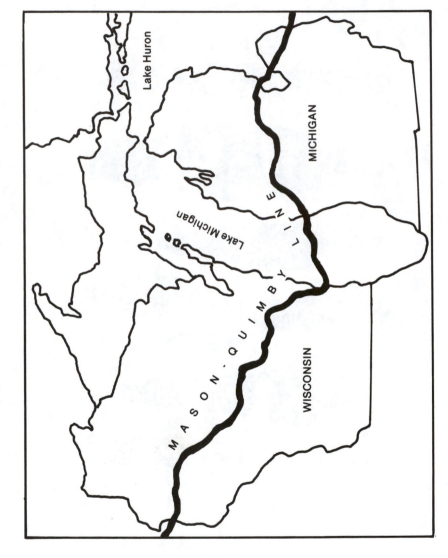

Mason-Quimby line indicating northern distribution of fluted points (after Martin 1967).

spuds and celts; stone and bone points; tubes made of the long hollow bones from the wings of trumpeter swans; copper, pearl, and shell beads; a gorget and toggle of marine shell; a copper headdress; and a netted fabric.

The first lesson from Reigh is that the users of the cemetery were people whose society lasted a long time, long enough for them to keep coming back to the same burial site year after year. Several generations of the same group were buried there. Enough time passed between burials for people to forget where older ones were; they sometimes disturbed those older burials by putting new ones into them. Another fact about the people at the Reigh site is that they followed an orderly round of life with long-lasting ideas of what was right and proper, ideas that persisted over time as cultural traditions. They were nomadic and in the winter left their dead in trees or on scaffolds until the ground thawed and they could return to gather the bones and bury them. Their funeral customs included the use of red ocher sprinkled in the graves. From this point onward, red ocher is often a part of Indian burial ceremonies.

What was put in the graves at the Reigh site is not easy to interpret. Some of the things might have been put in the ground because they belonged to the people who died: they were part of personal equipment. Other objects seem to be tools that people might have used in daily life. The tubes made of swan bone are different. Were they something owned by people with special status? Or were they religious objects? Perhaps they were only blanks for whistles, on their way to becoming someone's courting flute or noisemaker. The marine shell objects speak volumes. The shell itself had to come from the Gulf Coast and had to come through trade. Shell probably came to Wisconsin in exchange for something that was abundant locally but not common to the south. The most likely trade item is copper, although where it went and how it moved is still unknown. People can carry trade goods long distances themselves or they can exchange things hand to hand between people in nearby villages. In this case, trade is often carried out as part of a ceremony, trading partnership, or kinship tie. The value of an object rises as the distance between it and the source of supply increases. Marine shell, when found in Wisconsin, must have been valuable to the people who received it.

The skeletons of domestic dogs were found near the human burials at the Reigh site. Among the earliest dogs found anywhere near Wisconsin are from northern Minnesota with a date somewhere before 5,000 B.C. (Shay

1971). Hunters, guards, pets, eaters of garbage, and occasionally food--dogs were probably all these things. The dogs from Reigh do not seem to be special in any way; about the size of coyotes, they were of no particular breed. Why they were buried in a cemetery might be explained by their being pets or by some role they had in the burial ritual or even because of their outstanding careers as hunters. No one really knows.

What is clear about Old Copper and cultures like it is that they had a complex and varied adaptation to the land and its resources. This pattern of resource use lasted a long time even though a number of different groups appear to have been following it at different times. For people who lived in places where farming could not be a reliable source of food, the Archaic pattern of intensive food collecting, hunting, and fishing survived into historic times. The Old Copper culture, however, went the way of most human endeavors: it became extinct or developed into something new. In either case, by about 500 B.C. in Wisconsin, Old Copper and other Late Archaic complexes were gone.

Early Woodland Transitions

Much of what happened next must be understood in terms of what was happening somewhere else. New ideas and new things, mostly from the south, had an effect on what Indians did in Wisconsin. This time of transition, of new ideas and things coming to change life, is called Early Woodland (Griffin 1978). The important new developments include domesticated plants. There is no evidence for farming at this time in Wisconsin, but people further south were planting gourds, squash, and perhaps some native species such as sunflowers or amaranth (Yarnell 1976). Eventually, of course, corn was added, but in the beginning only a few plants appeared, and they were additions to the diet rather than being staples. Perhaps Wisconsin people met a growing need for food by processing more acorns and collecting more hickory nuts and butternuts rather than taking to crop raising. People were still hunters and gatherers although, through trade ties with the south, they must have been aware of change.

Another new development was the appearance of pottery. The earliest known pottery in America north of Mexico appears far to the south of Wisconsin, and why it ever succeeded is a mystery. The earliest pots were crude, heavily tempered with fiber, and very heavy. When pottery first appeared in Wisconsin (possibly by 700 B.C.), it was also coarse and heavy. One of the names archaeologists have given to this early ware--*Marion Thick,* for example-- gives some idea as to what it was like. If women made the pottery, why did they ever begin to use clay vessels for whatever they had before pottery arrived? Clay pots were very heavy and seem ill-suited to the life of hunters and gatherers who had to move around.

Mound burial also appears for the first time in the Early Woodland in Wisconsin (Green, Stoltman, and Kehoe 1986). Why ceremonies for the dead began to involve building mounds is an unanswered question. Mound burial means complex organization and clear lines of authority. The labor needed to build a mound has to be arranged and the work coordinated so that everyone comes to the cere- mony at the same time. The beliefs behind the elaborate mound burials of more southernly people may have influenced Wisconsin. They might have come over the old trade routes of Archaic times or perhaps more direct contacts played a role.

The Early Woodland complex of farming, pottery, and mound burial did not spread quickly throughout Wisconsin. It is as if these ideas moved into the Carolinian Zone but not into the northern forests beyond. Even in the Carolinian Zone, little seemed to change. Only a few mounds were built, only a little pottery appeared, and the spread of garden crops is suspected, not proven. Whatever was promising in these new ideas did not develop into new ways of life right away. Perhaps the older Archaic pattern of hunting and gathering was still supporting the good life in northern Wisconsin, and population was still small enough to live on what nature provided. Whatever was happening, it looks as if the same people were still in Wisconsin; no new populations were moving in to absorb or replace the old.

Middle Woodland Cultures

By about 100 B.C., elaborate new ways of life spread across eastern North America. This was the time of the fa- mous Hopewell culture of Ohio and Illinois (Prufer 1964), when really large societies began to appear along the major rivers, and village life became common. Why all this happened at this time is not clear. Perhaps a new source of food, reliable farming, was responsible. Perhaps more com- plicated trade and the need to manage it played a role. Certainly the Hopewell culture is more than just village life. It included widely shared ideas, similar art, burial rituals, beautiful ceremonial pottery, and increased trade

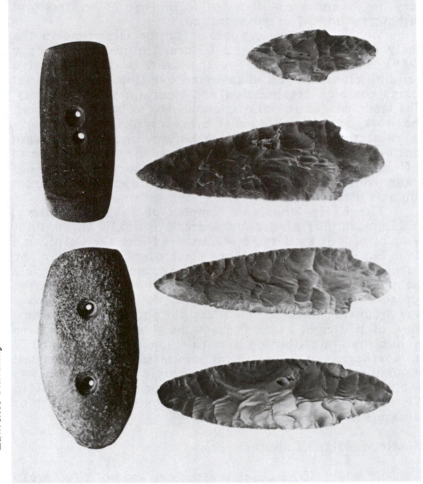

Early Woodland Stone: drilled bar gorgets (top); spearpoints (bottom)
Lawrence University

across distances. There are even signs of unequal ranks of people, probably based on some kind of family statuses.

The objects made by Hopewell people include little clay figurines, obsidian knives, copper artifacts, stone pipes, marine shell ornaments, exotic stone blades, bear canine teeth with inset pearls, sheet mica effigies, and cut animal jaws (Griffin 1978). Almost all of these things appear to have been made especially for putting in graves. Whenever they are found outside the Hopewell areas of Illinois and Ohio, they mean some sort of contact with it. Hopewell copper artifacts are of special interest since Wisconsin is an obvious source for the copper. Hopewell copper objects are not at all like the traditional tools of Old Copper, and it seems clear from this that if the raw copper came from Wisconsin, no ideas as to how it was to be used came with it. Hopewell people made few everyday tools from copper; instead they beat it into sheets and used it to cover elaborate ornaments and to make cut-out decorations.

The Hopewell period is called Middle Woodland, and during this time the prehistory of Wisconsin becomes much more complicated. Hopewell affected northern people even though the people of the north were of little direct interest or importance in the everyday life of Hopewell. The north was a source for raw materials, copper and perhaps fine furs, but the scattered population would not have made much of an impact upon the better organized life of the south. As Hopewell population grew, its people expanded north into what was for them an empty land. They may have moved north in a temporary warm phase between 300 B.C. and A.D. 300 when the southern Wisconsin climate was more like central Illinois. Hopewell groups moved into the southern part of the state, but not into the Transition Zone nor into the Canadian Zone beyond. The spreading settlements moved along broad river valleys and into areas where later peoples grew good crops of corn.

Wisconsin Hopewell

Wisconsin Hopewell sites are found along the Mississippi River (Cooper 1933), where settlers could move by canoe from one spot to another. Trempealeau County has the greatest number of them with between 1,000 and 2,000 mounds and earthworks recorded. The mounds are found in groups, sometimes more than 25 or 30 per group, and some of them stand 10 feet high and are over 60 feet long. Like Illinois Hopewell mounds, they were for burials of the dead; but because they were along the frontier, they did not have some of the elaborate features found to the south. Typical Hopewell burial goods, however, were present, although not in large quantities. The people were rural Hopewellians living in small communities on the fringes of their civilized world. Perhaps they saw their movement north as a kind of exile or perhaps they found it useful if they were part of the copper trade. Hopewell people moved north along other waterways as well. The Rock River and its branches were a means for spreading Hopewell into southern Wisconsin in the area below Fond du Lac. In some respects, these eastern Hopewell settlements seem more "classic" than those along the Mississippi. Perhaps they were only more conservative.

Northern Middle Woodland

During the time of Hopewell in the south, the northern two-thirds of Wisconsin began to change, too. The first Early Woodland pottery and burial mounds had not moved this far north, and the older Archaic ways of doing things lasted with few changes. Yet by the Middle Woodland, the north began to look very different. Population increased, and places that were not lived in at all by Archaic people, filled with settlers. The scale of human society became suddenly greater as large settlements appeared. What happened in the north may have been population growth as well as migration of new peoples, perhaps from the northwest, perhaps from the east. However, there is a strong continuity in which new ideas seem to have been added to older ones (R. Mason 1970).

One of the things that caused changes was a greater emphasis on Great Lakes fishing. Middle Woodland people did not invent the fishing techniques they used; people of the Old Copper culture, for example, had many useful tools for catching fish. Yet Old Copper was gone, and whatever skills its people had and passed down were turned toward fishing of a different kind. Sites along major waterways are found at places good for fishing during spawning runs and produce so much fish bone that gill nets, not just hooks and lines or harpoons, were probably used. A pattern of intensive, seasonal use of fish began with the Middle Woodland, and as a way of life, it continued with few changes into the twentieth century (Cleland 1982).

In the north, Middle Woodland people were the first to use pottery in any extensive way. In Wisconsin, Middle Woodland pots were heavy and had pointed bottoms. The

Northern Middle Woodland Pottery: Hopewell (top, left); various stamped surfaces *Lawrence University*

potters decorated them in several ways, most often impressing or stamping into the soft clay over a plain or cord-marked surface. Patterns of stamped designs were often put in rows around the rims. There is a wide range in how well the potters managed these decorations. Some are famous for tiny, neat stamped designs, but other Middle Woodland people were less expert in the way they embellished their pottery.

The tools and weapons from northern Middle Woodland sites have strong ties with the past. The chipped stone tools consist of simple stemmed or notched projectile points, stone wedges, and scrapers. Heavy ground stone axes were replaced by lighter ones, perhaps as birchbark became an important raw material and lighter axes could handle it. The many bone tools mean basket-making, mat weaving, and making clothes. Beaver incisor chisels point to fine scale work in bone or wood. The old theme of copper use was continued, but the use of pounds and pounds of it for large, heavy-duty tools was over. Middle Woodland people were thrifty producers of little copper fishhooks, beads, rivets, and tiny slender awls. It is as if obtaining copper was harder. Perhaps float copper could not be found anymore; perhaps copper deposits were now in the hands of people who would not allow others access to it.

Between 500 B.C. and A.D. 500, Wisconsin was archaeologically a divided land. Hopewell Middle Woodland cultures were to the south, edging their way northward; in the north, the Canadian forest Middle Woodland populations were growing larger, perhaps as their way of life more successfully used what the environment had to offer. How the two cultures of Wisconsin interacted with each other is not known. The north was a source for copper, and perhaps Hopewell interest in copper played a role in making it less available for everyone else. But what came from Hopewell to the north in exchange for copper? Trade probably went over the old routes that for thousands of years had carried things all over eastern North America. Marine shell, obsidian, special charts, galena, and copper were traded, and many perishables might have come with them: food, feathers, tobacco, medicinal herbs, nut oils, children. Perhaps some of the exchange was in ideas and opinions given for free along with whatever was traded for copper.

By about A.D. 500, Hopewell in Illinois and Ohio had declined. The northern centers were abandoned; and throughout Hopewell lands, mound building and the use of big ceremonial enclosures had ceased. The art style faded away, and the beautiful Hopewell artifacts were no longer made. Many explanations of the decline of Hopewell have been considered over the years--warfare, disease, changes of climate, crop failure--but there is no agreement among experts. The Hopewell decline touched Wisconsin Indians in several different ways. Hopewell people may have moved from the north, leaving behind a place in the Carolinian Zone where new people might settle. Perhaps the people scattered in smaller groups as village life of a Hopewell sort was no longer possible. With no more demand in the south for copper and furs, the people who still controlled the sources would have to look for others willing to trade. The decline of Hopewell must have been an intellectual loss for Wisconsin people whose lives were influenced by what they saw and heard of it.

Effigy Mounds

In the years following Hopewell, the southern half of Wisconsin became the center of a new mound building culture called Effigy Mounds (Hurley 1975; Rowe 1956). Much of early archaeology in Wisconsin was an effort to record effigy mound sites before they were destroyed by plowing. The maps and drawings made then show that thousands of them once existed. The most northern examples were near Green Bay and the most southern ones in northern Illinois and Iowa. Some fine examples are preserved in Effigy Mounds National Monument in northern Iowa and in many state and county parks (such as Lizard Mounds) in Wisconsin.

An effigy mound is seldom found all by itself; more often the mounds are in groups of 10, 20, or 30 and sometimes even more. Low and very long, they stand only a few feet above the surrounding land and stretch sometimes to 100 or 200 feet. Many mound groups were put in places that seem to have been chosen for their view: on high ridges or bluffs overlooking rivers. The mounds at Effigy Mounds National Monument, for example, stand in long rows high above a splendid view of the Mississippi River.

What gives them their name is the fact that many of the mounds are in the forms of birds or animals. Effigies of panthers, deer, turtles, dogs, birds of prey, and bears have been identified in the shapes laid out by the mounds. These interpretations are all modern ones, not necessarily those of the builders, and they may not be accurate. A few mounds are shaped like people, and many others are simple conical or linear forms. Each mound was put up in one operation rather than in a series of layers, and they seldom contain very many grave goods. In fact, sometimes they are empty, without either human bones or grave offerings. When there are burials, they may be of a single person or several people placed in a hole under the mound, on the ground surface before the mound was put up, or even somewhere in the mound fill. The burials themselves might be simple cremations, indicated by a small pile of burned bone. If grave goods are found, they are most often useful things, and sometimes they look as if they were merely forgotten rather than deliberately put with the dead. Ceremonies evidently took place at funerals since fireplaces have been found with the burials, dogs were sometimes buried in the mounds, and stone-lined pits were occasionally put under the mound floors.

Makers of effigy mounds

A major puzzle about effigy mounds is figuring out who made them (Rowe 1956). The mounds are usually not in village sites that might provide more information. Even the artifacts from effigy mounds are not very helpful. Stone spearpoints, so often a key to identifying people, have been found in the mound fill; but they run all the way from Archaic types to the little triangular points of very recent periods. Which of them were made by the mound builders cannot be learned from the mounds. Chipped stone scrapers or drills in the mounds are of ordinary forms found in all time periods and are of no help. The same is true of bone and antler tools, copper awls, simple pipes, and the few ground stone tools that sometimes come from the mounds.

The most helpful artifacts are clay pots, which could bring together the mounds and the village sites where the builders lived. The best information comes from whole pots that were crushed in place. A few sherds in the mound fill might be an accident, but a whole pot sitting smashed on the mound floor is not likely to be there as a result of careless shoveling. The pottery that comes with Effigy Mounds is called Madison Ware: thin;, hard pottery decorated with a cord-wrapped stick or a twisted cord. Between at least A.D. 600 and 1200, Madison Ware was widespread and very important in Wisconsin, and at least some of the makers of Madison Ware also made effigy mounds (Green, Stoltman, and Kehoe 1986).

How were the makers of Madison Ware related to what had happened earlier in Wisconsin? Since Effigy Mounds occupied some of the same space as Wisconsin

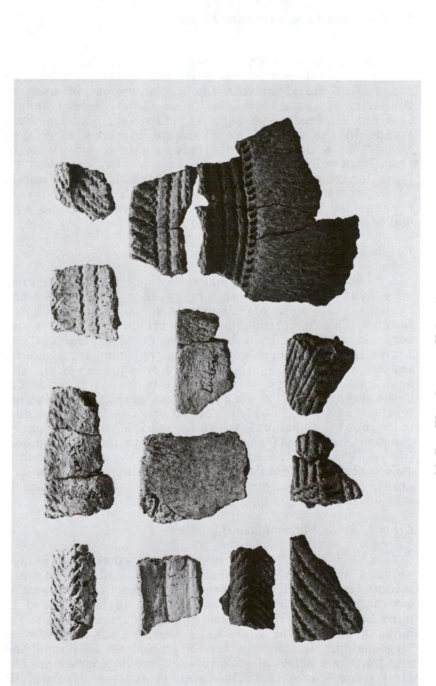

Hopewell, an obvious inference is that the sons and daughters of Hopewell also built the effigy mounds. The presence of burial mounds, the use of cremation, and the similarity of the effigy idea to the Great Serpent Mound of Ohio all lend some support. However, Madison Ware stands in the way of any attempt to think of Effigy Mounds as a descendant of Hopewell. It is too different from Hopewell pottery and not likely to have been derived from it. Its nearest possible ancestors lie to the north, perhaps with the non-Hopewellian Middle Woodland. Perhaps its line of descent is from northern people who moved in when Hopewell went away.

The meaning of the effigies

The question of the nature of the mounds remains: why did people build in effigy shapes? People once thought they were clan symbols of modern Wisconsin Indians. This is reasonable if the effigy mounds are not very old and were built by the Winnebago, Menomini, or Santee Dakota. It turns out, though, that comparing mound shapes with clan symbols will not work even if the problem of the age of the mounds is not considered. Symbols of modern clans do not match the figures represented by the mounds, and no one can figure out how the linear or conical mounds, which are even more common that the effigies, can fit in with the clan symbols (Rowe 1956). Other ideas include thinking of the mounds as expressing people's guardian spirits or marking the graves of important men or women. The whole question is still unanswered.

Clam Lake and other mounds

Other burial mounds in Wisconsin come after Effigy Mounds and carry the mound-building tradition forward into at least the fifteenth century. In the far northwest is a widespread complex of large mounds that are found in pairs or alone, often on lakes or near water. The most famous of them is the Clam Lake Mound (McKern 1963). A large mound, it stood 14 feet high and 90 feet long and was built in a series of stages over several generations. The first stage was 4 feet high and 34 feet in diameter. It contained no burials, but it was neatly covered with a layer of red ocher. After this stage was built, the mound was left to itself for a time when a layer of clean beach sand was poured on with 6 clusters of bundled bones put near the center. Over these, a layer of 3 feet of earth was added, and the mound was again abandoned for a long time. The surface was then cleaned and a new layer of sand was applied with 15 packages of human bones and another earth cap. The mound was then left for 20 years (as judged from tree stumps in the earth layer), and another burial ceremony with the same pattern of layering burials and sand took place. Only a few artifacts were found in the mound: birchbark containers, pipes, projectile points, and pottery. Most of these things were part of the burial ceremonies, not special grave goods added to the burials.

Clam Lake says a great deal about a lifeway that involved moving around in a hard land. The people were not in a rich hunting and gathering territory: they did not have the wealth of Great Lakes fishing grounds to exploit. Death in winter meant leaving the dead to be collected later as bones, which were saved for burial at one time at long intervals. Low in population, the people survived year in and year out to leave their record of a persistent, successful way of life at their places of death. A guess date for Clam Lake puts it between A.D. 1100 and 1400, later than the Effigy Mounds, but not historic. They might have been ancestors of the Santee, but no one knows.

Other mounds are found further east in the Canadian Zone. Most of them are small, oval or conical in shape, and they belong to several different cultural traditions. Two small ones are on top of Mosquito Hill in western Outagamie County and several larger ones sit on Chambers Island out in the middle of Green Bay. They are found in many places, often quite alone, without any village sites or other mounds nearby. In the north, people built burial mounds long after the practice was given up in the south. Building a burial mound is not just a solution to a universal problem; it is a means of bringing a community together. It expresses organization, orderly life, and tradition. Perhaps in the Canadian Zone of Wisconsin, community organization continued to exist partly through planning for mound building.

Farming Communities

If northern Wisconsin seems out of step in clinging to mounds for the dead, then it seems even more out of step in the way people earned a living. All across the northeastern part of North America, new things were happening. After A.D. 800, clear and abundant evidence for farming appeared, first for squash, pumpkin, and sunflowers and finally for corn and beans (Fitting 1970).

A new variety of corn was grown, one better adapted to
northern conditions. Corn became a practical crop in
southern Wisconsin and even for some parts of the
Canadian Zone. Most of northern Wisconsin remained
outside the range of reliable corn gardening, and people
continued to be hunters and gatherers long after people of
the Carolinian and Transitional Zones had come to think
of themselves as farmers since the beginning of time.

Farming had many consequences for social life. One
of these was an increase in population as more and more
people came to live on the same land. Greater food
production helped to handle more people, but there must
have been times when neighbors seemed uncomfortably
close, especially when new fields had to be cleared. An important part of population growth was greater pressure on
hunting lands. Men had to have forest lands for hunting,
and as time passed, certain forests came to be regarded as
the lands of certain groups. Conflict over hunting rights
and other resources resulted in warfare on a scale
unknown before; villages even came to be defended with
palisade walls. The world was different, and many things
that were once important were abandoned or changed. The
burial complexes of earlier days were forgotten, unifying
regional art styles disappeared, and diversity was the outcome of growing local concern.

Late Woodland cultures

The farming complexes of the period after A.D. 800
are called "Late Woodland," and they include a number of
different traditions (Fitting 1978; Griffin 1978). Many
similar tools and weapons, though, are found in all of
them and provide common threads throughout. Among
these is the bow and arrow, which becomes the main
weapon for hunting and for warfare. Bows may have been
present in Wisconsin earlier, but in the Late Woodland,
they are found all over. The bow and arrow represent an
important leap forward in technology: they use little raw
material and are lighter and more accurate than spears or
darts. They altered forever habits and styles in stone tools
that had been popular for a long time in Wisconsin. The
chipped stone points used on arrows were triangular in
shape and usually very small. The large stemmed and
notched points that Wisconsin Indians had used in the
thousands of years since the Paleo-Indian period were now
out of date. When one was found in the woods by accident,
it must have seemed as strange as Paleolithic handaxes
seem to European farmers who find them in their fields.

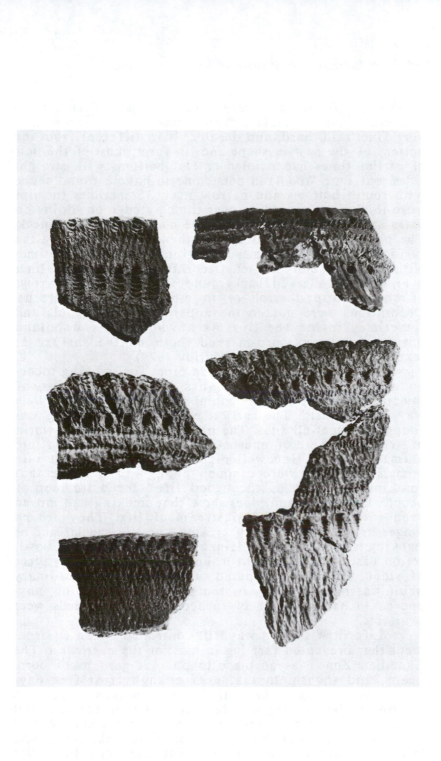

Late Woodland pottery comes in many forms, some still classified as Madison Ware. Most of it is technically very fine: thin, hard, and durable. It is different from the pottery of the past in shape and lip form; most of the pots of earlier times had pointed or flat bottoms with straight sides, but Late Woodland pots come to have a round shape with round bottoms and narrow necks. Sometimes the lips were thickened by folding over the clay edge or adding an extra strip of clay to form a little collar around the neck. The pots were almost always roughened by impressing the surface all over, sometimes with thin cords and sometimes with pieces of cloth or net. Decorations were corded lines over the cord-marked background in single parallel rows of cord-wrapped stick or in more complex patterns. Decorations were put on the upper half of the pots and sometimes inside the lips. As a whole, Late Woodland pottery is always cord-marked, both on the surface as texturing and as decoration (Hurley 1979).

Late Woodland people made pipes for smoking tobacco and probably other plants as well. Smoking of something, mainly for ceremonial reasons, goes back a long way in Wisconsin. The earliest evidence for smoking was found in Hopewell sites. The pipes made then were works of art; many were of unusual stone, cut and polished into animal effigies. Hopewell pipes were evidently not rare possessions; they were common enough to indicate that smoking was part of the "good life" for a number of people. Late Woodland pipes show that smoking had moved even farther into the mainstream of life. They are no longer art objects lovingly created for the special act of smoking; they are small, plain, and shaped like little bowls set on bases. Anyone might make one out of a handy piece of stone. Perhaps the spread of smoking as an ordinary habit was made possible by the presence of farming; anyone could have a patch of tobacco as long as seeds were available.

Life in Wisconsin was still controlled by an environment that prevented farming in most of the northwest. The Canadian Zone was no place to put out gardens of corn, beans, and squash. In that area enough frost free days were never going to be available for Indians to give up hunting and gathering and become full time farmers. Yet signs of change occurred there, too. Across the central lakes country, pottery shows influence from the south, and little triangular stone arrow points replaced the older forms. Perhaps some of the harvest from village farming in the southern part of the state moved along the old trade routes in exchange for copper and furs. Northern

Wisconsin Indians were also influenced by the coming and going of people, ideas, and things through Lake Superior, the Straits of Mackinac, and Lake Michigan.

Mississippian farming communities

One of the most important influences on Wisconsin Indian life was the Middle Mississippian culture that developed about A.D. 700-900 (Griffin 1978). Its major location was the Mississippi River drainage, but its influence spread more widely and was more powerful than anything else since the days of Hopewell. The distribution of the sites is wide; they are present along the Mississippi River as far south as Louisiana and all the way north into Wisconsin and Minnesota, and they occur along the rivers into the East and Southeast. The sites themselves are very impressive and rank among the most remarkable of the remains left by American Indians in the lands north of Mexico. Many of the towns were laid out according to a definite plan, and all of the larger ones have huge mounds that were used as platforms for temples or the houses of chiefs. At least some of these sites were still being used at the time of the earliest European contacts with parts of the Southeast, and Spanish records from that period have aided in interpreting how Mississippian people were organized.

The people who lived in the towns were mostly farmers. They raised corn, beans, and squash in quantity, sometimes by planting more than one crop on the same land in good years. They spent their lives in a society with powerful hereditary leaders at the top; and in addition to farming, they served as workers for whatever the chiefly family thought needed doing. With all this labor, Mississippian towns could have major public works: temple mounds, defensive ditches, big open plazas. Some of the people were craftsmen who made so many fine things that it seems likely they were specialists, excused from doing any of the work in the fields. They used raw materials that came from trade: copper, shell, special kinds of stone and flint. The quantity of the things they made--thousands and thousands of shell beads in a single burial, for example--means that trade was not on the small scale of Archaic times, or even the enlarged one of the Hopewell period. It had become a system that moved large quantities of raw materials regularly from one corner of the Mississippian world to the other.

The pottery made by the Mississippian people is important to Wisconsin prehistory (Griffin 1978). While Late

Woodland people continued to make cord-marked pots in Wisconsin, Mississippians preferred plain ones with smooth and even polished surfaces. Some of them were rounded on the bottoms with wide mouths, and others were bottles with high necks and small openings. The decoration was done with narrow trailed lines arranged in patterns of interlocking scrolls. A very unusual trait of most of the pottery is the use of shell mixed into the clay for tempering, a procedure that improves it when it is fired. Shell used for tempering requires salt as part of the complex chemistry producing shell-tempered pottery, and salt had to be traded from elsewhere. In Wisconsin, with few exceptions, pottery made by Indians in Middle and Late Woodland cultures had always been grit-tempered: shell tempering was a dramatic change, at least in the eyes of archaeologists.

Cahokia and Aztalan

Cahokia, a site near East St. Louis, Illinois, is the largest Mississippian settlement. It was so large that it was a true "urban center" (Fowler 1978), and by A.D. 1000, it may have had a population of 40,000. The rich bottom lands of the Mississippi floodplain encouraged farming and let Cahokia grow and expand along the river, and many small satellite communities were built. There was good farming land to the north, perhaps with the added attraction of being closer to the suppliers of copper. Cahokia Mississippians moved north in the same way as the Hopewell people had done earlier, building towns along the rivers. They went up the Mississippi as far as what is now St. Paul and Minneapolis and made small settlements with temple mounds in several locations. The Illinois River and the Rock River are natural roads into Wisconsin, and a large group made its way as far as the Crawfish, a small tributary of the Rock. On this little river, they built a palisaded town complete with temple mounds; and later people gave it the unlikely name of Aztalan (Barrett 1933).

No one knows whether or not the Mississippians at Aztalan settled there with permission of the Late Woodland village people who were already there. They may not have, for Aztalan was strongly fortified, an outpost in what was apparently dangerous territory. It was protected by single, double, and even triple rows of palisades formed of 6 inch tree trunks over 12 feet high. The walls were plastered with clay to protect them from arrows and fire. The entrances were overlapping, and enemies might be trapped there before breaking inside.

The core of the site was a large rectangle laid out with one of the long sides parallel to the Crawfish River. Measuring about 17 acres, it was both a place for ordinary houses and a center for political and religious life. Two and perhaps three temple mounds stood in a small open plaza. They do not look very large today: their original size and shape have been worn away by years of plowing and erosion.

Aztalan presents a number of problems for archaeologists. One of these is explaining the numbers of Late Woodland artifacts found there. Maybe Late Woodland people lived there after Aztalan was abandoned, re-occupying a site that was once their own. The Late Woodland materials might mean that the Aztalan people, rather than being invaders from Illinois, were actually Late Woodland people taking on the ways of the Mississippians. In any case, the evidence speaks of troubled times at Aztalan. Those big palisades were intended to protect people inside from other human beings, not creatures of the forest. Evidence of cannibalism also exists at Aztalan. It is not known who was eating whom, but it might have happened during a siege when food was scarce or it could have been religious cannibalism or part of terrorism during warfare. Aztalan itself was eventually burned down, either by its own people or by enemies. The puzzle of its decline and fall is as great as the problem of its origins.

The troubles at Aztalan were only a small part of a general decline in Mississippian life after A.D. 1200. Many of the larger centers in the north were no longer expanding, and some of them did not even survive. The decline might have been caused by a slight climatic change, one that shortened the growing season by only a few frost-free days. Corn, very susceptible to frost, would have then become less reliable and less able to support large numbers of people at places like Cahokia. If Cahokia were in trouble with its corn yield, then Aztalan, so much farther north, could not be far behind. It would have become a more and more marginal operation. The actual fate of the people of Aztalan has been debated for many years. Perhaps the people themselves burned their village and then withdrew by boat back into Illinois. If the town were destroyed in war, its people could have been killed or taken prisoner. Or maybe Aztalan only quietly declined with fewer and fewer people able to grow enough corn there. Perhaps as life became more and more difficult, they had to live as their Late Woodland neighbors lived, in a cycle of farming combined with hunting and gathering.

Whatever happened, the Mississippian movement into Wisconsin had failed, and the political and religious life of its temple town vanished as if it had never been.

Wisconsin Oneota

Oneota is the last prehistoric and the earliest historic culture in the southern part of Wisconsin. It is related to a whole series of similar complexes that are widespread in the Upper Mississippi Valley at about the same time. In some ways, Oneota looks more like Mississippian than it does Late Woodland, but its relation to either of these traditions is still uncertain. In the early days of Oneota study, it seemed clear that Oneota must represent the descendants of Mississippian people, rural survivors of places like Aztalan, but more recent work has made its origin a much more complex story (Overstreet 1978).

The people of Oneota culture were people of rivers and lake shores, of farmland and forests (McKern 1945). They followed a way of life that exploited many resources, some of them entirely the bounty of nature and some of their own making. They hunted in the forest and on the prairie, taking such game as deer, bison, elk, beaver, bear, raccoon, and muskrat. Wherever it was possible, they were skillful fishermen. They also gathered many wild fruits: blueberries, raspberries, wild plums, and nuts; and grew corn, beans, and squash in gardens. At certain times of the year, they lived in good-sized villages, but their settlements were not on the order of Mississippian towns with temple mounds and plazas. They did not trade widely or have the arts and crafts that were so much a part of elite Mississippian life. Oneota pottery, while thin, plain, and shell-tempered, was made mainly in only one kind of pot: a big jar with a piecrust decoration around the lip. Sometimes these jars had little loop handles and sometimes they were decorated with trailed lines, chevron designs, or patches of simple punctations.

What Oneota represented in prehistoric Wisconsin remains something of a puzzle. The older view is that it came from Mississippian roots, the kind of society to be expected as the great temple mound culture declined. Oneota people might also have been Late Woodland Indians who learned to make their pottery in Mississippian styles and lived on the northern borders of Mississippian life. Another view is that Oneota culture was a separate adaptation in its own right, a vigorous and successful way of life in very productive areas. The people lived where the biotic provinces intergraded and took advantage of the

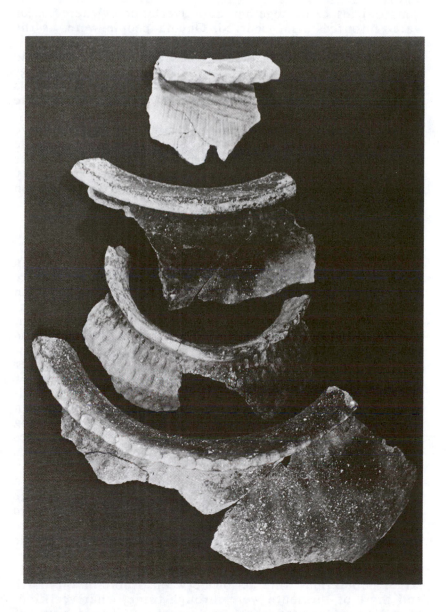

Oneota Pottery *Lawrence University*

"edge effect." It could have given them a boost in places where the fringes of the major plant and animal communities came together and overlapped. Where major water resources also occurred, Oneota people were, as the saying goes, "sitting pretty."

What Oneota eventually became as the historic period approached is not known for sure. All other things being equal, some of the Indians met by early Europeans must have been Oneota in culture type. Since some Late Woodland people also passed from prehistory to history, things are not as simple as they might be. People move around, and archaeological work has not as yet been able to match all the historic Indians with their ancestors. As far as is known, Ioway and Winnebago are the likely survivors of the Oneota tradition in Wisconsin (C. Mason 1976).

Summary

The twelve thousand year record of Indian life in Wisconsin began in a climate still dominated by the Ice Age. People moved north, hunting and gathering within range of the last of the retreating glaciers. From that time to historic contact, the story is one of change, as environmental conditions for life altered and people learned to do new things. The pace of change was generally very slow until the coming of farming, when populations were larger and village life became more widespread. By the time of the Oneota culture, Wisconsin Indian life included complicated patterns worked out over thousands of years in a land whose resources allowed farming, hunting, gathering wild plants, fishing, and collecting shellfish. In places where these resources were plentiful, populations could be large and village life complex.

In general, when Europeans arrived, they found a land populated by farming-hunting-gathering village people to the south and nomadic hunters and gatherers to the north. Populations in the northern Canadian Zone were smaller, and there were fewer places where many people lived at once; the other biotic zones had more extensive village life and farming communities with correspondingly larger populations. Interaction between people of the north and those of the south were through trade, whatever kinds of alliances existed then, and warfare. The arrival of Europeans ended prehistory and began the most far-reaching period of change for Wisconsin people.

CHAPTER 3
Wisconsin Indians of the Seventeenth
and Eighteenth Centuries

European contact reached Wisconsin fairly late. Settlement of the New World by Europeans began in the late
fifteenth century. Champlain founded New France in
1615, and Wisconsin Indians appear in historic records only
after that. The first written words about Indians in
Wisconsin were early in the seventeenth century, well over
a hundred years after European arrival in the Americas. In
many respects what happened in Wisconsin was on the
ripples caused by dropping the stone of European contact
into the waters of the east coast.

Two separate processes acted on Indian life and
changed what was there in the fifteenth century. The first
of these was the fur trade (see Chapter 8). No discussion
of Indian culture after European contact can slide by the
fact that from the very beginning the fur trade caused
changes in every facet of life. No one was untouched by
it, and it operated so early that it is often hard to know
what life was like before it began. The second process was
nineteenth century American settlement in Wisconsin,
which not only replaced Indian cultures but also altered
the land through lumbering and farming (see Chapter 9).
Over more than three hundred years, the fur trade and
then American settlement were responsible for greater
changes than had taken place over the preceding twelve
thousand years. The history of European-Indian contact
has to be considered with both of these processes in mind.

French Contact

Officials of New France and French missionaries
were the first Europeans to record the presence of Indians
in Wisconsin. Their interest in what was then a faraway
country fluctuated with the directions sent by the
government back in France and with the fortunes of New
France. In general, though, they thought of distant
territories in terms of the trade that could be arranged
with them, the missionary work that might be carried on
there, or how information about them might help in the

long-standing French hope of outmaneuvering the English in the New World. The very earliest mention of Indians in Wisconsin occurred after 1620 when the Winnebago were spoken of as possible participants in the fur trade (Lurie 1978). Beyond these concerns, early French officials and missionaries included men who were curious about where the rivers came from and whether or not they might provide a northern passage to take travelers from the Atlantic to the Pacific.

Huron

The major focus of official French records before 1650 was a people known as the Huron, an Iroquoian-speaking people of the Georgian Bay area in Ontario. The Huron are of importance to Wisconsin because they were for many years the means of European contact with the western Great Lakes. They controlled access through their lands and over the canoe routes; and through Huronia, as through a funnel, the bulk of Indian trade goods had to move on the way west. The French understood the importance of the Huron villages and promised them military help as well as European trade. Military help was needed since the Huron tried to exclude everyone else from a share in the trade and made many enemies in the process (Trigger 1976).

How did the Huron organize their trade? They had things that were useful to people of the north, their food crops, for example, and tobacco. The Huron were able to raise impressive corn crops in the mild climate of eastern Ontario, and they produced more than they could consume themselves. Through the Huron, corn and other produce found its way to those who could not grow crops of their own. In prehistory, and before the French demand for furs created a market, the amount of trade was probably small. With the development of the European fur trade, the Hurons also gave European goods to their partners in exchange for furs. Through these networks, European goods came to places like Wisconsin long before the Europeans themselves arrived. All during the early seventeenth century, the Huron did their very best to keep the French from trading on their own. For a long time they were successful in standing as a barrier to French movement west. In the long run, though, they could not put a complete stop to explorations by the French trying to directly tap the sources of furs.

Early records of Wisconsin Indians

The knowledge about Wisconsin Indians that moved around the Hurons into the hands of French officials was only bits and pieces (Lurie 1960). Champlain had heard of the Winnebago as early as 1629, when he learned of a faraway and powerful people who spoke a language different from the familiar Algonquin or Iroquoian of the east. At that time they were called "People of the Sea" or, less attractively, "Puans," people of the stinking water. Champlain was interested in them and the lands beyond, and he sent Jean Nicolet west to contact them. The motives behind Nicolet's voyage are complex, not quite a simple notion of "discovering China." Granted that Champlain knew about the search for the famous northwest passage, but he had more immediate goals in mind for Nicolet's voyage. For one thing, Nicolet could make a separate trade contact with a distant people, one that did not depend on Indian middlemen for success. And for another, who knew what raw materials there were in that distant land? Champlain had heard about copper and may have thought that the People of the Sea controlled the sources. Champlain also tried to make "peace" among the western peoples, perhaps with the idea of putting the French in a position of peacemaker and holder of the balance of power among the western tribes.

Information about Wisconsin Indians from Nicolet's voyage west is only indirect since his own journals were lost. The information was recorded secondhand in the *Jesuit Relation* of 1640 (Thwaites 1896-1901, vol. 23). Several Indian groups were mentioned as living in an area whose boundaries were not described: Naduesiu, Assinipour, Eriniouai, Rasaouakoueton, Pouutouatami. It is not known where Nicolet made his famous landfall in Wisconsin nor is it known for sure which Indians he met there (Lurie 1960). Among them were Winnebago, but the people who gathered to feast with him seem to have included others as well.

The Winnebago, the People of the Sea, were not ignorant of the French in Quebec, and they were well aware of European trade goods controlled by French sources. Years before Nicolet's voyage they had regular trade relations with the Ottawa, who brought them a small supply of European goods in exchange for furs. At this time, the Winnebago were "Early Historic." That is, they had some European goods but no direct contact with Europeans. Winnebago archaeological sites of this period would look much like late prehistoric sites except for the presence of a few things made by Europeans: beads, iron knives, brass bracelets, and glass bottle fragments (Quimby 1966). Most of Winnebago material culture was still being made and used locally.

The Winnebago of 1634 were a "very populous" people (Lurie 1960). Their numbers, political power, and warriors were common knowledge among the Algonquin-speaking people of the east. Estimates put their numbers at nearly ten thousand, a large size for the time and the place. For twenty years after Nicolet's voyage, however, no contacts at all existed between the French and the Winnebago. Because of Huron policy, no one was able to follow up on Nicolet's voyage, and no one could make maps of village distribution or even describe Winnebago villages. Trade continued during these 20 years of French silence, but it was again in the hands of the Ottawa, who were probably relieved that the French could not pursue their initial advantage. When the French returned to Wisconsin, the Winnebago had dwindled to a people of little importance. By the end of the seventeenth century, much of their former lands had been taken over by others.

What happened to reduce the once powerful Winnebago to only minor importance is not known. Historical sources mention a series of disasters that brought their population down to only 600 by the end of the seventeenth century (Blair 1911). Some of these disasters seem reasonable, but others sound less possible. For example, one account of 600 warriors being drowned in a lake all at once seems unlikely to have been a major reason for the whole population to decline. The most often repeated disaster involved Winnebago treachery to Illinois ambassadors who had come to offer help to the Winnebago during a famine. According to this story, the Winnebago murdered and ate their guests, fleeing then to Doty Island in Lake Winnebago where they would be safe from the vengeance of their victims' kinsmen. The Illinois waited until winter, crossed on the ice, and killed or captured most of the Winnebago (Lurie 1960). The most likely explanation, however, is that epidemic disease reached them and reduced the population within a short time. Everywhere in North America, European diseases spread to people who had no built-in biological defenses. The results were often so sweeping that whole groups perished and large areas were emptied of people (Dobyns 1983).

Even with the benefit of the better maps of the late seventeenth and early eighteenth century, it has still not been possible to find a single early historic Winnebago archaeological site. As far as physical remains are concerned, the Winnebago have not left signs enough behind them to show they had ever once lived in Wisconsin at all. The latest Oneota phase was probably Winnebago, using linguistic evidence and comparison with sites belonging to the Ioway, but no certain historic Oneota sites, apart from one component on Rock Island in Door County (R. Mason 1986), have been found in eastern Wisconsin. The Oneota sites are there, but as yet only the one on Rock Island has been found to have any of the proper kinds of trade goods; even that site is suggestive and not definitive.

The Menomini were among those mentioned by Nicolet. They were "neighbors" of the Winnebago, and no one is certain where their villages were located then. By the late seventeenth century, they had a "Grand Village" on the Menominee River, and this may have been the center of their homeland for a long time (Keesing 1939). They were the original Algonquin-speaking people of Wisconsin; but it is not clear how big their range was nor how large a population they had. They seem, by comparison with the Winnebago, to have been a small group, much like the little bands that were to become Chippewa in the eighteenth century.

Menomini archaeology is as unknown as Winnebago, and no reliable culture history can be reconstructed for them either. Some research into Menomini prehistory began with a few excavations on the Menomini Reservation. Out of this work, archaeologists defined what they thought was prehistoric Menomini culture (Barrett and Skinner 1932). However, artifacts found on the Menomini Reservation are likely to be almost anything, especially since the Menomini moved there only in the nineteenth century. Since the Grand Village of the Menomini was at the mouth of the Menominee River, future work should be attempted there.

The third native Wisconsin people who were there when Nicolet arrived were the Santee Dakota, who were called the "Naduesiu" (Thwaites 1896-1901, vol. 23). They were in the neighborhood of the Winnebago, but, as in the case of the Menomini, the "neighborhood" is hard to define. Nicolet said that he had visited most of the people he listed, but in the case of the Santee Dakota, it seems more likely he only heard of them or met some of them when feasting with the Winnebago and their guests. The Santee Dakota or Naduesiu are not mentioned very often in the early records; when missionaries wrote about them, it seems they were located near the Mississippi River, "18 days west" of Sault Ste. Marie. As time passed, the Naduesiu appeared more often in the reports sent back to France as European knowledge took in more remote places. As seen through the eyes of their enemies to the east, the Santee Dakota appeared to the French as a fierce, warlike people referred to with feeling by the Chippewa as "snakes," and eventually by the French as the "Iroquois of the north." No more heartfelt tribute to their military might could be expressed than to compare them to the Iroquois.

A people of importance, located on the upper Mississippi in early Historic times, the Santee Dakota are another archaeological mystery. Their ancestors could have built some of the conical burial mounds that continued to be put up even when mound burial had been given up almost everywhere else. Perhaps the Clam Lake Mound was built by ancestral Dakota (see Chapter 2). No real archaeological evidence exists from Wisconsin to show where they lived in prehistory or what their archaeological remains looked like. So far the data come from sites in Minnesota and support mound building into the historic period and the presence of pottery that is plain, shell-tempered, and Oneota in style (Johnson 1985).

For the earliest period of European contact in Wisconsin, the archaeological record is weak and the supporting historic sources are few. Adding to the problems in trying to figure out what was going on is the nature of the Indian societies themselves. With the possible exception of the Winnebago, Wisconsin Indians did not live in strong tribes with firm boundaries and powerful leaders. They often lived as independent villages or even single families with only local leaders and local concerns; tribal government was a development of the historic period, and the prehistoric local groups can only be an approximation of what came later. Prehistoric boundaries must have changed, too, making archaeological identification very complex, especially as older and older time periods are examined. The best guess as to which Indian groups were in Wisconsin at the time of contact includes only Winnebago, Menomini, and Santee Dakota. The historic evidence is very limited because Nicolet's visit was a short one, intending only to open relations with people in an unknown land. If he did the basic tasks of information gathering that would come before sending missionaries and traders, his records are lost.

The years following Nicolet's 1634 voyage were of great importance to the Winnebago since their population losses occurred then, but only rumors exist in European sources of what was happening at that time. The political result of the Winnebago decline was a softening of the control they had in their own area. The Winnebago of the 1650s were not the same power they had been; they were in no position to resist pressures put on them by others moving into the vacuum created by their collapse. What made the Winnebago situation so unfortunate for them and so lucky for other people was what was happening farther east.

The refugee period

Pressure by eastern people on the Indians of Lower Michigan was of long standing duration. When the French first arrived in Canada, they heard tales of Algonquin-speaking people to the west of the Huron, Petun, and Neutral. These Algonquin people were often called "People of the Fire," and they were traditional enemies of the Iroquoian-speaking tribes. "People of the Fire" does not clearly refer to any one group of historic Indians; sometimes they are identified as Potawatomi or Mascouten, and at other times scholars despair of ever learning who was included in the term (Fitting 1970). With the growing political power of people like the Neutral, the Lower Peninsula of Michigan became a dangerous place to be. Gradually the "People of the Fire" withdrew westward, and thanks to the weakness of the Winnebago, they were able to move into Wisconsin. By the 1640s, some of them were already at the mouth of Green Bay.

The collapse of the Huron gave an added push to what was to become a major movement of Indians into Wisconsin. For years, the Huron had been enjoying their location squarely on the water routes for trade to the west and northwest. For years, they had cannily resisted French attempts to reach inland for trade, and it was their efforts that prevented the French from doing anything with their connection west through Nicolet. However skillful the Huron were with the French, they were not successful with all their Indian neighbors. The Huron had trade ties with the Petun and the Neutral, who were not neutral when it came to groups such as the "People of the Fire" to the west. Both Petun and Neutral confederacies, however, became part of the great disaster that overcame the Huron at the hands of their enemies, the Five Nations of Iroquois, mainly the Seneca (Trigger 1976). The Five Nations (Seneca, Onondaga, Cayuga, Mohawk, and Oneida)

are often called "the Iroquois," a name that has been given
to the language family shared by many different groups in
the East: Huron, Neutral, Erie, Petun, etc.

The Iroquois were old enemies of the Huron, but
over the years their warfare had not been very costly. It
involved a pattern of blood feud between local groups in
which a life was sought to avenge a kinsman's life lost
earlier. The quarrels never ended. Relationships stood at
the simmer until a single act, a single captive taken and
burned, put both groups at the ready for raiding. This perpetual feuding pattern set the stage for Huron destruction
and was the means for upsetting the balance of power in
the eastern lakes and eventually in Wisconsin as well.

Escalation in warfare with the Huron came about
for the Iroquois as a result of their early contact with
Dutch traders and entry into the fur trade through New
York (Norton 1974). Unlike the French, the Dutch were
generous in supplying guns to Indians. This new weapon
had great potential, not especially for hunting beaver, but
for warfare. In order to get guns, furs had to be gathered,
ultimately meaning the disappearance of beaver from the
Iroquois home range. In their eagerness to continue
trading, the Iroquois were forced to look for other sources
of furs, and the most obvious one was north. The northern
supply, however, was in the hands of the Huron, whose
role as middlemen in the trade was now of many years
standing. The Iroquois built upon their traditional blood
feud with the Huron, enlarging and intensifying it. They
descended upon Huronia like the poetical wolf on the fold;
and between 1648 and 1649, they rapidly transformed the
old pattern into a war of conquest. The final Iroquois
raids into Huronia were not simply for the purpose of
snatching a few Hurons but to ambush trade canoes, create
terror among the Huron as a whole, and to destroy
villages. This is quite unlike simple revenge raiding and
indicates that the Iroquois knew very well what they were
about: to break the Huron hold on the fur trade and gain
control of it themselves (Hunt 1940).

The Huron were not a powerless people. They had
many experienced warriors and understood as well as anyone how to carry on traditional feuds. Yet they were totally defeated by the Iroquois, their villages were burned,
and the people were scattered across the Northeast. Part of
the success of the Iroquois may be laid at the door of more
frightening and deadly weapons; they were plentifully
supplied with guns or, at least, they had more than the
Huron. Perhaps more than their weapons was the strategy

adopted by Iroquois war leaders; it showed an understanding of both short term tactics and long term goals: they sought and won a vast new beaver territory in Ontario. In addition, they attacked missionaries as if to show that French religion and French soldiers were both helpless. Several missionaries were martyred during this war, tortured to death in an honorable fashion alongside the Hurons whose fate they had come to share. The surviving Hurons, disorganized and frightened, fled their villages and scattered before the Iroquois. By 1650, the Huron homeland had been abandoned.

The fate of the Huron was dramatic. At first, many of the Christian Hurons took shelter on an island in Georgian Bay, but fear of the Iroquois drove them away. Many fled into the forests where they starved or were given refuge for a time by sympathetic neighbors who as yet had not felt the hot breath of the Iroquois themselves. Some, however, joined by Petuns and Ottawas, went north by canoe into the waters of Lake Huron, along the shores of Manitoulin Island, through the Straits of Mackinac and down across the islands at the mouth of Green Bay into Wisconsin. Some of them continued their flight until they came to rest on Prairie Island in the Mississippi River, hundreds of miles from their homeland. Eventually they wound up along the south shore of Lake Superior at Chequamegon. Ironically, still others back in Ontario were adopted by their enemies and merged with the Iroquois in New York (Trigger 1976) while another group fled to the St. Lawrence to place themselves under the protection of the French.

The effects of the Huron diaspora on Wisconsin were profound. For one thing, the scattering of the Huron opened the whole route into Wisconsin to Europeans. The French no longer needed to keep one eye on the Huron in their westward voyages; the route was free and clear as long as the Iroquois could be avoided along the way. What was open to the French was open to others as well, and the Iroquois could come and go as they pleased. The scattering of the Huron meant that Wisconsin was now part of a potential battleground: French and British opposing each other, both of these against Indians, Indian groups with each other, and the Iroquois as enemies of everyone else. For better or for worse, a new chapter was opening for Wisconsin; by 1650 the sheltering effect of distance and intervening people was over.

A factor of lasting importance in the years both before and after the defeat of the Huron was the fear

people had of the Iroquois. There is no question but that
the Iroquois inspired a degree of fear that no other Northeastern people ever achieved. The Iroquois seem to have
made such feelings a deliberate policy, for they practiced
a studied terrorism far out of proportion to the ends
achieved by it. The fear they created among the people of
the Northeast was increased as they attacked the Erie,
Susquehannock, Neutral, Petun, and whoever else stood in
their way (see, for example, Wallace 1970).

As the Huron went west, fleeing before the Iroquois,
they inspired whole groups of people to move to what they
thought to be a safer land. During this time, many old
alliances and relations that had been present among Indian
societies became unbalanced. Some places were emptied as
people shifted out of the way of possible Iroquois attacks.
Like a wolf driving sheep, fear of the Iroquois sent people
north, and as they went through the Straits of Mackinac,
they were funneled down into Wisconsin, which became
the principal refuge for displaced people. The defeat of
the Huron resulted in a major flow of refugees across the
northern lakes into Wisconsin, accelerating a movement
that had begun earlier. But the northern route was not the
only road--other people curved around Lake Michigan and
entered Wisconsin from the south (Silverberg 1957).

Besides the Huron, Petun, and Ottawa, the groups
known to have moved west in the seventeenth century include many who became Wisconsin residents: Potawatomi,
Sauk, Fox, Kickapoo, Mascouten, Miami, and Chippewa.
Many of these people came from the Lower Peninsula of
Michigan, but others came from Indiana or Ohio. For the
refugees, coming into Wisconsin was not simply to take up
new lands and begin again the kind of life they had
before. They needed land for raising crops, certainly, but
beaver hunting territory and contact with a source for
European trade were now necessary parts of life. Much of
their restless movement during this period is tied into one
or another of these goals. For many of them a strong
westward impulse eventually brought them to the
Mississippi River or even beyond. North and south in
Wisconsin, east and west they moved, not as whole groups
but as sections or even households. During the years
following 1650, few Indian societies that once had been
village people living together in one place survived as
single units; scattered, eager to create new alliances, and
quick to follow up any advantage, they form a kaleido-
scope of changing locations and loyalties.

For the most part, native Wisconsin groups were unable to withstand this wholesale invasion of what had been their territory. The Winnebago, reduced in population, were simply by-passed, and eventually they, too, saw advantages in the westward movement of these troubled times. The Menomini moved south and west, and with their looser social structure, they broke into small groups that infiltrated other people's new claims to the west and south. The Santee Dakota, as became the "Iroquois of the north," took up arms against many of the newcomers and disputed their passage.

Early French accounts of Wisconsin

Because of the Iroquois, the French withdrew their missionaries from many places in the west, and information during the years following the defeat of the Huron is very scarce. Not all Frenchmen were missionaries, however, and by the end of the decade, traders were in Wisconsin, feeling out the lay of the land. The most famous of these were Pierre Esprit Radisson and Medard Chouart, known as Sieur des Groseilliers. These men ran a gauntlet of Iroquois interference along the way and explored the shores of Lake Michigan and Lake Superior as well as an unknown stretch of land in between. Radisson wrote a memoir of his trips into the interior in his old age when he was living in England. This chaotic narrative of his journeys (Adams 1961) is frustrating because it tells so little of all there was to be told, but it is full of information on seventeenth century Indian life in Wisconsin.

One of the things that Radisson says is that people still feared the Iroquois even this far from their homeland. Again and again, fear of the Iroquois turned people aside from journeys or pushed them farther west. When traveling, they saw Iroquois behind every tree and often threw up crude fortifications to protect themselves, even when stopping overnight. Radisson and Grosseilliers traveled with Huron and Ottawa, both of whom knew firsthand what had happened in Huronia.

Another fact that comes through Radisson's accounts is how invisible the Winnebago had become. In spite of going back and forth at least once over the Fox-Wisconsin route to the Mississippi, Radisson scarcely commented at all on the people who once dominated eastern Wisconsin. The pages of Radisson's account are filled with Hurons, Ottawas, Mascoutens, Potawatomis, and Chippewas but not with Winnebagos. The only mention of this once important people is the appearance of the name "Ouinipisoeck" in a list of Indian nations living in the north and the single comment that the people were "sedentary and do reap" (Adams 1961: 160). The Menomini are likewise given little notice: they appear only as a family living along the south shore of Lake Superior, an old man and woman with many children who give shelter to the Frenchmen. The Santee Dakota appear more prominently, perhaps because they successfully resisted incoming Indians and perhaps because Radisson and Groseilliers were the first Frenchmen to actually reach their country and try to establish trade ties with them.

Radisson's view of Wisconsin is a confused one as far as its Indian population is concerned. The coming and going of people here and there made it impossible to have a clear picture of tribal claims or boundaries. Perhaps most moving are Radisson's descriptions of Wisconsin. He had never before seen a "kingdom" so fair, and he described Lake Michigan as the "delightsomest lake of the world" (Adams 1961: 91). Others who followed Radisson knew much more about the area, but none expressed himself with more simple charm than this French traveler in a land then unknown to Europeans.

Clearing the Hurons out of the way opened the road westward to many more people besides Radisson and Groseilliers. Many Europeans came between 1650 and 1715: military men, missionaries, and political agents as well as legal and illegal traders. Missionaries in Wisconsin tried to recover from the losses suffered in Huronia by following converts wherever they went. The first permanent mission in the area was at Chequamegon in a village of refugee Ottawa and Huron. Eventually the village included Potawatomi, Sauk, Fox, Chippewa, and Illinois as well. Other missions were located at Sault Ste. Marie and eventually Green Bay, where in 1677 Father Allouez settled at DePere in the mission of St. Francis Xavier. Father Allouez's reports indicate that the refugee people were settling into lands they now claimed as their own. The lower end of Green Bay was occupied by Sauk and Potawatomi combined in a single village; and to the west on the Wolf River, the Fox had a village of their own. Farther up the Fox-Wisconsin Rivers were Mascouten and Miami, Kickapoo and Illinois. The Menomini were still there in their village on the Menominee River.

Throughout the late seventeenth century, many missionaries came to Wisconsin (Thwaites 1896-1901); and from their accounts, religious work went well, at least at first. The Indians seemed to them to be more interested in conversion, their attitudes appeared more favorable, and they struck the missionaries as more docile than they had been before. How long this might last was another question, but for the moment, the mission effort had been revived.

European traders in Wisconsin were present even earlier than the missionaries, and in a real sense they were competitors. In the years following the Huron defeat, the role of middlemen in the trade was filled by the Ottawa, who arranged to transport furs back to New France and supplied trade goods in return. Because of their early middleman position as a source of European goods, the Ottawa were sometimes called "French" Indians, people with a special relationship to the French source-of-supply. Once French traders began to move into Wisconsin in larger numbers, Ottawa control slipped, and they lost their advantage as traders. Other Indians at various times sought to fill their place, but finally middleman status fell completely into the hands of Europeans.

Nicolas Perrot was prominent among the traders of the seventeenth century. His memoir of his experiences in Wisconsin is an important direct source on the Indian people of the time (Blair I: 1911). Perrot was a government agent and administrator in addition to being involved in trade. He not only made and maintained French alliances with the Indians, but also had real influence on the relations between Indian societies as well. At that time no single group in Wisconsin had boundaries that could be defended as traditional against all others. Jockeying for position among the refugee groups sometimes led to ruffled tempers and fighting. Perrot represented no single Indian people and was free to act as a judge and peacemaker among them all. As a French agent, it was his business to do so and in that way to further French interests. He seems to have been a man of courage and good sense, which, added to a gift for languages and a willingness--literally and figuratively--to go the extra mile, made him a useful man in the wilderness.

In 1689, Perrot took possession of Wisconsin in a ceremony on the Mississippi River. Similar ceremonies had taken place at Sault Ste. Marie and other places along Lake Superior, but the Mississippi River event was aimed at the regions bounded by Wisconsin's waterways. Perrot declared French sovereignty over Green Bay, the Fox-Wisconsin water route with its lakes, the Mississippi, and the land all around them. If the Mississippi ceremony was like the earlier one at the Sault, it was impressive and dignified, bringing together religious, military, and civilian resources in a pageant of song, speech-making, and firing of guns. The assembled Indians could not have known in full the implications of the gathering, but with their feel for ritual, they must have approved of the performance.

French military presence

The need felt by the French to publicly declare their right to the northwest resulted in French soldiers being stationed in Wisconsin. They were intended not only to stop British attempts to interfere in the fur trade but also to control French subjects, to protect them, and punish them if necessary. Illegal trading had to be discouraged and the behavior of traders regulated, insofar as possible. Soldiers were also expected by their presence to impress Indian allies and even offer help in their own warfare. Finally, soldiers could be used to punish enemy Indians for any actions taken against the French.

Soldiers needed bases, and a number of forts were built at strategic locations. Perrot was responsible for forts built along the Mississippi at Prairie du Chien, Trempealeau, and Lake Pepin (Blair 1911). Other people later put up more substantial structures in many of the same places used by Perrot. As time passed, Prairie du Chien was the most important place on the Mississippi, balanced on the north by Chequamegon and on the east by the mission of St. Francis Xavier and later the fort at La Baye, the future city of Green Bay. Dominating the entire region, however, was the military settlement at St. Ignace. Later it was moved to the opposite shore where, as Ft. Michilimackinac, it controlled access by water through the Straits of Mackinac and into the western lands (Maxwell and Binford 1961).

Middle Historic Period

After 1670 and before 1760, French influence in Wisconsin reached its greatest extent. For the Indians, it was in this ninety-year period that European influence became widespread. Everything was affected by the sameness of European goods that came to all Indian societies, no matter what their language or background. For archaeologists, this is the time when native artifacts were finally replaced. Archaeological sites during these years are the last chance anyone has of identifying historic Indians with their own prehistoric traditions. This is called the Middle Historic Period (Quimby 1966), recognized in the ground by the flood of European artifacts that suddenly appears. Compared to the few beads, iron knives, and brass bracelets found on a site in Wisconsin of 1650, the riches of the post-1670 period are remarkable. Excavating sites of this period, archaeologists can expect a great variety of European goods: brass trade kettles, iron axes and hoes, bottle fragments, white clay pipes, bale seals, large numbers of trade knives, gun parts and gunflints, fire steels, Jew's harps, Jesuit rings and religious medals, and trade beads. Beads of this period change to an emphasis on tiny seed beads and a variety of larger many-colored beads--raspberry beads, oval white beads, many-sided beads, and lovely translucent beads of milky blue-white. The Indians, if nothing else, did not look the same as the people who met Nicolet only a few years earlier.

Indians had few difficulties with the trade as it was carried on by the traders: they understood what each side could expect and tried to use the trade and the traders to their own advantage. Each Indian group in turn attempted to serve as middlemen for people farther in the interior, and each in turn was by-passed by the French. When Indians attacked the traders or other Frenchmen, they understood both retribution and the need to have dependable allies. One thing they saw clearly was the impossibility of ever going back to stone tools and clay pottery once they had adopted trade goods. They realized that they could not do without the French or someone else who could supply them with goods. In this sense, they had become locked into trade as a necessary part of life.

The French period in Wisconsin came to an end with the French defeat by the British at Quebec in 1760 and the loss of Canada to the victors (Kellogg 1925). The conflict between these two European powers in America is called the French and Indian War, and the fate of Wisconsin rested on its outcome. If the French forces had been the stronger, Wisconsin might still be part of a Canada French in language and tradition.

British Period

The British victory meant a change from French to British goods in the trade and a change in the way the trade operated. When the flag of France was taken down along the Mississippi, on Lake Superior, and at Green Bay and the Union Jack run up the flagpoles, more than just a change in government occurred. The British were not the French, and their ways of doing things were different. Trade was to be reorganized, and the old image of traders living in Indian style was replaced by the shopkeeper image as trading with Indians was to be standardized, civilized, and regulated. Rules came to the frontier that could not be enforced, but their intent was in the direction of more rigid organization. The military side of life was dominant at first, and trade began under the British with traders assigned to military posts where they worked under the fort commandants.

The French mission system ended with the coming of the British. Missionaries were withdrawn from Wisconsin and not replaced. However much the British were concerned in theory with the souls of the people in the Northwest, they did not supply missionaries of their own. No British mission system replaced the French one, and no clergymen were encouraged to live on the frontier among the Indians. Protestant missionaries came to Wisconsin much later.

During the years of British rule, Indians saw the trade shift its focus several times. British authorities changed their minds often enough to discourage customers who needed a dependable supply of goods. At times the British allowed a flood of unregulated traders to operate in Wisconsin; at other times, they clamped down on the traffic in furs and made trading more difficult. They began with the idea of regulating the fur trade, but the effect of their policies was to make it more competitive and to force Indians to look for other trade sources. Indians took advantage of whatever was reliable, and they began to deal with traders from the new Spanish settlements at St. Louis. Some of them were even willing to go all the way down the Mississippi to reach familiar French traders in New Orleans. Prairie du Chien, already an important location, became a pivot for control over the Mississippi/Missouri area. The struggle for Prairie du Chien outlasted the British in Wisconsin and was finally settled only after the Louisiana Purchase in 1803.

The Revolutionary War should have ended British concern with Indian affairs in Wisconsin. After 1776, the territory was supposed to belong to the new United States. In practice, however, the British, through rights granted them in the Jay Treaty of 1794, continued to trade there. They secured Indian customers by giving out rich presents every year; and through skillful delaying tactics, they refused to give up their share of the market. Only well after the War of 1812 were British goods and British traders finally excluded from Wisconsin.

Late Historic Period

Archaeological sites between 1760 and about 1820 show greater change from hand-made to European artifacts. Pottery, stone projectile points, copper awls, and stone scrapers are entirely gone. Even bone awls and antler harpoons, which could be made so easily with the new iron knives, are no longer an important part of the tool kits of sewers and fishermen. It is very difficult to tell whether a site of this period belongs to one Indian society rather than another without solid historic identification. The cultural remains are now uniform and mean that people far in the interior had as good an opportunity to get European goods as those closest to the sources of supply. The trade materials were no longer French but British or British-Canadian: factories in Sheffield or the pipe works of Bristol made things that wound up lost or broken in the forests of Wisconsin. Even English china made its way to the frontier, bowls and plates, often fancy with decoration. Most important in terms of what it meant for patterns of wealth and property was Canadian trade silver, found everywhere in the Late Historic Period (see Chapter 5).

As the British period ended, the Wisconsin frontier began to appear more often in books and journals. Firsthand accounts of Wisconsin as it was in the nineteenth century were published, often filled with descriptions of Indians and their ways of life. Official reports were required of military observers, and even traders wrote their memoirs (Gates 1965). By the end of the nineteenth century, serious anthropological work was being done in Wisconsin, and scholarly studies were well under way.

One result of so many descriptions, photographs, and even paintings was that the Indians of Wisconsin have become nineteenth century people. They are frozen into a visual image that was true in the nineteenth century and not before. How they looked and earned their living then, what they thought then, and how they worshipped then all became "traditional." It is as if all Americans when asked what traditional American life was like had to choose the village life and attitudes of 1860. People have lived in Wisconsin for a long time, and many changes have taken place: where should traditional life be located? "Typical" or "traditional" are very slippery terms to apply. "Traditional" sometimes refers to a period when Indian life was unchanging, but no such time ever existed. If "traditional" simply means before Europeans affected Indian life, then the seventeenth and early eighteenth centuries are more appropriate.

Historical Summaries: Original Groups

The first 150 years of European contact involved events that changed where Indians lived and how they managed their affairs. The defeat of the Huron, population losses, and the flood of eastern Indian immigrants were the important events affecting the people already in Wisconsin. The coming of traders, soldiers, missionaries, and government officials provided new agents of change. Through these 150 years, individual Indian groups, reacting to the things that touched them, moved around.

Winnebago

After immigrants came to Wisconsin, the Winnebago were possibly pushed south or were already south of earlier settlements near Green Bay. A few families persisted there into the seventeenth century on the parish lists of St. Francis Xavier (Thwaites 1902). Others pressing on them pushed the main population into the Upper Fox, where they had villages well into the American period. The Upper Fox and the lands on Lake Winnebago are the core of the early Winnebago range. They never moved permanently out of the Transition Zone, but this westward drift included more prairies than before. By the eighteenth century, the Winnebago had reached the Mississippi River, where they claimed an area bounded on the north by the Black River, on the south by the Wisconsin, and on the west by the Mississippi itself (Lurie 1978). They even extended into lands near the St. Croix and Chippewa Rivers, but, caught in the crossfire of other peoples' claims, they never confidently pressed their own.

What moved the Winnebago westward was more than just pressure on them from the north. The resources of the western lands, of the Mississippi River and the rivers entering it from the east, drew them in that direction. Even while they kept villages on Lake Winnebago and the Upper Fox, they hunted westward on the prairies and in the forests in between. At times they even crossed the

Mississippi to hunt bison on the Plains. The Winnebago were hunters in the west and at the same time corn growers in eastern Wisconsin partly because they had horses. With horses, they could hunt far from home and still communicate with their villages.

Another factor moving the Winnebago westward was the convenience of European trade along the Mississippi River. By the early nineteenth century, settlements such as Prairie du Chien were places of rendezvous for traders. The Mississippi trade connection was reliable no matter what governments were in power or what rules were in effect. The great gatherings at Prairie du Chien for trading fairs, for outfitting traders, and even for military action were exciting for people whose ordinary lives involved only their own families.

By the time of the Revolutionary War, the Winnebago were still ranging widely into lands bordering the Mississippi. By 1805 some were at Prairie du Chien, but their major settlement was in seven villages on the Wisconsin River, the Fox, and near Green Bay. Eventually they gave up their claims to the Green Bay area and moved out of the lands where Nicolet first found them.

Menomini

What is known about the earliest Menomini locations is very consistent. They were first recorded in the 1640 account of Nicolet's exploration west. Nicolet did not visit their "Grand Village" on the Menominee River, but he met some of them at the feast given in his honor by the Winnebago. Through known history, Menomini settlement continued to be northeastern Wisconsin. How much of this vast area was actually Menomini land or whether others shared it with them is not clear. Even the size of the Menomini population before war and disease took their toll is unknown.

The coming of eastern Indians in the seventeenth century left the Menomini untouched, mainly because of their location out of the major traffic patterns and in lands less suitable for growing corn. However, the same forces that were pushing and pulling other people westward affected the Menomini, too. Gradually, they moved into Lower Green Bay, attracted by the mission of St. Francis Xavier and access to trade. Menominis were included in missionary lists of Indians in the area, and as others moved on, the Menomini remained. The Lower Fox came to be their principal homeland, and their villages were on the old fields of the Winnebago. The Menomini slowly assumed title to what had been large sections of former Winnebago range, and by the nineteenth century their claims were strong enough that they could offer to give some of the land to others.

At times, Menomini hunting and trading interests took them into the west as far as the Mississippi River. During eighteenth century warfare between the Santee Dakota and the Chippewa, the game-rich lands between the two groups could not be safely hunted by either one of them. French traders who wanted to harvest furs there in spite of the war imported Menominis to hunt and trap for them. Menominis used these debatable lands for many years, and gradually they grew into a right to be there. Sometimes, Menominis wintered in the western forests, freely using birchbark and sugar bushes. Zebulon Pike in his 1805 exploration of the Mississippi met Menominis in a number of places: one group had stayed the winter on the Rum River and was on its way to descend the Mississippi as far as the trading center at Prairie du Chien (D. Jackson 1966). Menominis were moving as individual families far from their original northeast Wisconsin home.

Warfare also took them away from northeastern Wisconsin. In the western lands, they joined with others to fight the Fox, the Illinois, and even the Dakota. During the French and Indian War and Pontiac's War, they went east as mercenaries, and they fought in both the American Revolutionary War and the War of 1812. In the nineteenth century, an attack by the Sauk and Fox on some Menominis near Prairie du Chien and their need for revenge was an early event of the Black Hawk War (D. Jackson 1964).

Santee Dakota

Very early comments on the location of the Santee Dakota appear in Nicolas Perrot's memoir (Blair 1911, I). He had heard of their hunting along the Mississippi far from their homeland, a place of lakes and marshes, 50 leagues square, southwest of the St. Croix River. They did not have European trade goods then and wanted a safe and reliable source. Perrot said they were hunters and wild rice gatherers with a large population. Perrot's most significant comment was that the Dakota were constantly at war and not just with the Chippewa, who were by that time their principal enemies.

By 1663 Radisson visited the "Scioux" in their villages "seven small journeys" from his winter camp on Lake Superior and found they were still without a reliable trade source. The elaborate attention they paid to Radisson's party meant that they knew they needed Frenchmen of their own if they were to get trade goods in any quantity. Radisson was followed by other Frenchmen in 1665-1666, who came from Chequamegon with Ottawa middlemen to set up regular trade. At that point the Santee Dakota were not used to hunting furs for trade and had few prepared (Blair 1911, I). They had not yet become professional fur hunters.

The next major glimpse of the Santee is through the eyes of Father Hennepin, the companion of LaSalle. In the spring of 1680, LaSalle sent Hennepin to explore a possible route to the Mississippi and make trading connections with the Indians he found there. Hennepin and his companion were captured by the Santee somewhere on the Mississippi near the DesMoines River (Hennepin 1966). The Indians were on their way down the river to raid someone else when they fell upon the French instead. They took their captives to their villages, possibly near the mouth of the St. Croix. Brought overland to Dakota country, somewhere west of Lake Superior, the Frenchmen did not enjoy the same hospitality once shown Radisson. After great hardship, they were finally rescued.

When Perrot took possession of Wisconsin in 1689 in the name of France, he specifically included the land of the "Nadoesioux" as part of the claim. From this time on, the Santee Dakota had many more contacts with the French, mainly missionaries and traders. A priest was assigned to them by 1689, and the French trader LeSueur, a witness to Perrot's taking possession, set up operations there also (Wedel 1974). By LeSueur's time, the Santee had 22 or 23 villages on both sides of the Mississippi River north of the Minnesota. However, they claimed the entire Mississippi, at least on the west bank down to the DesMoines River, as their hunting territory.

As time passed, Santee movement included greater and greater land claims to the south. By 1766 everything from Lake Pepin northward to the major villages on the Minnesota was part of their lands. By the end of the eighteenth century, the Minnesota River area was still the major location for their villages, but the southern limit was now the Upper Iowa River. Pike, on his nineteenth century exploration, first met them at the Wisconsin River, near Prairie du Chien, and he stopped at one of their villages on the Upper Iowa where it joins the Mississippi. Each of the bands of the Santee then claimed a sometimes overlapping segment of the Mississippi: one group controlled both sides of the river from the Upper Iowa to a point 35 miles north; a second group lived near the head of Lake Pepin and hunted northward; a third lived on the Mississippi between the Cannon and the Minnesota; and the fourth seems to have been on the Minnesota itself. By 1820, a British trader located them as far south as Prairie du Chien (Gates 1965); and by the end of 1834, their main settlements were north of Winona, Minnesota.

The persistence of the Santee in the Upper Mississippi region came about through long struggle. Century after century they were still there, but many other people tried to claim the same lands. The Santee were a barrier to the westward movement of all the refugees coming from the east. They controlled the Mississippi and the access it gave to the heartland of North America. Many of the refugee groups tried to remove them by force, and almost all Wisconsin Indians were at one time or other involved in fighting with them or raiding their villages. Their major enemies came to be the Chippewa, who eventually were successful in expanding their lands at Santee expense. In their own defense, the Santee were "generally at war with all kinds of nations" (Hennepin 1966: 374), and much of the energy of European and later American officials was spent in making peace between the Santee and their neighbors.

**Historical Summaries: Seventeenth
and Eighteenth Century Refugees**

Huron-Petun-Ottawa

The Huron who fled west away from the Iroquois were joined by a few Petuns and Ottawas. All of these people moved into Wisconsin in small numbers, not as whole tribes but as disorganized groups of refugees. The Huron, whose name means "head of a wild boar," called themselves Wyandot, a name that was seldom used by others. The Petun, or Tobacco Huron, were also known as the Tionontati. The term "Ottawa" (Odawa) means "trader" in Algonquin and came to be applied to a group of people who were important in the French trade.

By 1653 or slightly before, some Hurons and their allies reached the western lake country. The route they took is a very historic one since it was followed by travelers from Michilimackinac over several hundred years. By canoe, the refugees skirted the Garden Peninsula of Michigan and headed across the "Grand Traverse": from Summer Island past St. Martin's and then to Rock, Washington, and Detroit Islands. From there, they crossed through the Porte des Morts Straits and coasted along the east shore of Green Bay to the entrance of the Fox River.

The first Wisconsin stop in the flight of these people took place on the islands at the mouth of Green Bay (R. Mason 1974, 1986). Evidence indicates that they paused to build a large stockade on Rock Island, perhaps intending a long stay. They lived there only briefly, however, long enough to leave behind some Huron-Petun pottery, a few trade goods, and some special tools. Perhaps still fearing Iroquoian attacks, some of them moved to the mainland and eventually went over the Fox-Wisconsin water route to the Mississippi. At first they turned south to take refuge with the Ioway, who lived on the prairies beyond the river. The prairie was not a suitable place so they finally left, going up the Mississippi and hunting along the way.

At this time, hunting on the Mississippi was controlled by the Santee, who used it as their major highway north and south. They captured some of the Huron, evidently thinking they could supply trade goods. The Huron and their allies had lost their own sure trade sources and were now useless as middlemen, a role they had filled so well in the past. The Santee let the refugees settle on Prairie (or Pelee) Island in the Mississippi opposite what is now Red Wing, Minnesota. They did not stay there long although they built a small village within a stockade. Perhaps the island was too small or too close to the Santee with whom they soon quarreled. They then scattered north from Prairie Island in separated communities, but they all came together again to settle at Chequamegon Bay on the south shore of Lake Superior (Blair 1911).

Before the Hurons arrived, Radisson and Grosseilliers spent the winter alone at Chequamegon in 1663. At that time, it seemed simply a stopover point on the way to somewhere else, but it soon became a magnet drawing refugees from all over for trade and also to its mission. For the Hurons and their allies, Chequamegon was an uneasy home. It was too close to the Santee Dakota, and war with them continued off and on for several years. As more and more people came to live there, Chequamegon acquired a cosmopolitan character, and it eventually became identified with the Southwestern Chippewa, who came to regard it as their own.

The struggle with the Santee ended badly for the Hurons and their allies, and by 1671 they left Chequamegon and headed east once more. Some Hurons and Petuns established a village at St. Ignace and were no longer concerned with Wisconsin. In general, then, the role of the Hurons and Petuns in Wisconsin was as refugees who settled briefly here and there, first on Rock Island, then with other Indians near Green Bay, for a time on an island in the Mississippi, and for a few years at Chequamegon Bay. They did not become permanent residents.

The Ottawa continued to play a role in Wisconsin, mainly as middlemen in the trade. In the years between the fall of the Huron and the establishment of the French trade in the western Great Lakes, the Ottawa were important traders themselves. Ottawa families continued to appear on rolls kept by missionaries in Wisconsin, most often in villages of other Algonquin-speaking peoples. Eighteenth century Ottawa artifacts were found on Rock Island, and individual Ottawa were in and out of villages on Green Bay during that time. As late as 1763, Ottawa people were living near Milwaukee in a village that included not only Potawatomi but Sauk as well (Feest and Feest 1978).

Potawatomi

The first recorded location of the Potawatomi was in Nicolet's list of groups living in the "neighborhood" of the Winnebago. Where is not clear, but it was probably not in Wisconsin at all. In the early years of French contact and long before then, the Potawatomi had lived in the Lower Peninsula of Michigan. By very late prehistoric times, some of them were living along the east shore of Lake Michigan (Quimby 1963). How long they had lived there is unknown; originally, they may have been farther east in Michigan, pushed westward by the expansion of the Neutral. In the historic period, after Nicolet's voyage and before the downfall of the Huron, the Potawatomi were pushed north by Neutral raiding into the comparative peace of the land beyond Lake Michigan, where they took refuge for a time at Sault Ste. Marie.

The Sault was not the right environment for the Potawatomi. From the Carolinian deciduous forests and Transition Zone into the Canadian fringes was a leap of more than miles. They told tales of those years when spring was late and winter was very harsh. By 1648, they were on the move south again, across Rock Island and down into the area around Green Bay (Clifton 1977). For a short time they acted as hosts to fleeing Hurons, Petuns, and Ottawas; and all together they gathered themselves to resist the Iroquois. Together they built a stockaded village somewhere along the Lake Michigan shore between the Porte des Morts Passage and what is now Manitowoc. In 1653 they defeated the Iroquois, who besieged them in their village but were finally forced to withdraw. The site of this combined village has not yet been located, but it is of great interest and historical importance: it was called Mechingan, "Great Lake," the name that later became Michigan.

Fresh from their victory over the Iroquois, the Potawatomi enjoyed a new military position. Their settlements dominated the approaches to Wisconsin over the water to the north, and anyone coming across the Grand Traverse into the Door Peninsula had to meet the Potawatomis on their home ground along the lake shore. Eager for trade and anxious to control it, they went to Chequamegon Bay in 1667, as one of many groups then gathering there. The Chequamegon area was, like the Sault, not a welcoming place for them. Thanks to the lake effect, corn could be grown there, but farming could never be as reliable as it was farther south. They urged Perrot to come south with them to Green Bay; and in 1668 he came, setting the stage for French control and paving the way for the mission of St. Francis Xavier. The Potawatomi may have thought that they could control the trade by controlling agents of both church and state, and perhaps at this time they were not mistaken. By the end of the seventeenth century, they had become the dominant people in northeastern Wisconsin and a military force to be reckoned with in the changing fortunes of European powers across the entire lakes area.

A rare glimpse of the Potawatomi in Wisconsin comes from Father Hennepin (Hennepin 1966). In 1679, LaSalle went west with Hennepin and others in his sailing ship, the *Griffon*, to pick up furs gathered over the previous winter by his men. The *Griffon*, the first known sailing vessel in the Great Lakes, followed the northern shore, and came to anchor in a tiny sheltered cove on the southwest shore of Rock Island. A village of Potawatomis was on the island, right on the water routes to the south. No more strategic location could be imagined, and the Potawatomi controlled it. Father Hennepin recorded that the hospitable Potawatomis came out in their canoes, although the water was rough, and carried the party to shore. Rock Island, which once sheltered the Hurons and Petuns, was now a thriving Potawatomi village with corn fields on Washington Island and hunting territories south into Wisconsin.

They continued to spread south and then back east to their old fields in Michigan. By 1704 they were as far east as Detroit and in parts of Indiana. Major Potawatomi settlements were no longer in Wisconsin. In northern Illinois, they occupied lands that once were Illinois country, replacing the Illinois as far south as they could. The southward extension of the Potawatomi had a lot to do with the weakness of the people of Illinois, but it also involved their increasing political skill. Another factor was poor hunting along the shores of Lake Michigan. The game-rich prairies held by the Illinois drew them south and caused them to move on the Illinois and later the Miami. The same motives were behind Potawatomi efforts to acquire hunting lands along the Mississippi River. As early as 1720, they were hunting bison there, and they continued to claim land along the Mississippi into the nineteenth century (Clifton 1977).

In the eighteenth century, the Potawatomi became a mercenary force in the employ of the French. They served in the French and Indian War as well as in other conflicts between the British and the French. They also fought as allies of the Chippewa in their wars against the Santee in western Wisconsin. Nearer home, they joined the French in their campaigns against the Fox. When British and then Americans replaced the French, the Potawatomis fought against them for many years, but most of this frontier warfare was in lands east of Lake Michigan.

Fox

The original homeland of the Fox (also called Outagamie or Mesquakie) is thought to have been east of Lake Michigan, in what is now southeastern Michigan (Wittry 1963). The evidence consists of glimpses of them in early missionary records and Radisson's classification of them as a "northern" group (Adams 1961). They were part of the westward movement after the fall of the Huron, and they came into Wisconsin from the north. The presence of trade and missionaries attracted them first to Chequamegon Bay and eventually to the Wolf River somewhere in Outagamie County. Through time their range extended southward to Lake Butte des Morts and to the

Upper Fox River, where Father Hennepin found them in the late seventeenth century.

Life for the Fox in the eighteenth century was dominated by wars with the French. The original cause of the wars lay in Fox attempts to become middlemen in the trade west to the Santee Dakota. Because the Fox were on the Upper Fox River, they could interfere with French trade over the Fox-Wisconsin route to the Mississippi. They had no old loyalties to French suppliers and began to loot trade flotillas. The French could not tolerate direct attacks on the trade, and they moved against the Fox in force in campaigns that lasted until 1737.

One incident of the French-Fox wars is especially important since it resulted in the identification of a Fox village of 1716. This village, known as the Bell site (Wittry 1963), had evidence of a palisade and many artifacts of the Middle Historic period. Historic documents point to its having been the place where a French and Indian force of over 800 men besieged the Fox, bombarding them with cannon and grenades for three days and nights until the Fox surrendered. The picture of armies moving through Green Bay and up the Lower Fox, winding up on Lake Butte des Morts firing grenades at the main village of the Fox seems unlikely, but the testimony of the spade has even turned up fragments of the grenades fired by the French. Of great interest to Fox history is Bell site pottery, which can now be identified as belonging to the Fox. Some of this pottery has been found in Michigan and is a surer means of finding the early historic Fox than their brief mention in early written records.

Many Wisconsin Indians looked on the Fox as their enemies, but the Fox found help among the Sauk, with whom they became more closely allied. The late eighteenth century Fox, often with Sauks, moved west, first to villages on the Wisconsin and finally in 1776 to the Mississippi at Prairie du Chien (Parker 1976). At this time the Fox were allied to the British, but they traded with Spaniards from St. Louis and even with French sources in the south. Use of the Mississippi drew the Fox into conflict with the Santee, and by the 1780s they had moved north and were trying to get a piece of Santee Dakota hunting land for themselves. By the early nineteenth century, Fox villages were as far south along the Mississippi as the mouth of the Rock River and even into Iowa. By this time, they claimed hunting lands on both sides of the Mississippi from the DesMoines River to the Upper Iowa (D. Jackson 1966).

Sauk

The Sauk and Fox had very similar cultures and probably originally lived very near each other before the seventeenth century movements west. Like the Fox, they appeared first in the western lakes at Chequamegon Bay, brought there by their interest in trade as well as a need to move out of the way of enemies. Their first place of permanent refuge was around Green Bay, where they stayed for many years. Travelers over the Fox-Wisconsin route saw them there well into the eighteenth century. For a long time the Fox River was even known as the "Sacks" River, and early European settlers in the Green Bay area thought the Sauks were the original Indians there.

The ties of the Sauk to the Fox led to their joining in the French-Fox wars but only during the last few years (Calender 1978). Sauk support for the Fox was enough to make them flee west away from the French, and they never again lived on their old fields near Green Bay. For a time, they had villages on the Wisconsin and the Rock, and they finally joined the Fox on the Mississippi. Some of them were living in a joint Fox-Sauk village at Prairie du Chien by the end of the eighteenth century (Parker 1976).

Once on the Mississippi, the Sauk needed land for hunting and for planting crops. Their need for beaver caused them to look northward to the lands of the Santee, where they tried to gain a foothold by joining other refugees in raids. The Mississippi River became a war road for those raiding up the river as well as for those coming from its headwaters. The northward push included many others besides the Sauk, but they all ultimately failed to take any land away from the still powerful Santee Dakota.

The Sauk then turned south and began pushing at the Illinois tribes, whose land and trading connections they hoped to take over. Sauk conflict with the Illinois was helpful to the British, who saw trouble on the Mississippi as the best guarantee that the Santee Dakota would not be able to move freely down the river to contact French or Spanish traders, now as close as St. Louis. The Sauk were so successful in their wars with the Illinois that they pushed them from a part of their lands. Sauk claims in Illinois included most of the east side of the Mississippi south of the Wisconsin River to the mouth of the Illinois.

Kickapoo

Prehistoric Kickapoo may have lived originally in northeastern Ohio (R. Mason 1981) or around the southern shore of Lake Michigan (Silverberg 1957). The Kickapoo first appeared in Wisconsin (or at least in the "neighborhood") in those remarks attributed to Nicolet (Thwaites 1896-1901, vol. 18). At that time they seemed to be southeast of the Winnebago, lending support to the idea that they came into Wisconsin from the south along Lake Michigan.

In Wisconsin, the Kickapoo moved around from place to place. They frequently lived as small groups in the villages of their allies, or they set up independent villages of their own. In the unsettled times of the seventeenth century, the Kickapoo seem to have been more unsettled than anyone else. They moved here and there and never stayed long in any one area. Kickapoo were early visitors to Chequamegon Bay and were reported in the Green Bay area west of the Fox River by about 1667 (Blair 1911), but they did not stay in either place. Their usual location was the Mississippi River and even beyond on the Upper Iowa. The tie of the Kickapoo with the Mississippi was true at least by the time of LaSalle, who said that the Kickapoo language was needed by travelers on the Mississippi from north to south. This was probably before he knew of the Santee position on the river, but it is a sign--assuming that LaSalle was correctly informed--that for a while the Kickapoo were important river people.

The Kickapoo changed their alliances with other Indians and took advantage of whatever their alliances might bring them. They were once allies of the Santee in raiding people even farther north (Blair 1911, I), and they also joined the Chippewa to make war on the Santee. Eventually the Santee Dakota became their usual enemies. After the 1680s, the Kickapoo continued to move around as war and their yearly round of life dictated. They freely used much of southern Wisconsin as hunting territory, westward from the Mississippi and south into Illinois, but they continued to anchor themselves along the Mississippi. By the nineteenth century, they were farther south, and they had by this time given up any claims they had to the upper Mississippi region and Santee Dakota lands. They were moving into country formerly occupied by Illinois tribes.

Mascouten

Earlier in this century, the Mascouten were incorrectly identified as "Prairie Potawatomi" (Skinner 1924), and the confusion caused by this has made it harder to follow their history. During the seventeenth century, the Mascouten as a separate independent group shared the flight of other Algonquin-speakers from their homeland farther east. For the Mascouten, this may have been north central Ohio (R. Mason 1981). From there they moved into Wisconsin from the south and to the Mississippi River and beyond by the end of the century. Radisson visited them at that time and reported them at war with the Santee. Shortly afterwards, they saw an opportunity to trade with the French and moved back into the heart of Wisconsin where they had a "Grand Village" on the Upper Fox River. This late seventeenth century village of mixed Mascouten and Miami was near what is now New Berlin in Green Lake County. It was described as the largest historic village ever known in Wisconsin. Nicolas Perrot spoke of "thousands" of warriors there to greet him, and if at least three or four other people are represented by each warrior, the total population was enormous (Blair 1911). Missionaries, who probably did not actually count everyone, thought the village contained 20,000 "souls." A village of this size poses many problems in terms of hunting territories and food supplies in general. Even if the reported population size was exaggerated by ten thousand and the gathering was only a temporary one, such a large village was unusual during the historic period.

In the eighteenth century, the Mascouten lived in the Mississippi River area and on the prairie forest edges of the Carolinian Zone. They joined in mixed villages, first with one Indian group and then with another. Like the Kickapoo, they tried to push north against the Santee, but their general drift was southward from Prairie du Chien. They came to be enemies of the French, too, attacking them in the north country, and in 1712 they were defeated by French forces. From then on, they fought against anyone allied to French interests and joined in the French-Fox wars on the side of the Fox. By the end of those wars, however, the Mascouten changed their allegiance again and joined the French to fight the Fox (Goddard 1978b). In the years after the defeat of the Fox, many Mascoutens moved east again out of Wisconsin although they seem to have kept an interest in the hunting lands of southern Wisconsin. They were also part of raids against the Illinois people of the border areas. The Mascouten finally became extinct through merger with the Kickapoo in the nineteenth century.

Miami

The Miami were closely allied to the Mascouten and the Kickapoo during their years in Wisconsin, but they came from different cultural roots. They may have had the Oneota-like traditions of northeast Illinois and Indiana as ancestors (Brose 1978).

When they came as refugees into Wisconsin, the Miami moved into the southern part of the state and crossed it to the Mississippi. Perhaps for a time they even went beyond it into the lands of the Ioway. The explorer Joliet produced a map that put one of the sub-groups of the Miami on the west bank of the Mississippi south of the Wisconsin River in 1674 (Mott 1938). They fled, joined by some Illinois, across the "great river" just before Joliet found them there. Soon after, they left Iowa to settle on the Upper Fox, including in the famous "Grand Village" with the Mascouten. Nicolas Perrot persuaded some of them to follow him back again to the Mississippi River to help him during Santee raids from the north (Silverberg 1957). The Miami became one more on the list of enemies of the Santee, as they joined with Foxes, Mascoutens, and Kickapoos in raids up the river. By the end of the seventeenth century, the Miami were pushed east and southeast by the reactions of the Santee, and they gradually moved out of Wisconsin south into the Wabash area of Illinois.

The Miami and the other Algonquin-speaking Sauk, Fox, Kickapoo, and Mascouten, appear in seventeenth and eighteenth century Wisconsin in so many places that their movements are hard to keep track of. They were responding to several factors that should be kept in mind when trying to follow where they were going. First is the fact that they were displaced people, fleeing from enemies into a land where they had to push others in order to make room for themselves. The changing alliances and frequent quarrels among them reflect this instability. The presence of mixed villages, of bits and pieces of larger societies joining briefly together, is another sign of troubled times. A second factor is the French trade. All of them were anxious to have a reliable source and were wiling to travel halfway across Wisconsin on the mere chance of it being available. And they all tried in time-honored fashion to control the trade going to others. Another factor was the presence of the Santee Dakota. These powerful people resisted pressure put on them by the refugees and became the common enemy. Miami, Sauk, Fox, Kickapoo, and Mascouten were all caught in a triangle of difficulties: the Iroquois were behind them and the Santee in front of them; and they all wanted French trade.

Chippewa

The people who came to be known as Chippewa (or, in Canada, Ojibwa) began as small scattered bands with a similar language and culture. In the early French sources these groups have names such as Amikwe, Saulteur, and Outchibou; and in the seventeenth century they came to be regarded as a distinct people. Originally they lived north of Lake Superior and eastward into the country north of Lake Huron. When they emerged in historic records, they were in the midst of a general westward and southward motion.

The earliest location for them is at their fishing place at Sault Ste. Marie in the middle of the seventeenth century (Hickerson 1970), and they continued to be closely associated with that area. It was their base of operations for a westward drift along the south shore of Lake Superior to Chequamegon, where they had a settlement by 1695. At first, the Chippewa had an alliance with the Santee Dakota, but the later histories of both involved unending raids and counterraids. War between them was part of a long process of displacement that began as the Chippewa moved west from Sault Ste. Marie.

The reasons why the Chippewa expanded into the land west of the Sault are only partly explained by pressure from the rear. The Chippewa were hunters and gatherers and also farmers where they could grow corn. They depended on broad zones of hunting lands, and as they were more deeply involved in trade, their needs increased. The land north and east of the Sault was "hunted out," but the rich woodlands south and west of Lake Superior were apparently open to anyone. The presence of French missionaries and traders at Chequamegon also served to attract them in that direction. At first, the Santee, whose hunting lands were now being used by the Chippewa, had been persuaded to tolerate their presence there. The peace held only by fits and starts. By 1695 the French sent their agents to try to keep war from breaking out; in terms of peaceful trade, it was clearly in their interest to try to reach an understanding between the two groups. By the early part of the eighteenth century, all such attempts had failed. The Santee, weakened by raids from northern people, were seen by the Chippewa as ready to be pushed from the hunting lands of northern Minnesota and western Wisconsin. The long wars that followed put pressures on the Santee that were felt even in their heartland. By 1766, Chippewas had reached the Mississippi River as far south as the mouth of the Chippewa River, and they were raiding in the Lake Pepin area. Fear of war parties moving on the river kept the Mississippi north of the Chippewa River in a state of alarm.

By the beginning of the nineteenth century, the Chippewa were hunting as far as the headwaters of the Mississippi and controlled its eastern banks at least as far south as the Chippewa River. Raids by the Santee did not stop, and a broad area across Wisconsin and Minnesota became a "debatable zone" between them (Hickerson 1970). Attempts by the Santee to meet this pressure failed, and they were pushed out of Wisconsin. The Mississippi River then became a boundary between hostile groups, each struggling for what had been the hunting lands of the Santee Dakota. Warfare between these two is the most important fact of Indian political life in the eighteenth century and affected all other Wisconsin people, Indian and non-Indian alike.

Illinois

Movement into Wisconsin by refugee groups was made easier by the weakness of the seventeenth century Winnebago and also by the decline in the once powerful tribes of Illinois. These people lived near the Illinois River and east of the Mississippi. In view of their adaptation to the Carolinian Zone, they moved freely into what is now southern Wisconsin, at least for hunting. The most northerly group, the Peoria, were most likely the people whose war with the Winnebago after 1634 is often blamed for some of the Winnebago population decline.

The Illinois were mentioned in the French sources as one of the people in the famous "neighborhood" of the Winnebago, and they were involved in the fur trade very early. Many French accounts report meeting them on the move for trade in Wisconsin. Marquette saw some of them between Green Bay and Chicago in 1674 actually carrying European goods to exchange for furs with other Indians;

they had already become middlemen to people farther south. Even earlier they had been all the way north to Chequamegon Bay and French trade sources there. After that, the missionary at St. Francis Xavier mentioned Illinois Indians living in a joint village with Miamis in the woods west of the mission (Thwaites 1896-1901, vol. 58). The choice of this location must have depended on the presence of French traders at Green Bay at that time.

In the late seventeenth century, the Illinois joined the Miami and other Indians in raiding the Santee, using the Mississippi as their route north. The Santee attacked Illinois villages in the south in retaliation. Well into the eighteenth century, the Santee were the main enemies of the Illinois, but by then they were also at war with the Sauk, Potawatomi, Kickapoo, Mascouten, and Fox. The Illinois could not withstand so many, and their fertile country was opened to the expansion of others, most of whom then claimed large parts of the Mississippi drainage in Illinois as their traditional homelands. The surviving Illinois had no choice but to move south, leaving their land to settle somewhere else.

Summary

When Europeans came to North America, the Indians living in Wisconsin included only Winnebago, Menomini, and Santee Dakota. Their cultures were end products of ancient traditions in the western lakes country, and for a while the people were shielded from the full impact of European contact by their distance from the east coast and the Indians in between. European trade had its effects on Wisconsin as eastern people looked for new sources for furs and began to move against their neighbors. Refugees from troubled areas moved to Wisconsin: Potawatomi, Huron-Petun-Ottawa, Sauk, Fox, Mascouten, Miami, and others. People originally north and east of Wisconsin came south to hunt in beaver and deer rich woodlands. In general, their movement was west, bringing many of them eventually up against the Mississippi River. The original people of the area became part of a large new population.

During the seventeenth and eighteenth centuries, refugee people experienced many changes as they tried to find places where trade, hunting, and ordinary life could be carried out. Often these things could be managed only at someone else's expense, and intense rivalry was the result. Stability in human affairs became the matter of a few years, not the normal condition of life. Competing

European powers and their attempts to control Indian societies through trade, use of force, or bribery changed political alignments and allowed no lasting balance of power to emerge. Indians found themselves on one side or another and were often part of military expeditions that had become full-scale wars.

Part II: Wisconsin Indian Life

CHAPTER 4
Ways of Making a Living

Wisconsin Indians lived by hunting, gathering, and gardening. No strict line can be drawn between those who hunted and gathered and those who raised crops: the over-all picture was more a range from those who were more likely to grow their own food to those who were more likely to hunt and gather. From one extreme to the other, there was every shade in between.

What could be grown, gathered, or hunted depended on the resources of the different biotic zones. These zones do not have sharp boundaries: the Canadian forest does not end abruptly in a line across the state. It grades slowly through a broad, irregular Transition Zone into a Carolinian province that contains elements of the more southern prairies. The landscape is a mosaic of possibilities, allowing farming in times and places where it ordinarily might not have been possible and rich hunting and gathering by people whose crops were very important. Farming people, when they had the choice, preferred the Carolinian or Transition Zones and were uneasy transplants into northern areas, but hunters and gatherers adapted well to all parts of the state.

As far as different groups are concerned, the *general* division of lifeways includes Santee Dakota, Menomini, and some Chippewa as the major hunters and gatherers. All of them lived in the Canadian Zone, where hunting and gathering had to be the mainstay of life. The lake effect near Lake Superior made it possible for some Chippewa to garden, but it was not enough of an effect to let them plant extensively. Radisson was given some corn by the Santee when he was living on Lake Superior in 1663 although by 1670 the *Jesuit Relations* describe the Santee as without any horticulture at all (Thwaites 1896-1901, vol. 20). By the nineteenth century, the Santee had fields of corn and beans in their villages, perhaps because they were then living farther south. The name "Menomini" means "wild rice people," and it suggests that they were living as hunters and gatherers in the sixteenth century. As they moved into the Lower Fox, they entered land where corn would grow well and wild rice was less plentiful. They added horticulture to their older patterns, and their corn fields became a familiar sight in the nineteenth century.

Gardening people include Winnebago, Miami, Illinois, Potawatomi, Fox, Sauk, Kickapoo, Huron, Petun, Ottawa, and Mascouten. A few of these were more intensive farmers than the others. Winnebago, Illinois, and Miami had the reputations of growing more and planting larger fields. In good places, the Potawatomi also grew impressive corn crops to sell to other Indians and to Europeans. The Hurons and Petuns had been expert farmers back in Ontario, but during their short stay in Wisconsin, they never grew enough to supply corn to others as they once did in Canada. Sauk, Fox, and Kickapoo were not famous for their gardens, but their unsettled lives in historic times may have made horticulture more difficult for them. As a general rule, gardening became more and more important the farther south people lived. A major reason behind the effort to push aside the Illinois tribes in the eighteenth century came from an understanding of how good their lands were for farming.

Hunting and Gathering

Hunting and gathering means living on what nature provides. As a lifeway, it is not a matter of simply collecting what falls: it requires skill, planning, and a good knowledge of the land and what it produces. Hunting and gathering groups ordinarily have to be nomadic: they have to go to food supplies as they ripen or can be caught. They do not wander around looking for a stray berry or wild plum; they know when things are going to be ready in a territory they know well.

Hunting and gathering usually works best in large areas with few people. Most hunting and gathering groups are smaller than farming villages, and when the land can support people by both techniques, hunting and gathering is usually replaced by crop growing. Once people come to depend on gardening for a living, they do not ordinarily go back to hunting and gathering again. The population supported by farming becomes too large to be fed by hunting and gathering alone on the same land.

All of Wisconsin's most ancient Indians were hunters and gatherers. The Paleo-Indians, Archaic peoples, and all of the Early and Middle Woodland Indians gathered the resources of land, air, and water. These ancient communities were small, scattered, and conservative. They changed slowly with their numbers keeping pace with what the land had to offer, given the tools they had to work with. The coming of farming profoundly affected them, and those that did not adopt the new way of life were people who lived in the Canadian Zone; there the shortness of the growing season made their choice of lifeway for them. Only in the historic period, when populations seem larger, is there evidence that the northern people were trying to grow crops. Perhaps they had received corn in trade and were trying their hand at it; nowhere in the north could it become a reliable crop.

The best descriptions of hunting and gathering are from the earliest part of the historic period, but even then it had been changed by the fur trade. Hunting for profit hangs over any understanding of what hunting and gathering might have been before the fur trade began. Almost all the accounts that have survived treat fur hunting as if it had always been a major part of life. No doubt it always a *part* of Indian life, but in the fur trading period, it dominated almost everything else. In addition to fur hunting, the yearly hunting and gathering cycle included fishing, hunting, fowling, wild rice collecting, using maple sap, nutting, and gathering wild plants. Most of these were important in prehistory as well.

Fishing

Fishing on Lake Michigan and Lake Superior was productive and very reliable from one season to the next (Cleland 1982). Europeans commented on fishing and Indian dependence on it as early as the days of Champlain, and year in and year out, it continued to be a major source of food. The contribution fishing made to the food supply and its steady reliability are important factors explaining how some Indian societies survived the ups and downs of the fur trade. As long as fishing in the Great Lakes and inland waterways was possible, people could continue to feed themselves no matter what happened to the price of furs.

The really productive parts of the lakes are the south shore of Lake Superior eastward from the Keewenaw Peninsula and the northern shoulder of Lake Michigan, including most of Green Bay. Within this natural fishery, fish were caught in great numbers at certain seasons. Some groups, the Chippewa, for example, could support large populations and villages in one place during fish runs. The Menomini Grand Village on the Menominee River was made possible by rich fishing on Green Bay. Other Indians used fish as much as they could, and their reliance on them sometimes reached a point as great as the Chippewa and Menomini.

The nature of the lakes has a lot to do with the way Indians fished. Both Lake Michigan and Lake Superior are cold, deep lakes; and, in general, fish are scarce. They have to hunt around for their food, and for most of the year they are scattered throughout the waters. The lakes are not easy places for fishermen to work in. The waters are very cold, liable to be rough or stormy; and for as much as three or four months of the year, the lakes are covered with ice. Fish could be taken in quantity only during breeding seasons, but at those times, they were present in truly unlimited numbers. They gathered near the shore in crowded spawning grounds, and Indian fishermen could harvest as many as they wanted, depending on their equipment and their persistence.

Luckily, the fish did not all spawn at once. In the spring, the shallow bays along the shores were filled with breeding sturgeon, white and red suckers, catfish, bullheads, perch, pike, and bass. These spring fish runs came at just the right time: people were weakened coming out of winter, and the fish were an immediate relief. From wherever they had spent the winter, people came to the spring spawning grounds to gather fish. The spring runs did not last long, but a lot of fish were there to be caught. The great problem with the catch, of course, was the coming of summer: spring fish could not be preserved. Drying and smoking were not enough to save fish over the warm weather without spoiling, and the spring fish had to be eaten as they were caught. By the end of the spring runs, though, people left the fishing grounds well-nourished and ready for what the summer might bring.

The fall spawning fish were mainly lake trout and whitefish. They need cold water to start breeding, and the season itself lasts from September through December. Indians coming back to the lakes in the fall had a long time to fish, and the danger of summer heat spoiling what they had caught was behind them. The fall spawning fish were more nutritious, too; their calorie count was twice that of the spring spawners since they had body fat built up for the coming cold of winter.

Many people came together to fish at one time during the fall runs. These groups often included a set of sisters, for much of the work was done by women. Paintings or drawings of places such as Sault Ste. Marie usually show men standing upright in canoes netting fish, but the more invisible labor of women made up the fishing industry. Making and caring for nets and setting them fell to women. Once the catch was on shore, all the work was done by mothers, wives, and sisters, not by the men in the canoes. Processing fish involved cleaning, gutting, and putting away for the future. Freezing, drying, and smoking were all important techniques used to save some of the fall catch for a snowy day in January.

The fish themselves were admired by European writers. Whitefish was a "most excellent" fish in the words of one missionary, so much so "that it furnishes food, almost by itself, to the greater part of all these people" (Kinietz 1940: 323). "Better fish cannot be eaten," stated another, and it was "very nourishing" (Blair, 1911, I: 276). The flavor of whitefish is "above all comparison whatever" (Quaife 1921: 56), and a barely literate trader of the eighteenth century called it an "Exquisseat fish" (Gates 1965: 32). Early comments made about Great Lakes Indian life indicate beyond question that the main protein source for those in reach of the lake shores was fish, not meat.

Many techniques were used to catch fish. Both men and women used hooks and lines, generally with barbless hooks or fish gorges attached to hand held lines. Fish gorges are little rods pointed on both ends with a line attached to the middle; when a baited gorge is swallowed by a fish, it traps him as effectively as a hook. Archaeological evidence for hooks and gorges goes back to Old Copper, when the hooks were made of copper, to the more recent versions in bone or shell on Oneota sites. Historic peoples used iron hooks, which gave them the added advantage of barbs. Spear fishing was done both from the shore and from canoes and even through the ice in winter. The heavy equipment of Old Copper included large gaffs; and other prehistoric complexes have some sort of spearpoint or, later, harpoon for landing sturgeon. European trade added stout iron harpoons to the fishing kit, and iron knives were used to make harpoon heads from bone or antler. A harpoon was a very long spear with a line tied to the detachable harpoon head. When the harpoon hit a fish, the spear section floated free to the surface leaving the harpoon head in the fish and the line in the hands of the fisherman. He could then pull it in by means of the line.

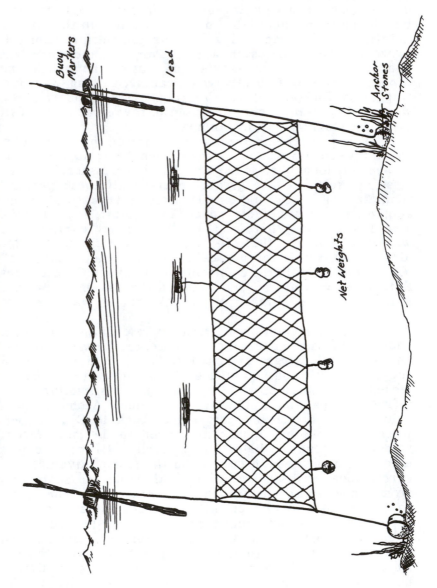

Gill net (courtesy of Charles E. Cleland, permission of *American Antiquity*).

Netting was more important than any other technique for catching fish. The early historic descriptions mention nets of many kinds, from dip nets all the way to simple seines. The famous description of Chippewa catching fish from their canoes at the Sault (Kinietz 1940) involves small dip nets on the end of poles. Dipping fish during the fall runs might produce 500 for a few hours' work. Using dip nets has become so famous that it overshadows the importance of seines and gill nets. These nets were used in the water off-shore and collected their fish with less fanfare but with more fish for the amount of work. Seines are long nets with very fine mesh attached to poles on either end and weighted along the bottom with netsinkers. A seine is used to surround fish in shallow water and pull them to shore where they can be picked up by hand or speared. It will only work when the net is handled well enough to prevent the fish from slipping under it and getting away. Seines have to be tended constantly during use and work well only in shallow water. The gill net, because it can stand by itself and can be used in any depth, is a great improvement. Gill nets consist of large-meshed nets attached to poles held vertically in place underwater by anchor stones on the bottom edges and by floats on the top. They function, as the name implies, by entangling fish by their gills. No one knows exactly when seines or gill nets were first used in North America, but hundreds of netsinkers in Middle Woodland sites in Wisconsin show that some kind of nets had become part of fishing by then.

Fishing in the productive fisheries of Lake Michigan and Lake Superior had many benefits for people of the Canadian Zone. With local exceptions, the Canadian forests are not good places to hunt and gather, and fish made the difference. This is especially true when winter food sources are considered. Fish, because they could be kept for months, helped people face the harsh Wisconsin winter with more confidence. Larger groups of people gathered along the shores to fish, and new kinds of organization came into being as new kinds of working groups operated. Long underestimated as a food source for northern people, fish and fishing had effects beyond subsistence.

Hunting

Fishing depended on access to water, but hunting was universal. For hunters and gatherers, it was an activity carried on most intensively at certain seasons and less intensively at others. A common pattern was to scatter in winter hunting territories. The groups of people who had been together at the fisheries separated to live a more solitary life during winter, the time of the most anxiety over food supplies: large groups had to break up in order to survive. Hunting success was often related directly to how well hunters could be scattered over as wide a territory as possible.

In general, the Canadian forest had few edible game animals. Nicolas Perrot described it as the "most sterile region in the world" (Blair 1911, I: 103). Some of the animals were moose, woodland caribou, lynx, porcupine, bear, and snowshoe hare (Cleland 1966). A number of southern species also ranged northward: deer, elk, bison, beaver, and muskrat. The question is, of course, which were plentiful enough to be hunted on a regular basis? The answer lies partly in their habits and in their numbers. A bear, for example, produces a lot of meat, but it is not a herd animal and is unreliable as a steady source of food once one or two are taken in a given area. The solitary moose and more gregarious woodland caribou are also good meat sources if they can be caught in number. The mature northern forest does not have enough of an understory to feed many browsers, grazers, or the animals that live on them.

Hunters and gatherers of the Canadian Zone could not hunt large numbers of deer either. Deer were never plentiful there: deer are animals of open forests where there are marshes, swamps, and other small habitat areas. What deer there were in the northern forests were rapidly cleaned out by human hunters and other animals who could catch them in their winter "yards" when they were least able to escape. Deer, never very common in the great virgin forests of the north, became less and less a source of food for people living there.

The northern people most directly affected by the low deer population were the Chippewa, pressing west and south from the shore of Lake Superior. What drew them in that direction was the excellent deer country in the Transition Zone (Hickerson 1970). This mixed forest/parkland area attracted hunters and gatherers who had exhausted stores of their fall fish runs. The only problem in Chippewa use of this zone was that the Santee, too, relied on it for deer meat over the winter, and they could not afford to allow free access to others. The fact that both groups came to regard it as a "debatable zone" meant that neither one could use it freely and in this way prevented over-use of the supply.

Techniques for hunting varied, depending on how much impact guns had made on peoples' habits. For animals such as bison, the bow and arrow continued to be preferred: its head was so "hard" as to make it effectively "bullet-proof" and, besides, bows and arrows were less likely to stampede herds. Beaver were snared or speared, often after wrecking dams and draining the water to force the animals to come out to fix the breaks. Moose were hunted with bow and arrow or with guns, but sometimes they were run down by hunters on snowshoes in deep snow and speared. Perrot thought that elk might be taken only with snares, but other sources say that elk, too, could be hunted in deep snows with spears. For many hunters, snow was a great help in the winter, and in years when little snow fell, hunting was more difficult. Deer were stalked and shot with bow and arrow or gun, and small mammals such as raccoon or rabbit were taken in the same way. Bear hunting was done in winter when the bears were still fat and other game was lean. Often it meant waking up a sleeping bear from its den and shooting it with guns or bow and arrow as it emerged. Many Indian hunters used dogs to help them. Dogs had to be fed, but they were a calorie bank against famine since they could be eaten if other resources failed.

When it came into camp, meat was treated in many ways. Much of it was braised in stews or soups with other things; some meat was roasted in pits with hot stones, and as much was preserved as possible. Meat could be cut into slices, hung near a fire, smoke-dried, and stored in birch-bark boxes. Sometimes dried meat was pounded with dried blueberries to make a kind of pemmican, and sometimes it was sealed in skin containers with oil made from rendered bear fat. Smoke-drying preserved meat as long as the weather was cold, and smoke-dried meat sealed in oil or tallow would keep even longer.

Meat was not the only thing that came from hunting. Skins, furs, sinews, bones, and antlers were important bonuses when an animal was killed. Once people became fur hunters, though, fewer things were saved to use: skin clothing was replaced by cloth, thread took the place of sinew for most uses, and the things made of bone and antler were bought ready-made of other materials. Hunting became more efficient through the use of guns and traps, but it also became more wasteful as once useful things were no longer kept.

Bird hunting

Evidence for hunting birds goes back into Archaic hunting and gathering sites in southern Wisconsin. At one rockshelter, for example, bones of passenger pigeons, ruffed grouse, turkeys, wood ducks, Canada geese, and mallards give some idea of the range of birds hunted by prehistoric Indians. Since Wisconsin is under the flyways of many migratory birds, it is likely that they could be caught in large numbers during migration. Some sites with the bones of many kinds of ducks confirm hunting at those times. Some sites, at spring or fall fishing spots, however, show little evidence of migrating birds, perhaps because fishing was much more important there.

It is hard to measure how much birds contributed to the diet. Lists of animals from archaeological sites (Cleland 1966) show many different kinds of birds whose bones wound up in the trash, but the percentage of meat from birds is usually very small: it never reaches what comes from large animals such as deer or elk. A duck, for example, looks very impressive, feathers and all, but it may produce less than a pound of meat. When birds could be caught in large numbers, they added to the diet, but considering the energy spent in hunting compared to what came from it, a hunter might be wiser to look for bigger game.

Historic records describe a number of ways to catch birds. Passenger pigeons were taken in large, bag-shaped nets, sometimes 500 at a time. Birds were netted as they came to eat wild rice. The nets were stretched in open water near the rice patches, and they entangled the birds, making it easy for someone in a canoe to pick them up. Other ways of catching birds included snaring, and, of course, bow and arrow. In some places, birds were hunted by the hundreds to sell to Europeans.

Birds were killed for other reasons besides food. Feathers were an important part of dress, and many birds were hunted for their feathers alone: woodpeckers, blue jays, eagles. Religious reasons may explain why some birds were hunted. Loons and eagles, for example, had ceremonial meaning for many people. The long hollow wing bones of birds were also used for flutes, whistles, or even beads.

Wild rice

Wisconsin and parts of the neighboring states and provinces of Canada have been called the "Wild Rice Area" (Kroeber 1953). In this region, wild rice was much like a domesticated grain crop: nutritious, productive, and able to be stored for a long time. Hunters and gatherers who had access to wild rice were sometimes as well off as many gardeners at harvest time: they had a crop provided by nature that could last through winter. Wild rice may have become an important food in this area because other plant foods were scarce. Having wild rice growing in a given place is no guarantee that people would use it for food. It grows all over eastern North America, but only in the "Wild Rice Area" was it important.

Wild rice, in spite of its name, is a kind of grass, and it is unrelated to the domestic forms of rice (Jenks 1900). It has some special needs: it has to grow in still waters with muddy or sandy bottoms. Given the many clear lakes and slowly moving streams in Wisconsin, wild rice was plentiful. It used to choke parts of the Upper Fox, encouraged by the gentle current, but it never grew well in the Lower Fox with its quickly moving water. As an annual plant, it does not persist if the harvesting takes too many seeds; not enough may be left to provide next year's crop. Some people were aware of this and sowed wild rice in good spots; others let nature take its course and learned to put up with the occasional years of low supplies.

Surviving descriptions of early historic wild rice beds are very impressive. They speak of stretches of miles of rice filling lakes and streams; in places it was so thick that even canoes could not be paddled through, only pulled along by tugging at the rice plants. The plants themselves sometimes rose in the water up to 12 feet high and with their nodding heads and fresh green leaves presented an unforgettable sight, even to those for whom the rice was a common part of the landscape.

Harvesting took place before the grains matured and fell off the heads. In late August or early September, women went out to the rice beds and tied the standing stalks into bunches. Tying the stalks made it harder for birds to get at the ripening grain, and it helped in the harvesting. It may also have been a way of claiming rights to certain rice beds and keeping more than one family from trying to harvest the same crop. Shortly after the tying, two people (nearly always women in the early accounts) went out in a canoe, one to paddle and the other to pull the stalks in and beat on the heads. The grains fell into the canoe, which had been lined with a mat or blanket to receive them.

Since the rice was gathered before it was mature, it had to be ripened or "cured" by sun drying, smoking, parching, or a combination of the three. Sun-dried rice was left in the full sun until it was dry. Smoking was done by putting the rice on a low platform covered with mats and building a slow fire underneath to heat it until the rice was dry. Both sun-dried and smoked rice then had to be parched. In the historic period, parching was done in trade kettles, and pottery probably served the same purpose earlier. Rice parched without first being dried popped as it was parched.

Threshing was done by men, often in holes in the ground. The holes, lined with skins or blankets, were filled with grain, and men with moccasinned feet stamped on it until the hulls came off and it was ready for winnowing. Women tossed it on blankets or birchbark trays and let the light husks blow away in the breeze. After this long process, wild rice was ready to be stored in bags or in birchbark boxes, often in special pits in the ground.

How much wild rice could be harvested depended on many factors. People had to compete for it with birds, and early frost or hail might ruin the crop in some places. Local failures meant that other rice beds had to be found. Ownership of the rice was not ownership of the stretch of shoreland where the rice grew but of the crop at the time it was tied. People with a poor crop or no crop at all near their own camps had to go where they could find rice not already claimed. Disputes must have arisen, especially as wild rice turned into a cash crop, but the system, common among hunters and gatherers, gave greater benefit to more people than individual ownership of the wild rice beds.

The amount of wild rice gathered by Indians changed from year to year, and it is hard to estimate how much they usually ate. There was so much of it available that they could have used it for food during most of the year, storing it away for winter. However, few Indians relied on it as a year-round food. Perhaps processing it was too much trouble when more easily prepared foods could be found. Perrot thought that the rice was too heavy to carry around for people who moved a great deal, and having stored rice hidden somewhere would mean long trips back and forth to get it (Blair 1911, I). As wild rice became part of commercial trade, it was gathered in larger quantities, and many Indians supplied it to fur traders or other Indians. Production apparently could be very easily increased once there was a reason for doing it.

Wild rice was eaten in many ways. Radisson had it among the Santee cooked like oatmeal, thrown into hot water and boiled in a pot. Most other uses of wild rice meant simmering it in soups or stews or even mixing the cooked rice with dried berries. Some wild rice was even eaten dry, probably the parched and popped rice.

Next to nothing is known about wild rice through archaeology. Only a few examples have been found in Great Lakes sites, perhaps because the seeds are so fragile. The earliest excavated wild rice comes from a Late Archaic cremation burial in northwestern Michigan (Ford and Brose 1975). Other ancient wild rice has come from a Wisconsin rock shelter and a late historic Winnebago site. A wild rice processing area in Minnesota included prehistoric threshing pits; the presence of these special holes may be as sure a way of identifying wild rice users as the grains themselves (Johnson 1969).

Maple Sugar

Maple sugar and maple syrup are high on the list of things added to world culture by American Indians, but neither seems to have been important before European trade. There are no references to maple sugaring in the early accounts nor are maple sugar or maple syrup described by the early explorers or missionaries (C. Mason 1985). The only use for maple sap in these sources is as a famine food in the early spring when nothing else was available (Keesing 1939).

By the nineteenth century, the equipment used was almost all European in origin: from the axes used to cut the trees to the kettles used to boil the sap down. Even the shoulder yokes for carrying buckets of sap from the trees to the boilers were standard European form. Only the birchbark sap collectors, trays, and the bark boxes used to store the sugar were of local origin.

The big expansion in maple sugar production was in the eighteenth century. Maple sugar camps became common during the springtime, and preparing maple sugar was part of the yearly gathering round. The Indians did not think of maple sugar as candy or as a syrup topping for pancakes or ice cream. Once they had the tools to make it in quantity, they used it as a dietary staple: it was a food eaten as the main part of the diet during April at the rate of about two pounds per person per day (Quimby 1966). At other times when it was less plentiful, maple sugar was a seasoning, eaten with everything from fish to wild rice. In some respects, it was treated very much like salt today, as a universal condiment. However, its real importance was as something that could be sold or traded to others.

Processing maple sap was different from most wild food gathering. The maple trees, the "sugar bushes," were permanent fixtures. In many respects they were like orchards, and as larger numbers of people came to use them, customary ownership became more and more common. As maple sugar and syrup grew in importance in the trade, rights to the maple groves became important, too. Among the Menomini in the nineteenth century, such rights came to belong to women and were handed down to their daughters.

Processing maple sap into sugar and syrup has been described many times (Hoffman 1896). Early in the spring, usually when there was still snow on the ground, people would move to the sugar bushes and set up camp to remain there for the month of the sap run. If birchbark dishes and buckets had not been saved from the year before, new ones had to be prepared. The first step in making sugar consisted of slashing the trees with an axe; a small piece of wood was wedged in the cuts to guide the sap as it dripped into containers on the ground. As they filled, they were emptied into larger buckets, which were carried by shoulder yokes to the boilers. The boilers, sometimes up to a dozen in one camp, were large kettles, each of which could hold up to 30 gallons at once. The sap was boiled slowly until it began to granulate, and then it was poured into wooden troughs and worked until it was fully converted into sugar. It is like making fudge--a good eye and an experienced hand has to judge when each step must be taken. The cooled sugar was stored in birchbark boxes, some holding up to 50 pounds. Maple sugar was also molded in small boxes, the forerunners of modern molds, making little "sugar cakes."

Sugaring time was surrounded by a spirit of fun, of celebration and pleasure as the end of winter. Yet, people worked long hard hours for days and nights on end. Much of the work fell to women, who prepared the birchbark boxes, hundreds and hundreds of them, and supervised the boiling. They also gathered the sap and stood over the kettles watching for the proper point for pouring. Men had the tiresome job of gathering firewood for the boiling, a task that became more difficult as nearby supplies were used up. Estimates of wood used in one eighteenth century sugar camp run as high as thirty cords to keep the kettles boiling day and night for the month of sugaring (Quimby 1966).

Other gathering

Wild foods include edible fruits, nuts, seeds, roots, and mushrooms (Yarnell 1964). However, the number of edible plants in the Canadian Zone is small compared to the wild resources of land to the south: even nuts were not plentiful. Many kinds of berries were important wild foods. They were welcome in their season, and many were dried and stored for the winter. The list includes some that are still common in Wisconsin: strawberries, huckleberries, raspberries, blueberries, blackberries, dewberries, cranberries, serviceberries, and grapes. The quantity of blueberries gathered from patches in the north brought people to camp there for long periods when berry drying was an everyday activity. In the late nineteenth century, berries became another cash crop, and they were picked for sale to others. Many berries used by Indians in small quantities include some not usually considered as foods today: holly berries, bunchberries, the berries from false Solomon's seal, and bearberries.

In the spring, hunters and gatherers were eager for greens. Early sprouting green plants were added to the soup kettle: fiddleheads, marsh marigold leaves, fresh milkweed shoots, wood sorrel, and the sprouts of the bracken fern. The list of useful greens is long, but the contribution of any one of them to the diet was small. They were welcome in the spring, adding needed vitamins and minerals, but they were not staples; people cannot live on greens alone, even for a few weeks.

Throughout summer and often into fall and winter, roots and bulbs provided a source of food when other things were scarce. The roots of lilies, spring beauties, jack-in-the-pulpit, cow parsnips, Virginia waterleaf, and American lotus provided food that could be eaten then or dried and kept for later. Such things as duck potatoes were often stolen from the stores of thrifty muskrats, and groundnut tubers were collected in as large quantities as possible. The bulbs of wild leeks and onions added their fragrance to soups and stews although Nicolas Perrot thought them dangerous to the digestion.

Hickory nuts, butternuts, and hazelnuts were the most important nuts in the Canadian Zone. They could be stored in the shell for a long time but they had to be cracked and picked before being eaten. Some of them were crushed and boiled to extract their oils. The acorns of burr oaks, red oaks, and white oaks needed even more processing than other nuts since they contain bitter tannins. In Wisconsin, shelled acorns were leached of tannin by soaking them whole in hot lye water made from wood ashes. Sometimes sweeter acorns could be dry roasted with ashes. Early French explorers thought acorns fit for human food only in famines, but Indians regarded them as an important wild crop.

Perrot added a final word on the diet of hunters and gatherers (Blair 1911, I). He noted, as had many others, that at times during the year, hunters and gatherers could not survive without the lichens growing on the rocks of the northern woods. Sometimes not all of their stored food lasted, and lichens and mosses became starvation foods. The northern zone, thanks to its short growing season, did not have many plants for people to eat over a difficult winter.

In general, Indians used wild plants in a predictable yearly round. In early spring they ate tubers and sometimes the inner barks of trees. As spring came, they added greens, and by early summer, they picked berries. By high summer, berries were the main plant food. In late summer, the first nuts and seeds were ready; and as early fall approached, fewer berries and more nuts were added to the diet. Once again in the fall, roots became important. During winter, people ate whatever stored vegetables they had, and sometimes ate lichens and tree bark (Yarnell 1964). Without wild rice, living just on collected plant foods would have made life very hard in the Canadian Zone.

Considering hunting and gathering as a whole, a good question to ask is how well such a regime worked in Wisconsin. On one hand, hunting and gathering is an ancient way of life. It persisted through time, changing as environment altered, technology evolved, and populations grew. On the other hand, as a success story, it has to be judged at the times of the year when the least amount of food was available. In Wisconsin, this was late winter and very early spring. Perrot felt that starvation was a severe problem then, sometimes causing many deaths and even starvation cannibalism (Blair 1911, I). The fur trade caused enough change in the old round of life that it may have been responsible for problems in the food supply by taking people away from hunting for food. Yet Radisson almost starved on his Lake Superior voyage while living among hard-pressed Indians before the fur trade was very important. He counted hundreds dead after a winter when people ate not only their starvation food of tree bark but also the skins they had put away to save for clothing. How often this happened before the French arrived is not known, but the lean part of the year must have been hard on the old, the very young, and the sick.

Chippewa Hunting and Gathering

The earliest comments on the way the Chippewa fed themselves come from French sources in the late seventeenth century (Blair 1911, I). Inland shore fishing provided their major food, according to these accounts. The French watched Indians dipping nets into the waters of the Sault and pulling out salmon-sized whitefish during the fall run. Fish was smoked and dried, and at least some Chippewa lived on stored fish through the fall while others left the Sault for hunting westward into Santee Dakota lands. These hunters, after beaver and deer according to the French, spent the entire winter in the woods in small groups, living off what they could catch and what they had stored. In the spring they returned to Lake Superior to plant corn and squash wherever the lake effect and the soil permitted. Once the harvest was gathered, they scattered again for hunting until the fall fish runs began again. The French missed the spring fish runs, and they did not notice any gathering or processing of wild plant foods.

An intimate view of Chippewa life from a later time comes from the memoir of Alexander Henry, a young American-born English trader who came to the Great Lakes in the eighteenth century to seek his fortune. In 1763 he was at Ft. Michilimackinac at the Straits of Mackinac when the fort was attacked by Indians. Henry, hiding in one of the houses, watched as the soldiers were killed and the stores looted, and he was saved through his adoptive ties with a respected Chippewa man, Wawatam. For the year following the attack on the fort, Alexander Henry lived with Wawatam's family in Michigan, doing as they did, and he left a vivid account of what Chippewa hunting and gathering was like in the eighteenth century (Quaife 1921, Quimby 1966).

Henry's family consisted of a number of people: Wawatam and his wife, their married son and his wife and baby, and Wawatam's younger son and daughter. Including Henry, this group consisted of seven working adults who carried out the tasks of providing food, making clothing, and preparing tools and weapons. The family was completely independent; it came and went according to its own ideas of what needed to be done. The yearly round was based on past experiences and pooled knowledge from other years.

The hunting and gathering cycle began in summer with fishing and hunting birds in several places, depending on what was available. Sturgeon was the major fish caught, and there was enough to feed the whole family from June through August. This also would have been the berrying season, but Henry, a hunter and not a gatherer, did not comment on this important summer work of women. During the summer season, the Wawatam family lived with other families in small temporary villages where there was a larger social life.

By the end of August, the family broke camp and got ready to go to the "wintering ground" where they would lead a more solitary life, hunting and eating what they could. They were not totally alone since members of Wawatam's band were nearby, but they were spaced out to improve chances in hunting. Wawatam's family, unlike most Chippewa, did not go to the fall fish runs; perhaps their involvement in fur trapping made them do other things. On the way to their winter quarters, they killed beaver and birds, which presumably were the major part of their food then. The winter house was built, and the adult men of the family spent their time hunting elk, bear, deer, raccoon, beaver, and marten. Henry hunted raccoon, and he helped to add over a hundred raccoon skins to the family's store of furs. By the end of December, the men had also collected 100 beaver skins, all processed by women. In December, the family moved to another hunting ground, this time an inland spot where game was plentiful. The animals hunted there included more beaver, elk, bear, and otter. Hunting was very successful since the family killed many of the large animals, mainly elk, and had a surplus of 4,000 pounds of dried meat by the end of the winter. A lucky bear kill added six whole porcupine skins filled with bear oil and strips of bear meat.

The Wawatam family never used wild rice nor any other plant foods except for corn. They did not grow any of their own; they received some corn as a gift, and they bought two bushels from a trader. They either did not use much in the way of dried plant foods over the winter or Henry simply did not mention them. Perhaps women were too busy preparing skins to gather whatever roots there were in the winter. Perhaps supplies of dried berries and roots were too ordinary for Henry to list just as modern people describe meals in terms of the meats served, not the vegetables.

By the early part of March, the family returned to the place where they had begun the winter and picked up their skins as well as the dried meat. Their intention at this time was to move to their sugar bush to begin making maple sugar and syrup. How they moved themselves and their belongings from one place to another is interesting. The Wawatam family had thousands of pounds of dried meat, bear oil, and furs to move, plus the family's equipment. They were deep in the woods of late winter without canoes or sleds, and they did not have horses. Henry described the move as a series of stages, carrying heavy packs a certain distance and leaving them while returning to camp for another load. One after another the stages were managed until the whole had been moved from the wintering grounds to the sugar bush. Henry spoke of it as "patient toil" (Quaife 1921: 143), and indeed it was, but very effective for moving quantities of goods from one place to another.

The sugar bush was a rendezvous for other families of Wawatam's kinsmen, and many people were there to make sugar. All during April, the boilers were filled and the syrup turned out to granulate. Although Henry did not say exactly how much sugar he and his Chippewa family made, he described in his memoir another sugaring time when a family of eight prepared 1600 pounds of sugar plus 36 gallons of syrup in one month. In addition, they had eaten 300 pounds more of sugar. In his words, "sugar was our principal food, during the whole month of April."

When maple sugar and syrup were ready, Henry's family moved again, this time to Ft. Michilimackinac to deal with the French traders there and sell their surplus. They had hundreds of skins to trade as well as large quantities of maple sugar and syrup. All of these things went to pay off past debts and let them buy supplies for the coming summer. After dealing with the traders, the Wawatam family began the yearly cycle again with fishing and bird hunting in about the same place as the year before.

The Chippewa of Alexander Henry's time had changed from the people who fished in the rapids at Sault Ste. Marie less than 100 years earlier. Their tools and weapons had changed but more important was the commercialization of hunting and gathering life. It was no longer tied to need but produced a surplus that was traded to Europeans. Even part of their food was no longer taken directly from nature; they bought corn in the same way they bought iron knives or trade beads. They were hunting intensively, killing hundreds of animals, and making the most of European trade. How long such a pattern could have continued is a good question.

By the nineteenth century, Chippewa subsistence had changed again. It preserved the framework of hunting and gathering but had shifted to a yearly round that included other things. Big game such as elk were now extinct, and deer, bear, and wolf had become important. Men had a regular fall trapping season as well as a season of hunting in the winter, and sometimes hunting took them away from their families for a long time. The heyday of the beaver trade was over, but what skins they had they still brought to the traders. As in the past, fish formed a major part of the diet, year round, with special emphasis on fall and spring runs. Fishing was done mainly by women, who tended nets and dried fish as they had done in the seventeenth century. Maple sugaring still occupied early spring, and maple sugar was still an important food.

The nineteenth century was different in other ways. The yearly round of hunting and gathering involved many of the same things as in earlier years, but Indians could not produce such large surpluses from their foraging. Hunting furbearing animals was not what it used to be, and men had to go farther to catch fewer animals. Maple sugaring no longer was as profitable outside the community since cheap white sugar was now mass-produced in factories in the East and sold to those who once bought maple sugar from the Indians.

What helped to fill the place of lost income was government annuities provided by treaties. These were given out by Indian agencies and provided a certain amount of manufactured goods to each person, according to age and sex. A man might receive a blanket, lengths of broadcloth, calico, a knife, a gun, a comb, and lead for making bullets. A woman received a blanket, calico, flannel, a comb, broadcloth for a dress, sewing equipment, and tin dishes. Food was also distributed--flour, pork, and baking soda--as well as cash, which was spent at trading houses as before. When the annuity payments stopped, many Chippewa were without any income at all and were not able to sell or trade what they hunted and gathered. Other sources of income--land and lumbering rights--eventually took their place.

Farming

The important crops raised by American Indian gardeners were corn, beans, and squash. These three plants were so important that they came to be known as the "three sisters," and they were often grown together in fields where beans wound up corn stalks and squash grew in between. The story of Indian horticulture in the Northeast ended with the three sisters all growing together in the same fields, but it did not begin that way. All three of them originated in Mexico, and they had to travel a long way and undergo many changes before they came to be grown together in places like Wisconsin.

The first of them to arrive was squash, which appears as charred seeds and pieces of rind in several early archaeological sites in the East. Most of these are Early Woodland or even Late Archaic sites from places like Kentucky or southern Ohio, and they have radiocarbon dates of nearly 2300 B.C. Squash may have arrived just as people were beginning to experiment with growing their own crops, trying out such local plants as sunflower, pigweed, goosefoot, or marshelder. For well over 2000 years, squash was alone, restricted in its distribution and hardly causing a ripple on human life. It was not until the corming of corn that farming really came into its own.

Corn was grown in Mexico as early as 5000 B.C., and it took many years to arrive in Eastern North America. Part of the reason for this slowness rests with the variety of corn. Some of the earliest corn was a kind found in Hopewell, resembling more tropical forms from Central America. It was certainly grown then, but judging from the few examples that are surely Hopewell, it was neither widespread nor dependable. Hopewell probably relied mainly on hunting and gathering, and farming was only a marginal activity. It was not until the Mississippian cultures began to spread that corn became a staple, a staff of life for many Indians. Mississippian corn and all later historic corns are Eastern Complex maize, a hard flint corn with eight rows of kernels arranged in paired rows. This corn may have originated in the east, perhaps by selective breeding from earlier Hopewell corn, and it grew well in the more northern climates. By A.D. 1000, Mississippians and their corn were already a powerful force throughout the east.

Beans do not seem to have been around nearly as early as corn and certainly not as early as squash. They are high in vegetable proteins and would have been very beneficial, especially in areas where animal protein was scarce. If they had come early, they should have quickly become part of local gardening. Instead, the third sister was the last to join the family. Not until A.D. 1000 were beans part of the diet and a common part of the seed collections recovered from archaeological sites.

The movement of domesticated plants into eastern North America presents some interesting questions. For one thing, what kept them all from coming together much earlier than they did? Why did they move separately and at such different times? How they came is another problem. Whether they came from Mexico in trade or hand to hand as curiosities or slowly as one group heard of the idea from another are all unknown. The evidence so far is insufficient to describe a route of diffusion or to suggest a model for moving crops north from Mexico. Another question is why only corn, beans, and squash came from Mexico in prehistory. Mexico was home to many domesticated plants, some of which were linked together as far as nutrition is concerned. Chile peppers, for example, are important in providing vitamins not found in beans and corn. It is hard to understand why they never came north with the other corps. Or, for that matter, tomatoes. In their prehistoric strains, neither one may have survived the short growing seasons of the Great Lakes area, but it is hard to imagine that they would not have grown well in Louisiana or Florida.

Once Mexican crops reached the Indians of the north, they were prepared differently from the techniques used in Mexico. Most striking is the fact that Indians used corn in many ways, not one of which was the universal tortilla, the basic Mexican bread. Corn was usually not ground on stone by eastern Indians. It was pounded into bits, cooked in soups and stews, parched, popped, and eaten green; but no one ever made tortillas. Corn came alone without the cultural setting that surrounded it in Mexico: not even the corn god came along.

Tobacco was another crop. Smoking is thought to be very old in America north of Mexico, and pipes in archaeological sites seem reasonable evidence for it. However, many things can be smoked, not just tobacco; and only the seeds are reliable proof that tobacco was grown. No early evidence for tobacco is known in the Northeast, and it may not have spread any earlier than beans. When Wisconsin people first had it is unknown, but in historic accounts it was considered "special," not just another crop. It was often raised in little plots apart from the regular gardens, and it was often men who grew it, even where almost all farming was done by women. This probably means that tobacco was not an everyday pleasure; it was for ceremonial occasions. Besides tobacco, Indians smoked a variety of plants, sometimes mixed with tobacco and sometimes alone: shining willow bark, sumac leaves, red osier bark, dogwood bark, bearberry leaves, arrowwood bark, New England aster root, and others (Yarnell 1964).

Prehistoric Wisconsin farming

Wisconsin Indians became farmers long after farming had become a way of life elsewhere (see Chapter 2). The earliest possible farming sites were the Hopewell villages of the Mississippi Valley, the moundbuilders of Trempeleau County. No seeds or plants have been found in their villages, however, and the earliest good information is from the Middle Mississippian site at Aztalan. Both corn and squash were found there but not beans. This fits the picture in the Northeast where Mississippians are often the source for the really important crops.

Prehistoric Oneota sites set the pattern for historic gardening across the southern half of Wisconsin. They have produced the charred remains of corn, both cobs and kernels, plus the seeds of beans and squash. The sites also show continued collecting of wild foods. Around the northwest shoulder of Lake Winnebago and down into Lake Butte des Morts, Lake Winneconne, and Lake Poygan, gardening and rich hunting and gathering supported large villages of Oneota farming people. Right in the Transition Zone, Oneota people had the best of what both biotic zones had to offer.

Besides plant remains in sites, other evidence for Oneota farming includes hoes and ridged fields. Many of these fields, called "garden beds," have been found in Wisconsin and elsewhere (Moffat 1979). The Wisconsin examples are part of all the Oneota stages from earliest to latest. They look very much like small plots of plowed lines with up to four or five feet between the furrows. Each ridge was built up with a bone hoe, forming a pointed ridge with a U-shaped furrow between the ridges (Peske 1966). As archaeological sites, ridged fields have not survived modern land use. They are hard to see and often are destroyed by people who do not even know they are there. Ridged fields may be most easily seen today in early winter when a dusting of snow throws into relief the ancient parallel rows.

Ridged fields were once thought to be a means for draining marshy or swampy ground so that corn could grow there. Garden beds, however, are found everywhere but in marshy or swampy areas. The best explanation for garden beds so far is that they were a way to deal with early frosts where the growing season was nearly too short for corn. Planting the corn on ridges with depressions in between protected the plants by raising them above the cold air at ground surface. Oneota people had a good idea of how to manage on the northern fringes of Wisconsin's corn belt. Why such a useful bit of information was lost is puzzling: no garden beds were ever made by historic Indians, even in places with short growing seasons.

Historic gardening

Learning about Wisconsin gardening from the earliest days of French contact is harder than finding out about fishing or hunting of the same period. The French, although they knew that the Indians "do reap," were not nearly as interested in how they did it as they were in how Indians did other things. The very best descriptions come from missionaries in Ontario, and much of what was true of crop raising there was also probably true in Wisconsin, with allowances for the smaller population and the less favorable environment.

One major effect of farming was stronger ties of people to villages. Life was regulated by the needs of crops growing in one spot, and permanent villages were the result. Permanent villages were permanent only in a relative sense, however. They had to be moved every ten to twenty years, depending upon how long the soil remained fertile and enough firewood could be found close by. Crops were planted over and over in the same fields, and the plots yielded less and less as the years passed. A point finally came when people had to move their fields and homes to another village site.

Moving a village presented some problems. A village might be relocated on "old fields," lands that had once been farmed but had been abandoned for years waiting for soil fertility to be restored. In this case, clearing the land to put up houses or prepare fields was a matter of cutting down small trees and brush. These would be piled up and burned, producing wood ash which benefited the soil. If they had to clear new fields, Indians cut down large trees or at least killed them so they would not shade the crops. This was difficult before steel axes: large trees could be girdled to kill them and fires started at the bases to begin removal. Sometimes this took years, and Indian fields continued to have large dead trees standing in them. Dead trees did not stop planting, growing, and harvesting of crops in and around them.

Once the men had opened the land to sunshine, women could begin to plant. They took corn, often soaked for days to make it sprout, and put several kernels in holes about a yard apart. A field with its bunches of stalks growing together at intervals looked quite different from modern fields of cornstalks growing in equally spaced rows. Beans were sown in the same fields at the bases of the sprouting corn so they could use the stalks as climbers. Women also planted squash, sprouted by keeping the seeds moist in a birchbark box full of rotten wood kept warm near the fire.

At harvest time, women gathered corn to prepare it for winter. Most Indians celebrated the success of their new corn crop while it was still green and could be roasted; and the fall picking was simply winding up the farming year, not a time of special celebration. The husks were peeled back and braided together to let the kernels dry out. Later the cobs would be shelled and the grain stored away in bags or pits. Corn, with beans and squash, were the preferred foods of most Indians, according to Perrot. He said that "if they are without these, they think they are fasting" (Blair 1911, I: 102), no matter what else they had to eat.

A farming life meant that someone usually had to stay around to watch the crops and care for the fields. In most Indian societies, this meant women. Men did the heavy work of clearing, but the responsibility for everything else rested with women. This kept women near the villages but did not affect men. If men were gone for long periods of time to hunt or on war parties, their home life carried on as usual; men were not needed in the everyday running of things as long as the village was safe and the weather predictable. Farming added to the freedom of men from village life since a bag of corn made it unnecessary to look for food on journeys. Women were more restricted and could leave villages for long periods only during mid-summer and winter. Farming, while providing a reliable and dependable source of food, made the shape of human settlement different and perhaps less free than it had been, at least for women.

Winnebago subsistence

The earliest comments on the way the Winnebago lived were by missionaries in the seventeenth century. The missionaries described them as a settled people depending on the crops they grew, the wild plants they gathered, and the animals they hunted. By the eighteenth century, travelers through Wisconsin spoke of Winnebago farming in much the same way as the missionaries of earlier times. Nineteenth century travelers repeated what was said before, with references to cultivated fields but no really detailed descriptions. The most complete accounts of Winnebago farming are from twentieth century memories of the nineteenth century (Radin 1923), and they may not reflect the details of the seventeenth century. However, successful techniques in the hands of women whose families survived on their successes tend to be conservative, especially when the crops and the tools have remained the same.

In the earliest historic accounts, the Winnebago lived in small villages. The population was about 150 or 200 people, but some settlements were even smaller. Some of the nineteenth century villages were so small as to have only three or four "cabanes." Many of the Winnebago tales of those days mention a tradition of once having lived in villages so large that people at one end did not know people at the other. The same old stories say that the villages were circular and arranged in two complementary halves.

The subsistence year of the village people was flexible. For part of the year, during the spring planting season, both men and women were there. Women planted their crops by June, tended to the early weeding, and then some left the villages in the hands of older men and women while they joined men for the summer bison hunt. All of the women did not go along, but a large number was always needed to help process the meat. The usual direction for hunting was west to the Mississippi and even beyond on the Plains; other hunting lands were down the Rock River in places such as Dixon's Swamp. In late August, the crops were ready for harvest, and in early September, wild rice was tied, gathered, and prepared for storage. When that was done, the village was again abandoned for a while as people left for a late fall hunt. By the real onset of winter in late December, they returned to the villages to spend what was left of December and all of January and February living on their stored harvest and on wild rice. By spring, April and May, men began hunting around the villages to add to whatever was left of the stored food, and women began to think of the fields that would soon need planting.

A rough picture of the Winnebago year is reflected in the names of the months (Radin 1923). Several different versions of these month names have been recorded, but they are all similar: First Bear Month (January), Last Bear Month (February), Raccoon Breeding Month (March), Fish Becoming Visible (April), Drying of the Earth Month (May), Digging Month (June), Cultivating Month (July), Tasseling Month (August), Elk Whistling Month (September), When the Deer Paw the Earth (October), Deer Breeding Month (November), When the Deer Shed their Horns (December). Many of the month names refer to hunting and ignore wild rice, berries, and other plants; only farming appears as an important activity concerned with plants.

The crops known to the Winnebago included corn, beans, and squash. By the nineteenth century, they had three kinds of corn--sweet, red, and yellow stalked. Two kinds of squash were known: a large hubbard squash and one with very small seeds. The beans were small, much like Great Northern or pea beans. Both corn and beans were stored in underground pits, where they could be kept almost indefinitely. The below-ground storage pits kept food safe from insects and other animals as well as human thieves. Villages could be raided for their stored corn when most of the people were away on the late fall hunt.

Vegetable foods were prepared in several ways. Corn was eaten green in the summer, roasted in the husk, and, in its dried form, made into a number of stews or soups. Some of them were like a thin cornmeal porridge, enriched with whatever meat or fish was on hand. Pounded corn meal poured into hot water until it thickened slightly was one form; and others involved pre-treating the corn, soaking or roasting, to make it easier to fix. Most corn was steamed in pits with hot stones (Lurie 1971): the fully ripe corn would be layered with corn husks in a pit with a bed of hot stones in the bottom; water was then poured in and the whole thing sealed up with earth. The next day, the cobs were taken out, and the steamed corn scraped off; the kernels were spread out to dry in the sun and afterwards stored. This corn could be simply boiled with blueberries, meat, or whatever else there was to eat. Squash was roasted in hot ashes or boiled in corn stews. For winter use, it was peeled, seeded, and then cut into long strips or slices and left to dry. Beans were boiled, pounded, and mixed with other foods.

Wild food made a contribution to the diet in spite of the reliance on garden crops. A number of wild plants were gathered: Jerusalem artichokes, yellow water lily bulbs, chokecherries, and many kinds of berries. Fruit was preserved by drying and stored away in bags or boxes. The Winnebago also gathered wild rice (Jenks 1900). They are an exception among Wisconsin farming people since few who were known to grow corn ever bothered to gather rice, too. The Winnebago were in the midst of a wild rice paradise, and that was an excellent reason for their gathering it. Processing wild rice in addition to corn would have placed a strain on Winnebago families except that the corn harvest was over before the wild rice harvest began. Nevertheless, women must have felt the fall to be one of the busiest times of their year.

The division of labor that separated the world of the Winnebago into women's work and men's work had many effects on everyday life. One of them was a high level of skill on the part of both sexes. Little girls learned from childhood the proper ways of farming, gathering wild plants, and preserving food while little boys became experts in hunting many kinds of animals, each with its own special problems. Each sex was specialized in exploiting different things: their skills were joined together through marriage. The Winnebago division of labor also separated men and women into same-sex working groups whose bonds were often as powerful as those uniting husband and wife.

As hunters, the Winnebago took many kinds of animals; deer, elk, bear, and bison were the main species hunted. Many small mammals--squirrels, rabbits, and beaver--were also sought. In the late nineteenth century, Winnebago hunters said they did not eat otter, marten, weasel, or mink; they hunted them only for their fur. Very little is known of eighteenth century or earlier patterns of hunting, but there are some archaeological data. A refuse pit from the Crabapple Point site on Lake Koshkonong in Jefferson County produced a small collection of bones: the broken remains of beaver, dog, raccoon, elk, and deer as well as fish and bird bones (Spector 1975). Judging from these, most of Winnebago hunting was aimed at deer; over 70 percent of all the animal bones were from deer.

Hunting tools included bows and arrows before the introduction of guns. The Winnebago probably tipped their arrows with little triangular chert points as did almost everyone else during Late Woodland or Mississippian times, but by the nineteenth century, the memory of a time when people made their own arrow points had faded. The site at Crabapple Point, for example, did not have any chipped stone tools from the historic levels. The only hunting tools found there were guns, even down to the gunflints, which came from Europe rather than being homemade. Another nineteenth century site, the White Crow Village at Carcajou Point at Lake Koshkonong (Hall 1962) also had no stone tools; guns had replaced bows, and iron axes had replaced those made of stone.

Winnebago hunters used deadfalls and other traps for bear or raccoon. The simplest kind was built so that a heavy log would fall on the animal as soon as it jiggled the bait and released the trigger holding the log. Snares were used to catch rabbits and other small game, using a running noose attached to a sapling bent back to spring up when released. When the animal reached through the noose to get at the bait, it triggered the spring, tightening the noose. The late nineteenth century Winnebago did not recall the special techniques that had earlier been used to hunt beaver and reported only pitfalls dug on the beavers' regular paths between streams. During the fur trade, they had used spears and iron traps in the same ways as the Chippewa or Menomini. Deadfalls, snares, and pitfalls are sophisticated traps that do not need people to run them. In this way a hunter can manage two places at once as he leaves his traps and snares to work while he is somewhere else.

In the eighteenth century, the Winnebago hunted bison on the Plains. They moved in large groups in the only community-wide hunting they practiced. How old a pattern it was for eastern Wisconsin Indians to move so far to hunt bison is not known. At one time bison ranged into northeastern Wisconsin and were hunted by prehistoric people. In the historic period, bison became extinct as the area was crowded with refugees, who hunted both bison and elk. The populations of these slowly-reproducing animals could not recover from so much hunting pressure, and they disappeared. The Winnebago may have been following old custom in going after bison, but a need for meat seems unlikely. Their home range was good deer country and full of many other kinds of game. The bison hunt was not safe since it took place across the Mississippi in what was someone else's hunting territory. Sometimes the Winnebago went in company with other Indian groups, and they acted as if the bison hunt was a kind of hostile raid against the bison and the people of the Plains.

The bison hunt occurred in summer after the crops were planted and the fields weeded. The Winnebago were proud of their gardens, and they did not leave until the necessary work was done. The hunt included many people moving over the Fox-Wisconsin water route from eastern Wisconsin to the Mississippi River. The hunting expedition was organized like a war party: leaders gave feasts and chose men to act as scouts to find the bison. Warrior groups acted as soldiers, enforcing rules against hunting before the signal was given and keeping men from individual hunts of their own. Once the bison were located, they were driven with fire to where they could be killed with bows and arrows: fire was an important tool in hunting on the Plains. In the late nineteenth century, they had horses, and bison could be killed from horseback without the use of fire or bluffs over which they could be driven. Once the bison had been killed, women's work began. The meat had to be dried and packaged, the hides had to be treated, and bones set aside for tools. When the Winnebago came home from their summer hunt, they were loaded down with meat, hides, sinew, horn, and bone. They may also have carried war wounds; sometimes their movements into the Plains were not made peacefully or with the permission of the people who regarded Plains bison as their own resource.

The communal hunt may have been something that took shape in historic times as a result of the extinction of local big game, the coming of refugees, and general unsettled conditions. Such an effort would have been more important then. The apparently unlimited supply of bison on the Plains with no strong group in between must have been an attraction for Winnebago hunters. Another factor is the role of horses in the communal hunt. Perhaps before horses, the Winnebago were less free to hunt on the Plains and had to stay closer to home with an even greater reliance on local game.

Bear hunting was also important. The idea was to find a bear sleeping in a hollow tree or a cave during winter. Sometimes a fire was used to wake it up and drive it out. Hunters were ready and killed it as it left its refuge. Bears were hunted for their meat, fat, fur, and bones; and before guns, they were killed with bow and arrow or trapped in deadfalls or pits. The Winnebago, in common with other Wisconsin people, shared a belief that killing a bear was more than just killing a bear. Bears, perhaps because they were dangerous animals and could walk on two feet like human beings, were always treated with ceremony. The bear kill was surrounded by what is known as "bear ceremonialism," ritual treatment of the dead animal. The hunter sometimes received the head, breast, feet, lungs, and heart while the rest of the bear was shared in a special way. Feasts were given with the head of the bear receiving ritual attention as the remainder was being eaten. If people neglected the bear ceremonies, they thought bad luck was sure to follow, and it might be a long time before anyone caught another one.

The Winnebago hunted many kinds of birds. Migrating water birds, ducks and geese, could be taken in large numbers. In the early nineteenth century, Mrs. Kinzie (1975) saw an Indian hunter with a gun bagging 50 ducks in one hour on Lake Butte des Morts. The Winnebago also caught passenger pigeons in great numbers, knocking them off their nests at night with long poles (Radin 1923). The only archaeological evidence for birds in the diet comes from the refuse pit at Crabapple Point, where turkey bones were found. Bird hunting appears to have been a regular part of subsistence, but its contribution to the diet in terms of pounds of meat was very small.

The lakes near Winnebago villages were full of fish, and people used whatever they could catch. In the late nineteenth century (Radin 1923), spears or long arrows shot from ordinary bows were remembered as the way fishing was done in "the old days." No nets were mentioned at all, very surprising in view of how common nets were everywhere else. Perhaps the old people who remembered these things were all men and simply forgot the tools used by women in fishing. The Crabapple Point refuse pit shows that different kinds of fish were caught--catfish, bass, crappie, drum, and sunfish.

The picture that emerges for early contact Winnebago is of gardeners who also hunted and gathered. In the eighteenth century, they successfully combined this way of life with the fur trade, but by the nineteenth century, competition with new immigrants for land during the settlement of Wisconsin led to food shortages and even famines. The flexible economic system of the Winnebago could not survive loss of the lands to which it was adapted.

Other farmers

Some other Wisconsin farmers were even more dependent on their crops than the Winnebago. When Perrot mentioned these people in his memoirs, he lumped them all together as "prairie tribes." He admired their "cultivation of the soil" and praised the squashes of "excellent flavor," the beans, and the way the people prepared corn cooked green in its milk (Blair 1911).

The Miami were one of the "prairie people." They were described as living in the midst of plenty with corn, beans, and squash growing in large fields around their villages. The Miami yearly cycle stressed farming and hunting, with regular bison hunts out on the Plains. The sources mention little fishing or collecting of wild vegetables or fruits: Miami villages did not move to berry patches in the summer or gather wild rice in the fall. This is the basic pattern for the prairie people of the more southerly areas and includes the various tribes of the Illinois and perhaps also the Ioway.

If the Miami represent the more southerly farmers, then the Ottawa are a good example of the more northern ones. They had a cycle of balanced hunting, gardening, and fishing that changed as their involvement in trade, both as customers and as traders themselves, deepened. The Ottawa were also famous fishermen, relying more on fish than on meat. They gathered wild food when they could, but they did not use wild rice, at least on any regular basis. They were also sugar makers in the historic period although they originally used maple sap only as a famine food. Most of the other farming people of Wisconsin fitted into the Ottawa pattern: Potawatomi, Sauk, Fox, Mascouten, and Kickapoo.

Summary

Through time, farmers and hunters and gatherers changed older patterns of making a living and took on new ones. The fur trade put them in the business of supplying goods to outsiders, and they became buyers and sellers in a market system. Many things that they had collected or grown were harvested in larger quantities and sold: wild rice, berries, medicinal herbs. Maple sugar and syrup were produced for sale to traders or other Indians. Corn was grown in large fields so that hundreds or even thousands of bushels could be sold. Even dried fish became a commodity that Indians could sell to others. Expanding trade ended when loss of land in the nineteenth century reduced the area from which wild products could be taken, animals could be hunted, or crops grown.

CHAPTER 5
Material Culture

Wisconsin people shared many things in common. Their relatively small world belonged to what is called a "culture area," where a general similarity exists in the material culture of all the people who lived there. Once European trade came, the similarity was even greater; and as time passed, fewer and fewer objects of distinctly local character were made. Trade, intermarriage, and easy travel meant a greater sharing of ideas and objects.

Museum collections do not have many artifacts from the earliest years of contact with Europeans. Many early artifacts have not survived, and most museum specimens are mid- or late-nineteenth-century in date. Even things from the eighteenth or early nineteenth centuries are rare. Some specialists consider the mid-nineteenth century to have been a period of florescence in Indian art and craft work. Part of this was because of the enthusiasm of non-Indian collectors who wanted to buy elaborate or even non-traditional pieces. Thanks to the economic problems of the time, a commercial outlet for crafts was quickly appreciated. Indians moved into the production of handicrafts designed especially for sale. Many things were made in the late nineteenth and early twentieth centuries for this market: sewing baskets, beaded vests, wall hangings, Victorian visiting card holders, and buckskin gloves.

It is probably safe to say, however, that many of the *types* of artifacts made in the nineteenth century--unless they are obvious European forms--reflect *types* in actual use in prior years. The greatest changes came in decoration or in new tools and raw materials. Where entirely new techniques or habits were added to what people did from day to day, entirely new tools and ways of using them became part of the material culture, and older prototypes do not exist. For example, no prehistoric or early historic equipment used on horses or in lead casting or silversmithing can be expected.

Before European trade, everyday raw materials were easily obtained and locally processed. Indians often lived where they could find most of their raw materials in the land around them. Stone, bone, shell, bark, fiber, animal skins, wood, clay, antler, copper, and mineral pigments came directly from nature. Under special circumstances people used resources from distant places. Isle Royale and the surrounding copper country, for example, had copper deposits that were not officially controlled by any one group; the southwestern lead mines were claimed and used by almost everyone in the historic period. At the other extreme, catlinite, the red pipestone of Minnesota, was in the land of the Santee and controlled by them. Other pipestone deposits in Wisconsin were found in lands claimed over time by many different groups.

Houses and the Household

Ordinarily, a family's home during the late fall and winter months was the oval or round wigwam, the major house type throughout the Northeast. In form and function, wigwams did not change very much from their first descriptions by Europeans all the way to the twentieth century. They are still being made in much the same style today, although not with the same tools or always with the same materials. Archaeological evidence for wigwams is very old: Middle Woodland people lived in them around A.D. 100, and it would be surprising if Late Archaic people did not also use this adaptable house form.

Wigwams were made of a framework of saplings with the ends sharpened and stuck into the ground in an oval or round pattern (Skinner 1921; Densmore 1979). They were then arched across and tied to form a simple, dome-shaped structure about 12 or 15 feet across that was covered with cattail leaf mats or sewn rolls of birchbark or even sheets of elm bark. Wigwams could be made in any size, depending on the number of people they had to shelter. Materials for the frame were taken from local trees as were the basswood bark strips used to tie the frame together. The mats were propped and tied over and around the frame with more basswood strips. Except for the mats or the bark covers, which were carried from house site to house site in rolls, building a wigwam involved nothing that had to be brought from any distance at all. It did not need any special help in the building; a single woman could put together a small wigwam very quickly.

Inside, a central fireplace provided heat, and a smokehole overhead provided ventilation. Wigwams were often too smoky for the comfort of Europeans, but in the trade-off between letting out the smoke and at the same time keeping in the heat, fresh air must often have been the loser. Many older Indian people of today feel that the modern generation of wigwam makers are less expert in keeping the smoke under control. In the "good old days," women were more skillful, or so people think.

People sat inside a wigwam on beds of evergreens covered with skins or mats. These were put around the walls on a bench made of saplings or they were put on the ground. The family's possessions were hung from the frame of the house or tucked under the bench. Neat, compact, and energy-efficient, wigwams were well-suited to a life of frequent movement in a climate that was often very severe.

Like the wigwam, the summer house was built of local materials (Skinner 1921; Ritzenthaler and Ritzenthaler 1970), and like the wigwam, it gave people shelter appropriate for the season. This means more fresh air and cooler inside temperatures through higher roofs. Summer houses had peaked gabled roofs and rectangular floor plans that made them look quite different from the small, domed wigwam. The building methods were very similar with a framework of saplings covered with overlapping sections of bark. Both the wigwam and summer house had a similar floor plan: inside there were benches, a central fireplace, and personal possessions hanging from the frame of the house. The summer house was roomier than a wigwam, and with its gabled roof, it was cooler and better ventilated than a wigwam would be in the summer. It must have been a welcome change when the family moved from the one to the other at the end of the winter. Even the everyday cooking chores could be done outside in the open near the summer house. Both wigwams and summer houses often had tall decorated poles stuck in the ground outside. These were places to hang sacred bundles in the open air.

In the past, some people lived in other kinds of houses. Archaeological remains of pit houses, for example, have been found in some early sites in northern Wisconsin (Salzer 1974). At Aztalan, rectangular houses built of a basket-like framework of saplings coated with clay were in use around A.D. 1000 (Barrett 1933). Closer to the historic period, some people lived in large, long houses. A few of these long houses appear to have been like very long wigwams, but others seem to have been closer in style to Iroquois longhouses. The archaeological site on Rock Island, for example, contained two longhouses that were historic in age, probably belonging to the Ottawa (R. Mason 1986). The Santee Dakota often used skin-covered tipis when traveling out to the Plains to hunt bison, and bark covered tipis were a common kind of temporary shelter for almost all Wisconsin Indians.

Fiber mats

Inside wigwams, summer houses, longhouses, or tipis, the major household objects were two kinds of fiber mats (Skinner 1921; Hoffman 1896): made of bullrush reeds or of cattail leaves. These useful and decorative artifacts were everywhere around the home, on the floors or walls. Mats were part of every woman's possessions, made and owned by her and used for whatever she thought proper. The possible uses for mats were legion: within the home, they were used for sitting, for dining, for decoration, and for protecting the inner walls from drafts and the floor from damp. When the smokehole had to be covered, a mat was the means for doing it; when a door was needed, a mat could serve the purpose. Outside the house, mats were places for fixing food, for eating in the open air, and for storing whatever had to be kept off the ground. In death, mats could serve as burial wrappings. In the form of cattail mats, they were the usual covering for wigwams. When people moved from summer to winter houses and back again, the household equipment went wrapped in mats. When a wigwam was abandoned, the frame was left behind but not the mats that covered it.

Mat making probably filled up a good part of the time women spent in housekeeping. They must always have had mats in progress or were planning the mats that had to be put together in the future; mat making must have been more or less continuous. Old mats certainly wore out and had to be replaced, and new households had to have them. One estimate of the number of mats a single village made came from a mixed Sauk and Fox village of the eighteenth century. In that village, 300 were produced in a single summer (Blair 1911, II: 152-153).

Both the cattail and reed mats needed processing before weaving could take place. The raw materials for both grew in water and had to be picked or pulled up in marshy places. Reeds had to be cut, dried, blanched in boiling water, dried again, sorted, bundled, dyed, and only then used in finger-weaving a mat on a large upright frame. Since the reeds became very brittle when they dried out, the weaver always had to keep them moist as she did

Reed Mat: Menomini *Neville Public Museum* (1503/2193)

her work. Weaving itself was a matter of great skill, especially when geometric designs were woven into the mats. The decorated mats caught the fancy of early Europeans, who enthusiastically compared them to "Turkish carpets" (Kinietz 1940: 244). Cattail leaves for mats to go on wigwams had to be gathered, trimmed, and blanched to prevent drying before being laid out on a flat surface and sewed into mats. Women used long flat bone needles to pull basswood fiber threads through the cattails in stitched lines between four and six inches apart across the mats. Because these mats were sewn, not woven, they could be made in any length (Ritzenthaler and Ritzenthaler 1970). Six cattail mats were enough for an average-sized wigwam cover.

Perhaps because they were fragile or because they were such an ordinary part of life, few really early mats are in museums. The mats that have survived are good evidence that the household mat was a craft form of great skill and complexity. Women used many different techniques in making them, and they tried many variations on the same themes. The weaving is sometimes so complex that the weaver seems to have done far more than make a useful household object; the mats often approach being art objects as well.

Equipment for cooking, storing food, and serving was of wood, stone or clay before the coming of brass kettles and English china. Wooden bowls and ladles had graceful shapes, often with handles in human or animal form. Clay pottery was decorated with several kinds of cord-marking or was left with plain surfaces decorated with incised lines. Wooden mortars with their great wooden pestles were used to crush dried corn to prepare it for cooking. The everyday equipment used by women in the home changed quickly with European trade, and few of the older things have survived.

Birchbark containers and baskets

Women picked, sorted, stored, and cooked in birchbark, especially in the Canadian Zone. The important place held by baskets in other parts of North America was filled by birchbark containers of all sizes. A common birchbark container was a simple box with a rectangular bottom. It was made of one piece of bark folded and stitched up to an oval or round opening and lashed over a hoop of split willow that served as a rim (Schneider 1974). Making one involved heating the bark in order to make it pliable and cutting it out in a shape that had to be visualized as a finished box before the bark was cut. Bark containers could be round, rectangular, or square; they were shallow or deep, large or small, depending on the need, and sometimes they had lids that fit inside the wooden rims. Some of them were made watertight, and by adding hot stones, could be used for cooking. For maple sugaring, hundreds of birchbark containers had to be made; and when they could not be safely hidden at the end of a season, hundreds more had to be made again before the sap began to run in the spring.

Birchbark containers, particularly those intended for sale, were often decorated. The usual method was to peel off part of the bark on the outside. The design, often a floral pattern, could be either a negative image on a peeled field or a peeled figure on an unpeeled background. Many historic birchbark boxes were also decorated with dyed porcupine quills or even glass beads. Modern examples can be found with surfaces completely covered with quillwork, sometimes in the natural quill colors. Many birchbark boxes, trays, or other things were made for sale to non-Indians. Most of these are easy to identify since they include elaborate decoration and such bizarre forms as wall pockets, card holders, and Victorian hair savers.

The baskets that were made in Wisconsin were often coils of sweet grass sewed together with awl and thread to make a bowl or dish shape. Sweet grass is a plant whose stalks have a sweet and pleasant smell. Even when making other kinds of containers, women liked to add a coil of sweet grass somewhere along the rims or on the edges of lids. The sweet odor may fade with time, but it never seems to disappear. Even today, a whiff of the dainty sweet grass smell lingers in baskets in museum collections like a message from another century.

The splint baskets made more recently by many Wisconsin Indians are in wickerwork or checkerboard patterns. A twist is often put in the elm or ash strips that make up the basket so that modern examples have little projecting points around the rim or shoulder. Splint basketry techniques were learned from Europeans, apparently first in New England, and they may have been introduced into Wisconsin by some of the nineteenth century Indian immigrants: Oneida, Stockbridge, or Brothertown. They rapidly spread with the iron tools that made making the thin splints possible. As a rule, a single example of this type of basket cannot be told from similar baskets made by Indians all across the Northeast.

Fiber bags

Another kind of container was the flexible fiber bag. These bags were used to store hulled corn, wild rice, or dried roots; or to hold personal equipment that needed to be tucked away or carried from place to place. Most of them were rectangular with a drawstring at the top to pull them closed.

The history of the fiber bag is a key to appreciating the intricate interplay of old and new as crafts changed after European contact. Evidently, fiber bags have been around a long time, although direct archaeological evidence is scant. Indirect evidence--the cord impressing on pottery, for example--shows that fiber arts were present at least as far back as the Early Woodland. The bags collected from early historic periods presumably used prehistoric materials and techniques, and they are so complex that they imply a long development. The earliest known bags were made of many kinds of native fibers: basswood, slippery elm, cedar, or even animal hair (Whiteford 1977a); and they were finger twined by a weaver's passing weft threads back and forth through warp threads suspended from a single stick. The bags were small or large, plain or fancy, depending on how they were to be used.

By the middle of the eighteenth century, wool came to be a common material for making bags, and many new techniques were developed at the same time. Wool thread first came from cloth that Indians unraveled and later was supplied as yarn. The wool bags began to be made on a simple loom of two upright sticks set into the ground; the weaver hung her warp threads from a cord suspended between them and finger wove the weft threads around them. The bags woven with wool threads are much more variable in the type of weaving and the style of decoration. Like so many other things, the fiber bag exploded as an art form after European contact introduced only a few changes in materials (Whiteford 1977b).

Fiber bags may be both practical household objects and examples of textile art, depending on how the bags were made and decorated. Large, coarse-woven bags used to hold roots need not be as fancy as small bags used to carry a pipe or tobacco. Designs woven into some bags were geometric, and some were realistic: small animals, human forms, Thunderbirds, Underwater Panthers. These bags with their repeated parallel rows of figures often had symbolic meaning.

String

Women prepared thread, string, and binding as a
first step in mat-making, bag weaving, and sewing in
general. Thread was made from basswood bark, the inner
fibers of nettles, or the woolly hair of bison. Sometimes,
the inner bark of the basswood tree could be used without
any preparation at all. It was stripped, separated, and used
as is. This was the binding women gathered to put together
wigwam frames; the raw bark set as it dried and formed a
joint. For fiber bags and more general use, the basswood
inner bark had to be processed by boiling, pulling apart
the fibers, and, finally, twisting. The twisting meant
rolling the fibers along a leg until a string was formed
(Skinner 1921). Long lengths of string could be made by
splicing and then feeding in more fibers. Long lengths of
string were needed by every single household, considering
what it took to make just one woven bag or the many
yards used to sew together a long cattail leaf mat. Nets for
fishing alone must have required miles of threads.
Women's work in string making involved checking to see
what a household might need in the future and planning
for those needs. When ready-made strings and unraveled
European cloth could be used, women were relieved of
what must have been a never-ending cycle of string making.

Cradleboards

Women kept their babies on cradleboards. A
cradleboard is a broad board with a foot rest at one end
and a hoop at the other. The hoop protected the baby if
the board fell forward, and it supported a head covering
and little dangling objects to amuse the baby. A baby was
held on the board with many warm wraps in winter, few
in summer. Sometimes babies were laced into cradleboards
with thongs, and elaborate outer covers were put over all
the rest. Very young babies were often too small to fit on
cradleboards and might be put in little bark trays until
they grew bigger. A baby wrapped in a cradleboard could
not move while it was there. Arms were held down and
legs straightened with the whole body held securely
against the board; only the little face peering out was
active (Densmore 1979). As babies grew older, their hands
were freed to play with the objects hanging from the hoop
and more frequent periods off the cradleboard were
allowed.

Cradleboard *Neville Public Museum* (9210)

Cradleboarding had some very obvious advantages. It kept babies safely provided for while they lived in a small wigwam with large adults and active siblings. It made a mother's work easier by freeing her hands from holding the baby; and it kept babies warm and cozy. Mothers believed that cradleboarding made for straight limbs and backs, but this seems more a rationalization for a practice that was of great convenience. Cradleboarding does not seem to affect children's motor development: infants who have been cradleboarded do not walk appreciably later than those who have not spent long months on a cradleboard. Women also thought that cradleboarding had psychological benefits. Babies kept on cradleboards were secure and comfortable; sometimes they cried to be put back on their boards when taken out of them. From a safe and protected position on a cradleboard, infants could be part of all adult activities: they could be carried as mothers worked, stood upright to watch the life of the village, and hung in trees to be away from boiling kettles of maple sap or the skinning knives of working women.

Tools and Weapons

In addition to the tools used by women, household equipment included the things used for hunting, fishing, and the work of men. Men also used stone tools, antler and bone artifacts, objects of bark, and the fibers and mats made by women. Stone tools were quickly replaced after European trade, and what stone tools were disappearing for which people is not known. There may not have been any real tribal differences in these things then, and no one picking up a historic projectile point from a plowed field can really put a tribal tag on it.

When chipped stone tools come from historic sites, they are usually small triangular projectile points made of local cherts or quartzites. The stemmed or notched points from earlier times are completely gone. The small size and shape means a difference in weapons. The small triangular points are probably evidence for use of the bow and arrow. Bows were the common weapons in Wisconsin until trade guns took their place. The usual kind of bow was a simple one-piece weapon made of wood, rubbed and polished until it was smooth. Many bows were over four feet long, although they were scaled to suit the size of the hunter and the kind of animals hunted. Silent, efficient, and easily made, bows were the main hunting tools as well as the major weapons in war.

Fishing equipment (see Chapter 4) involved many things. A man spearing whitefish at the Sault stood up in his canoe and used a leister, spearpoint, or even a harpoon to land his fish. Once he had it, he killed it with a heavy wooden club. The fishing spear could be tipped with a stone point or a bone harpoon made by notching a long sliver of bone. Leisters are fish spears made with prongs; the prongs were made of bone or copper bound in groups of two or three with bark cord. In winter, people fished through the ice using many of these same tools.

Bark cord was an important part of all fishing: line fishing, traps or nets. The long lines attached to sturgeon spears were the same as the cord used in fiber bags and made in the same way. Bark cord went into the gill nets set in deep water and into the long seines that were pulled through shallow water. Some of the threads made for nets were coarse and others very fine, depending on the way the net was to be used. Some very ancient nets have left an imprint on pottery coming from sites of the late Middle Woodland or early Late Woodland. The fibers forming these nets are sometimes very fine with intervals of only half an inch and extremely tiny knots holding the mesh together.

Woodworking

Wood was a major natural resource: it was burned as fuel, cleared out of gardens, and used in one way or another in most of the things Indians made. Just getting at trees--killing and felling them--was a major job. The wood itself had to be split, shaved, smoothed, carved, sawed, bored, bent, or chopped. Before replacement by European trade, woodworking tools included ground stone celts, chipped stone knives, scrapers, wedges, and many kinds of stone drills. Woodworking went from everyday tasks of chopping and cutting all the way to such fine scale operations as putting holes through long wooden pipe stems or cutting a burl from a tree and turning it into a smooth cup or bowl.

After European contact, fine scale woodworking was changed by the introduction of the crooked knife. Crooked knives were made of metal, sometimes an old file or a section of gun barrel, and fitted into a pistol grip handle. The blades were short, often only four inches long, and they were beveled with the blade tip bent up like a farrier's knife. Crooked knives were used with a drawing motion pulling toward the user, and the bent tip served as

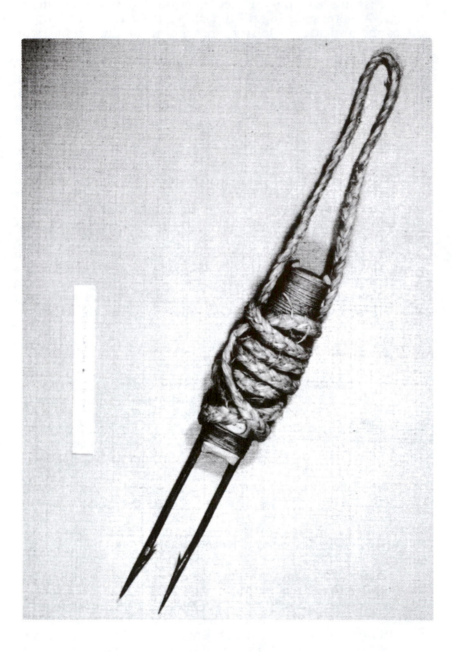

Harpoon *State Historical Society of Wisconsin* (1955.1097)

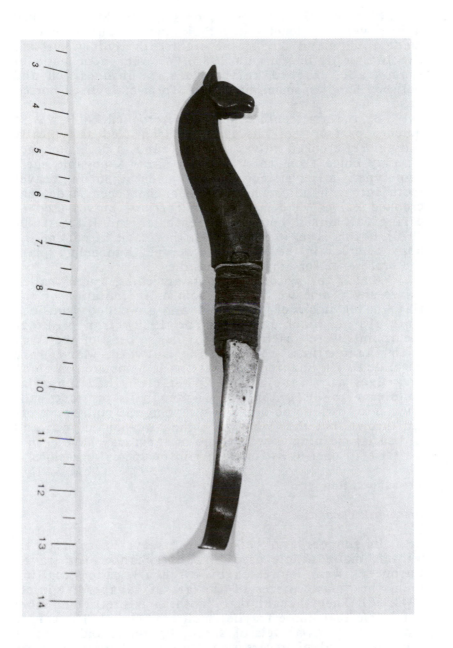

Crooked Knife *Neville Public Museum* (4076)

a tool for gouging, scraping, or splitting. Many crooked knives were put together by their owners, but some were made in England during the eighteenth century just for the Indian trade (Gilman 1982). Whether homemade or from trade, crooked knives were set into carved and polished handles, sometimes in the form of stylized horses' heads.

By the nineteenth century, the crooked knife was so much a part of tool kits as to be identified as typically Indian. Yet crooked knives are not found in prehistory nor do they come from early contact sites. A possible early prototype is a beaver incisor chisel made by putting beaver teeth into a handle. The suggestion has been made that crooked knives were modeled on farriers' knives used in caring for horses' hooves (Ritzenthaler and Ritzenthaler 1970). If this is so, it might mean they came as part of the horse complex in the eighteenth century and help explain the preference for horse head handles.

Among the wooden artifacts are clubs, usually called "warclubs." Some were made from or in imitation of the flat wooden stocks of trade guns and are called "gunstock warclubs" (Palmer and Camardo 1982). Iron or brass spearpoints were sometimes thrust in the bend of the stock with the business end sticking outward. Many were decorated with hundreds of brass nails hammered in along the edges as a fancy trim. Other clubs had long flat handles with inset stone or wooden balls or stone balls sewn into rawhide holders. As weapons, the clubs were often thrown, but they were more than weapons of war and had social meaning as well. Some of them may have been a matter of proper dress for a warrior on special occasions.

Transportation

Birchbark canoes

In summer and before waterways froze over in winter, many people used birchbark canoes for travel. Europeans were impressed by birchbark canoes, calling them the "masterpieces of the art of savages" (Kinietz 1940: 50). They thought that "nothing is prettier or more admirable than those fragile machines" (Ibid.). The canoes seemed to them marvels of speed, lightness, and grace as they moved along rivers and on lakes. They even were adopted by Europeans, and in the fur trade, they carried tons of freight over the long trade routes. In modern times, birchbark canoes are a symbol of the efficiency and expert nature of Indian transportation.

Not all Indians used bark canoes, though. Early observers cited the Winnebago, Fox, Kickapoo, Mascouten, and Miami as people without birchbark canoes (Kinietz 1940). The division into canoe and non-canoe people is based on the fact that people who lived outside the area where paper birch trees grew were less likely to cover canoes with the bark. However, birchbark canoes or the bark itself were traded over great distances, and sometimes southern people also had bark canoes.

Building a birchbark canoe (Adney and Chappelle 1964) was done by both men and women, in groups to make the work easier. While men selected the birch tree, women gathered roots for sewing and gum for pitch. Not any tree would do when making a canoe. A proper tree should be big enough, but it should have few "eyes" in the bark. Just choosing the tree often took hours of consideration as men weighed and judged one tree against another. After deciding on the tree, the bark had to be carefully removed. It came most easily at springtime when the flow of sap was strong, and it could be rolled and saved or used to make a canoe right away. Before European tools, canoes were made of small sections of bark because it was hard to remove birchbark in large sheets with stone tools. This made better canoes in spite of the piecing that had to be done since the smaller the bark sheets were, the more un-likely they were to include poorer, thinner sections near both ends. Other supplies needed to build a canoe included wood for the prow pieces, headboards, gunwales, ribs, and interior slats; many people also used a wooden form around which they shaped the canoe. Canoes were usually of the long-nosed variety, the kind with high curved bows and sterns. This type is the model for many modern canoes of fiberglass or aluminum.

Canoe building began on a level piece of ground. Everything was cleared away, and sometimes sand was spread to make a clean bed for the work. A canoe form or an old canoe was set down and a crib of stakes pounded in around it. Both form and stakes were taken away, and the bark sheet, white side up, was centered in the place marked by the stake holes. The stakes were put back in the holes, forming a support for the bark sheet. The top edge of the sheet then had to be joined to wooden gunwales with sections of bark sliced out much as tucks are taken in sewing. In this way, a rectangular, flat bark sheet could be joined to an oval opening. The tucks were sewn shut with awl and roots, and the bark sheet was lashed to the gunwales. Then the major inside fittings could be put in:

prow pieces, headboards, thwarts. All had to be laced into position using awls for piercing and roots for binding. As a final step, the whole inside was lined with very thin wooden slats, bent and trimmed to fit.

Canoes were made watertight by caulking the seams with pine pitch. Some seams were first covered with cloth before the pitch was applied, and sometimes charcoal was mixed with it, giving the canoe those characteristic black lines wherever it was put on. The first pitching was usually done by women, but when a man's canoe leaked on a journey, it was up to him to fix it himself.

Birchbark canoes were light and fast-moving, but they were often leaky and sometimes dangerous. Canoe users kept close to shore in case of accidents and skirted around lakes rather than crossing them. People felt more secure if they made offerings to water spirits before starting off on trips, a pinch of tobacco or sometimes a dog. The Underwater Panther, a supernatural being who caused canoes to upset, was a very important part of local belief, reflecting the uneasiness people felt in canoes. Problems with bark canoes were balanced by their advantages, but when other kinds of transportation came into use, bark canoes were quickly replaced.

Dugouts

Dugout canoes were used by people who had no birch trees and by people who also had birchbark canoes. Dugouts were made of logs hollowed out through burning and cutting away the charred wood. This technique was the same one used to make other things of wood; for making a dugout, it was simply a matter of doing it on a larger scale. Dugouts were often long with shallow draft and low sides, and they functioned best on slow rivers or in marshes. Compared to bark canoes, they were heavy, awkward, and slow. Once European tools were available, however, the birchbark canoe gave way to the clumsy dugout. With metal tools, dugouts could be made rapidly, and they were sturdier and less trouble to maintain.

Snowshoes

Winter transportation on foot over deep forest snow was by means of frame and mesh snowshoes, which let travelers move on top of the snow rather than through it. They were made of strips of wood, heated and then bent into snowshoe form. Added crossbars supported the frame,

Dugout Canoe: Potawatomi *Neville Public Museum* (830/552)

and the open spaces were filled in with woven sinews. Snowshoes came in several shapes and sizes, depending on local preference and function. The major types include the catfish, with a rounded tip and long tail, and the bear paw, a smaller oval or round shoe.

Snowshoes helped people move heavy loads in winter. A good hunt meant hundreds or even thousands of pounds of meat, and a successful season of gathering furs for trade meant a lot of weight to carry to trading houses or forts. During winter, camps were often moved, and people carried all their possessions with them. Considering just the information from Alexander Henry's life among the Chippewa (see Chapter 4), the heavy meat and furs had to be moved on human backs. Henry described packs, the heaviest being carried by women in stages from one camp to another. Even with a tump line across the forehead, carrying food, mats, tools, household equipment, and babies would be much harder in winter when deep snow was on the ground. Snowshoes spread the weight and made travel less difficult. Henry did not think walking on snowshoes was easy, especially day after day, and some Europeans found using snowshoes so exhausting that they could hardly continue traveling. Nevertheless, they were a great help in meeting the problem of walking where winter snow was deep.

Horses

Horses were introduced into Wisconsin in the eighteenth century. Many of them came back to Wisconsin with men who had fought in the French and Indian War, and they rapidly became part of Indian life. Horses changed life in many ways: they extended hunting territories and provided another means for moving goods. They could be used in indemnity payments, gambling, and gift exchange. Horse ownership freed women from many of the burdens that were carried--literally--on their shoulders. By their need for fodder, horses changed ideas of what a proper setting was for a village or camp: feeding horses became one more factor in deciding where people could live. During winter, when life was more difficult, horses and their care even determined what people did and where they went. As one Chippewa horse owner recalled in the last part of the nineteenth century: "we thought more of the horses than of ourselves when it came to feeding them" (Barnouw 1954: 97). In the spring, this family was so busy providing for the needs of their horses, they had no time at all to make maple sugar. Although horses in Wisconsin have not been given the same attention as horses among Plains Indians, it is clear that their effect on life was nearly as great.

The equipment used on horses included wooden-framed saddles, pad saddles, and bridles. Bridles were decorated with porcupine quillwork or beadwork designs, and saddle pommels were sometimes carved with horses' heads. Efficient packing equipment was slow to come to Wisconsin, a land without roads suitable for wagons or paths where travois could be dragged. For a long time, things were carried in fiber bags hanging from the saddles. Later, Indians used the same horse equipment available to everyone else on the frontier and no longer made their own.

Personal Equipment

Clothing

Before access to trade cloth and blankets, clothing was made of animal skins, mainly those of deer. Different techniques for processing had to be followed depending on whether the skin was to wind up as fur or a plain tanned skin without any hair left on it at all. The supple texture of both furs and skins came about by repeated scraping and stretching as well as rubbing the surfaces with prepared animal brains. The final result depended not only on the skills and judgment of the women who prepared the skins, but also on the age, sex, and condition of the deer. At certain seasons, skins were thinner to begin with and made less bulky clothing. Some buckskins were always too thick for anything except moccasins, and fawn skins were often too fragile for all but the most delicate work.

Clothing design was not unique to Wisconsin; the same general patterns were found across much of the Northeast. Ordinary dress for men consisted of a breechcloth, leggings, and moccasins of deerskin with robes or shirts added against the cold. All clothing was made by women and was an important place for their artistic expressions. For dress-up occasions, the flaps of the long breechcloths were decorated with quillwork; the leggings, too, could be quilled and perhaps fringed with tiny copper tinklers or dewclaws attached to the fringes. Leggings were set off with woven garters tied around the leg under the knee. These garters, intricately woven in geometric designs, are one of the most characteristic items of dress in the

Wooden Saddle: Menomini *Neville Public Museum* (772/1362)

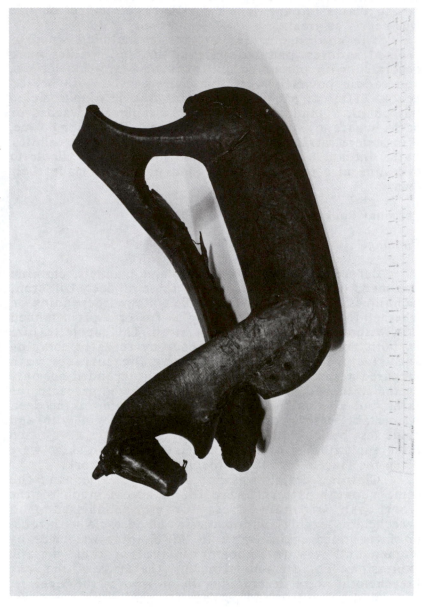

Wisconsin area. Long bands woven in the same way as the garters were used as headbands or as turbans. Among others, the Menomini used an otter skin strip, sometimes made with the whole skin, as a special headdress (Skinner 1921). Women's clothing consisted of a wrap-around skirt or sleeveless dress, leggings, and moccasins, all of which could be ornamented with quillwork for dress-up occasions.

Moccasins

Both men and women wore moccasins of a similar type, the soft-soled eastern style (Schneider 1974). They were made either of one piece of deerskin to form both sole and sides or with an added vamp over the toes and a separate piece forming a broad cuff or flap. They were often decorated with quillwork or beadwork on the vamps. Very fancy moccasins were made especially for trade or to be given away as gifts; moccasins sometimes wound up far from their place of origin.

It is not always possible to know if a particular moccasin was made by a specific group without having its history, but the general form certainly gives some clues about origins. The Menomini style had a broad vamp fitted to the body of the shoe with a line of very tiny puckers all around it. Menomini moccasins also had little heel tags for pulling a shoe off and strings attached to the ankle flaps for tying it on. Chippewa moccasins had a central seam on the toe with a small vamp surrounded by tiny puckers clustered on either side of the seam (Densmore 1979). Winnebago moccasins had no vamp, but there was a center seam down the front of the shoe. In the historic period, men and women wore slightly different styles among the Winnebago; women's moccasins had a single large wrap-around ankle flap, while men's had two cuffs, one on either side. Potawatomi moccasins had a single broad flap around the whole shoe with no vamp. Sometimes there were special styles for children: the Chippewa "partridge" moccasin, for example. It was made in one piece with a straight puckered seam across the toe and tiny fringe down the center seam (Flint Institute for the Arts 1973).

Clothing made of deerskin created problems for people who wore it every day rather than on special occasions. Deerskin stiffened when wet and became clammy and cold, needing reprocessing. Deerskin moccasins wore out under use, and a man might need five or six

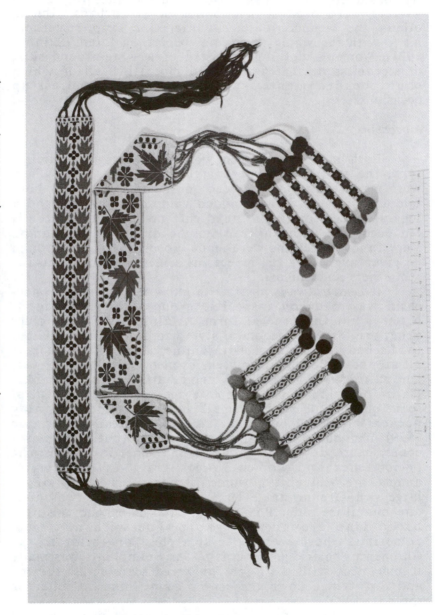

Beaded Sashes: Potawatomi, Menomini *Neville Public Museum* (1601/1979.62, 449/3330)

Moccasins Neville Public Museum (1418/1704, 1429/1759, 785/239, 421)

pairs for a long journey on foot. The handsome skin clothing wore out, too, and needed frequent mending or replacement. Women had to plan ahead for so many skins for a family's yearly needs, and men had to catch the deer, preferably when the skins were at their best. Without looking ahead, people might have to make do without good protection or proper shoes. In winter, such things were more than a matter of style.

What happened when European trade goods came was a classic case of cross-fertilization. Ideas took wing as more varied and flexible raw materials were introduced, and men's and women's clothing changed almost overnight. The old skin clothing of women simply disappeared and was replaced by a whole new costume. In general, the new fashion included a wrap-around skirt of dark cloth worn with a long-sleeved blouse, often without a collar. Under the skirt, women still wore leggings, but they were made of woolens held up by old style garters. With this dress, women wore a blanket or cape of the same dark color as their skirts and decorated to match. This costume, as museum collections and historic photographs show, changed through time as women developed new styles and new ideas about what was appropriate. They accepted and rejected, ordered and ranked, improved and changed things as they met new answers to their everyday needs, and each group developed its own local variation of dress. "Traditional" dress has to be judged in terms of a time period as well: pre-European dress is different from the dress of 1800, and both are different from the dress of more recent periods.

Men's costume underwent similar stylistic changes. The basic breechcloth, leggings, moccasins, and robes continued to be worn, but the materials were different and new things were added. Mackinac or Hudson's Bay blankets replaced fur robes; the raw materials for clothing were stroud, woolen, or cotton cloth. Most of the clothing continued to be made by the women in the styles that the men preferred, but the process was streamlined. Skins no longer had to be prepared for anything other than moccasins, and the sewing was easier and faster. The work of making clothing was as pressing as ever; machine-made cloth wore out, too, and had to be replaced each year (Marriott 1959). Later, men adopted clothing that came to them readymade, often as gifts or parts of annuity payments. Military coats, long trousers, ruffled shirts, and even hats became standard parts of male dress. Even these readymade clothes, though, came within the symbolic

Early 19th Century Woman's Dress *Neville Public Museum* (70/1948 - Theresa Rankin wedding dress)

world of the people who wore them: they became items of
Indian dress, decorated by women in what soon became
traditional ways.

Quillwork

Porcupine quillwork was one of the most widespread
of the earlier decorative techniques. Once a porcupine was
killed, the quills were plucked, sorted, and stored away in
birchbark boxes. They could be dyed lovely soft vegetable
colors by boiling them with natural plant dyes made from
bloodroot, sumac, or hemlock. Black could be made using
carbon from burned wood. After the invention of aniline
dyes in Europe and their appearance in the Indian trade,
very bright colors could go into quillwork. The shade of
the colors can sometimes be used as one clue as to the age
of a piece decorated with quills.

The main use for quills was in embroidery. The only
tools a quiller needed were an awl, thread, and a tool for
the final flattening of the finished work. First the quills
were softened by soaking them in water. The quiller began
by holding one end of a quill between her teeth and flattening it with her thumbnail. Each quill was sewn on with
one of several kinds of running stitches. Many of the
patterns were simple overall designs that lined up parallel
rows of quills. By putting enough of the rows together, a
quiller could produce the same effect as overall satin
stitch in ordinary embroidery. Each quill was applied by
sewing one end down with a tiny stitch, folding the quill,
and catching it somewhere else with another little stitch. If
the quill were long enough, it could be folded again and
brought back to be caught in another stitch. This process
was repeated, splicing in other quills as necessary, until
the work was finished. Besides using overall patterns, a
quiller could outline any shape she wanted with quills.

Even in its simplest, straightforward form, quillwork
is a highly skilled and imaginative craft. Quillers were not
always satisfied with the simple and straightforward: they
played with their art and made many complicated
variations on the basic themes. Some quillwork used quills
that had been braided in a very complex way. Quills could
be folded to produce different visual effects and textures.
Sometimes the quillers created checkerboard patterns. or
even wrapped quills around thin pieces of sinew to vary
the thickness (Orchard 1971). Quillwork was replaced by
glass beadwork, but a few women continued to work with
quills. Perhaps the effect produced could not always be
matched in glass beads.

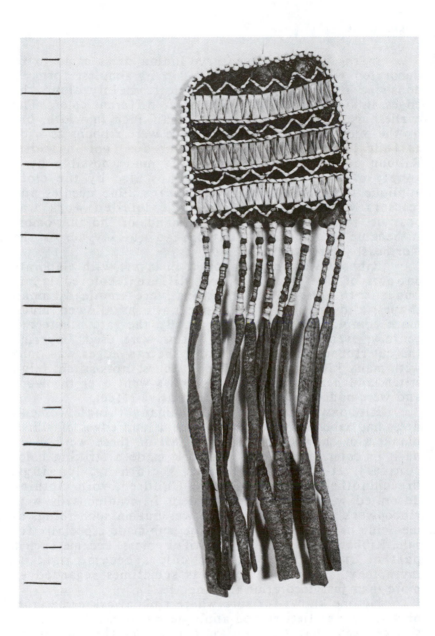

Bag with Woven Quillwork *Neville Public Museum* (854/461)

Ribbonwork

In the nineteenth century, Indian dress came to be decorated with ribbon applique. In its simplest form, it consisted of sewing ribbons to cloth, mainly along the edges, in single strips or in groups of different colors. The earliest were very narrow, only a half inch in width, but by the mid-nineteenth century, there were ribbons as wide as four inches. Later, some measured a foot in width. Ribbon applique was a new craft made possible by a supply of silk ribbons and perhaps also by the cloth applique techniques used by Europeans. Fine needles and scissors were needed before such detailed work was possible. Whatever its roots, in the hands of Indian women, it became a new craft that spread quickly across the Northeast (Marriott 1959).

Ribbons were often applied in layers with elaborate cut-outs of one color put over different colored layers underneath. The earliest designs were simple diamond shapes; and later bark or paper patterns allowed much more complicated cut-out forms. By the late nineteenth century, even elaborate floral forms were used. Layering the cut ribbons and sewing under the raw edges was done with many kinds of embroidery stitches: cross-stitch, blind stitch, and herringbone. Some stitches went over the work and were added just for their decorative effect.

Ribbonwork was applied to many things. Women's dress had ribbon work along the hems and edges of skirts, blankets or shawls, and leggings. All of these were often dark in color, and the ribbonwork made a striking color contrast. It appeared on men's clothing: leggings, breechcloths, shirts, and robes. Children wore clothing decorated with ribbonwork or slept in cradleboards with ribbonwork covers. Ribbonwork was put on such things as medicine bags, and it decorated objects made especially for sale. Ribbonwork, with its beautiful colors, became such a part of Indian life that the colors became part of mythology, and ribbonwork was sometimes regarded as more than just decoration (Skinner 1921).

No one knows for sure where ribbonwork came from or when the earliest ribbon applique was done. Some of the sources say that the Indian trade was the "dumping ground" for unwanted ribbons after the French Revolution (Marriott 1959). Ribbons were a favorite form of decoration for the French aristocracy, and after the Revolution, they were completely out of fashion. This would make most ribbonwork late eighteenth or nineteenth century.

Ribbonwork Blanket: Winnebago *Neville Public Museum* (1427/1759)

From that time, ribbonwork developed throughout the Northeast, with many of its finest examples from Wisconsin. Groups known for their outstanding work include Potawatomi, Winnebago, Menomini, Sauk, Fox, Kickapoo, and Miami.

Beadwork

Patterns in glass beadwork seem to be a translation of porcupine quillwork into beaded designs rather than being derived from earlier kinds of beadwork. Beads were present in prehistoric Wisconsin all the way back to the large, heavy copper beads of Archaic complexes, but most of these were worn as jewelry. Bead embroidery has left little prehistoric evidence, but shell or bone beads could have been sewn on skin clothing in patterns. When European glass beads came, however, they were used in ways resembling the quillwork that they almost completely replaced.

Glass beads were traded into Wisconsin before Europeans themselves arrived. The first beads were very large, and some of them could be pendants all by themselves. These beautiful "star chevron" beads, bright blue with red and white zigzag patterns, were the first in a flood of large, many-shaped, and brightly colored beads to arrive. They are known by curious names--raspberry beads, Man-in-the-Moon beads, pigeon's eggs, Cornaline d'Aleppo-- and some of them are still being made today. Along with them came tiny seed beads, which were the source for a new and vigorous art form. Seed bead embroidery quickly became the most important means of surface decoration on clothing and other articles. Glass seed beads, iron needles, and very thin threads held the potential for producing what may be the finest art form developed in the Northeast.

Women used beads for decoration in two ways: as embroidery or woven on looms. In direct embroidery, a design was put on buckskin or trade cloth by marking with an awl or with flour paste. Designs were sometimes done freehand and sometimes with a re-usable paper or bark pattern. Almost any design could be worked in beads. At first the emphasis was on geometric patterns, probably following older quillwork models, but designs quickly became curvilinear. The most popular beadwork patterns were floral shapes, often very realistic and usually in a number of different colors. Beadworkers could make their embroidered designs as outlines only or they could fill in the design to form an overall pattern. In many cases, the entire surface was beaded. Bead embroidery was done by threading several beads with a needle and then sewing them to the fabric with stitches that crossed the original thread. In this way, the beads could be firmly fixed in place. Possibilities using this technique are almost endless; many variations may be made in the stitching, the number of stitches taken, and in details of catching the beads. The result has great potential for decorating (Orchard 1975). Weaving of beads was done on little looms, most of which were portable and easily carried about. With these looms, women used many techniques, the most common being single weft weaving and double weft weaving (Schneider 1974). Single weft weaving secures the beads by passing a thread under one warp thread and over the next. In double weft weaving, the beads are held on by two threads, one passing above the warp threads, the other below, and both going through the holes in the beads. In these techniques, geometric designs are encouraged by the process itself. Loom weaving is not as suitable for rounded floral designs or other natural forms, but some women managed to weave them anyway.

Women decorated clothing with beadwork, particularly what was used on special occasions (Grand Rapids Public Museum 1977). Embroidered beadwork was put on leggings, breechcloths, moccasins, and blouses or shirts. Loom woven beadwork, because it was made in narrow panels, could be attached to clothing and then re-used when the clothing wore out.

Shoulder bags were an important place for beadwork. These bags, called "bandolier" bags, were worn by men to hold personal items or as a fancy addition to male costume. Bandolier bags are related to the ammunition bags Europeans carried in the days of matchlocks and end-loading muskets, and they spread widely in the historic period. The bags were square or rectangular, each with a long, wide shoulder strap that was also elaborately decorated. Some of them were made without openings or any means of practical use; their elegant beadwork was enough of a reason for carrying one or more of them. Some bags were made to be given away, and these are called "friendship bags." Friendship bags were taken on trading expeditions and sometimes wound up far in the West, long distances from their place of origin.

Beaded Bandolier Bag *Neville Public Museum* (1560/3165)

Floral designs

The origin of floral designs in embroidered work, on birchbark, and in ribbonwork is unknown. Floral patterns in historic Indian art might be the expression of older, native designs or they could have come from European contact. The difference of opinion ranges all the way from those who think floral patterns are very ancient (Skinner 1921, Ritzenthaler and Ritzenthaler 1970, Fredrickson 1980) to those who think they came directly from European models and even from deliberate European teaching (Feest 1980). The idea that floral patterns are ancient in North America is reasonable, given that people living in the forest were surrounded by leaves, flowers, trees,. and vines. These would be obvious models to turn into art. Others think floral forms came from teaching Indian girls embroidery and other needlework, first by nuns in Montreal and later in mission schools. Some of the most elaborate floral designs were worked by Huron women, geographically closest to the earliest European sources. In addition, no evidence exists for floral designs in prehistory. If Indians imitated plants in their art, it is reasonable to expect some of it on prehistoric objects. The only possible prehistoric ancestor is the widespread double-curve motif (Speck 1982), and it has only a vague similarity to plants or flowers.

Hair styles

Styles of dressing the hair varied from one group to another. Many men used to pluck much of their head hair and pulled the rest to the back where it was tied and decorated with beads or feathers. A scalp lock in the middle of the head was left by Sauk men of the eighteenth century (Ritzenthaler and Ritzenthaler 1970), and Menomini men of the same period kept a scalp lock on the crown. Men also wore their hair in braids, often tied with feathers or with painted lines where the hair parted (Densmore 1979). For special occasions, men wore roaches held in place by a scalp lock. A roach is a crest of hair that stands erect using a spreader; the effect is of a brush from front to back.

Women preferred a single braid down the back with the hair parted in the middle. The braid was often held by a binder, a strip of cloth decorated with quillwork or beadwork and wrapped around the doubled-up braid. From this binder, long streamers of ribbon or beadwork flowed nearly to the ground. The hair binder was not an item of everyday dress but a special costume for the most elegant occasions. The single braid is the timeless, classic look for Indian women, one seen as truly traditional, but it does not appear in the very earliest portraits. Early hair styles included free hanging hair parted in the middle or even banged across the forehead.

Silverwork

Silver jewelry was very popular after the French and Indian war. Silver armbands and wrist ornaments as well as gorgets, brooches, earrings, lockets, pendants, nose-rings, crosses, and silver coins were all worn, sometimes several at a time. Much silver jewelry was based on forms used earlier, and some even resemble prehistoric examples. The round silver gorget looks a lot like earlier ones in shell and stone, and the small silver beaver effigies may have replaced stone beavers. Some of the silver jewelry, however, is entirely new. The half-moon gorget, for example, came from European military uniforms, and the silver locket in the form of a spoon bowl with a lid came from European models. Crosses, religious medals, and other religious symbols were often worn as jewelry with no special sacred meaning.

Much of the silver came from the workshops of professional silversmiths, and some examples have little hallmarks to show who made them. A tiny "RC" stamp identifies Robert Cruickshank's shop in French Canada, while a "CA" stands for the Charles Arnoldi family and a "PH" for Pierre Huguet (Quimby 1966). The silversmiths often engraved their pieces with animals, geographic designs, or historical scenes (Frederickson 1980). The designs may have been what Indians asked for or what the silversmiths thought might appeal to them. Generations of silversmiths in Canada, the United States, and England made part of their living supplying silver artifacts for the Indian trade.

Some silver pieces were important for political and economic reasons as well as for jewelry. The half-moon silver gorgets were symbols of military rank and came to stand for being a chief or warrior (Frederickson 1980). Men of high rank wore so much silver that the importance of the individual could be judged by the amount: important men wore large collections at once. Armbands, many wrist ornaments, layers of gorgets, and hat ornaments indicated wealth and social standing. Medals given out by European governments to Indian

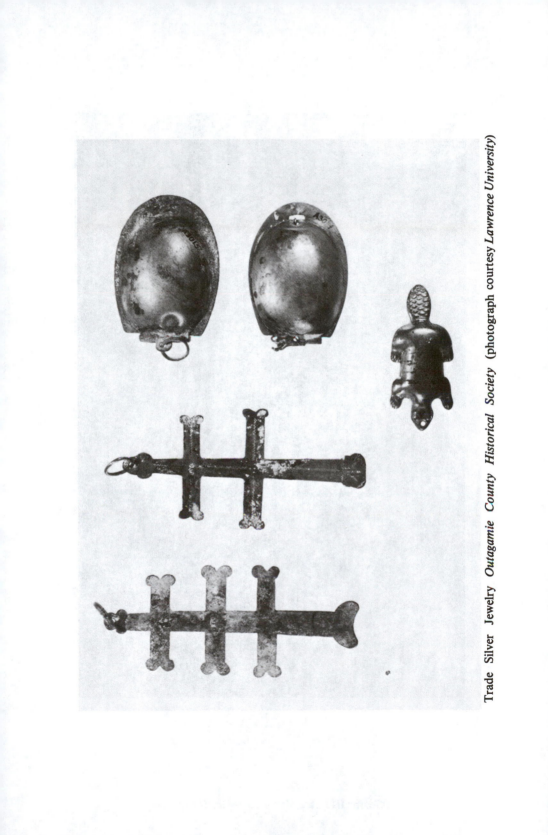

Trade Silver Jewelry *Outagamie County Historical Society* (photograph courtesy *Lawrence University*)

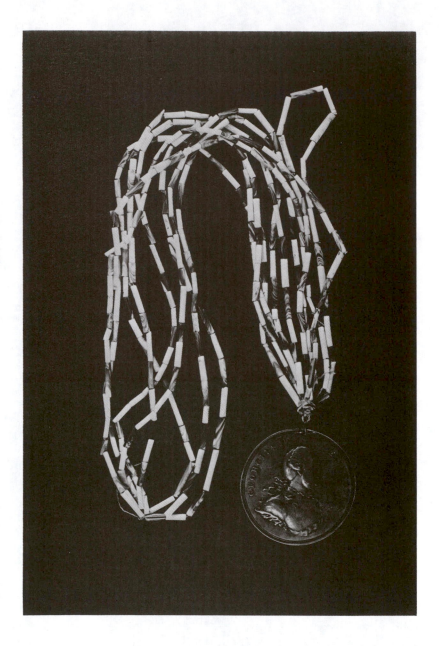

George III Peace Medal *Lawrence University*

supporters were important political symbols. These medals,
sometimes called "peace medals," were tokens of
recognition, friendship, alliance, and expectation of favors
in the future. When an Indian group shifted its allegiance,
the medals of one government were replaced by those of
another. When American expeditions moved up the
Mississippi River after the War of 1812, they tried to move
Indian loyalties in an American direction by giving out
American medals in place of British ones. In many
instances, they insisted that the replacement be made.
People with politically unpopular medals sometimes simply
filed away the offending royal heads and kept their
medals in spite of changes in the political wind.

Tattooing and painting

When Champlain first saw the Ottawa in the
seventeenth century, he noted that they were "much
carved about the body" (Kinietz 1940: 234), and tattooing
continued to be mentioned for the next 150 years. The
references are often detailed and indicate a lot of variation in form and design from one group to another. The
Miami, for example, tattooed young men over the body in
all kinds of patterns; the Ioway used tattooing selectively,
only as a means of identifying family and social standing;
Potawatomi tattooers covered the whole body with their
designs. Both men and women were tattooed, usually with
the women decorated only on the face, arms, or chest.
Tattooing was done with sharp pointed bones in a wooden
tool like a comb. The tips were soaked in paint, mainly a
mixture of charcoal black and water, and then forced into
the skin. By the nineteenth century, fewer references to
tattooing can be found. Perhaps the custom of wearing
more clothing summer and winter left less surface
available; perhaps newer kinds of decoration met the same
aesthetic needs more easily. In the twentieth century,
tattooing survived among some Menomini and Chippewa
people only as a technique for curing, not for decoration
(Skinner 1921).

Body painting was mentioned in the French sources
as early as tattooing, and it lasted longer. Like tattooing, it
might be only in certain places, sometimes on the face
only, or it might cover the entire body. Sometimes faces
were painted half green and half red; women often
painted their entire faces red with traders' vermillion,
imported all the way from China. Styles in painting often
reflected an individual's personal inspiration or

experiences; for warriors, it could indicate military honors or achievements. Looking at the existing portraits of Wisconsin Indians reveals a variety of body painting. For example, a famous portrait of the Sauk leader, Keokuck (Blair 1911, II: 159), shows several painted white stripes on his legs and three white hands painted on his breast and upper arm. The Winnebago leader, Four Legs (Lurie 1978), was painted with vertical stripes through his eyes, and George Catlin's portrait of an Ojibwa woman illustrates the use of vermillion on her face combined with parallel dark stripes on her cheeks (Frederickson 1980).

Body painting was done for many reasons. Clan markings were sometimes put on the faces of the dead before burial. The Winnebago in particular had a complex series of face paintings for the dead (Radin 1923: pl. 46). Body painting was also appropriate for other occasions. Fasting for dreams or after warfare meant that faces had to be blackened. People painted themselves before going out on raids and on their return home. Face painting symbolized levels of membership in the Midewiwin Society (see Chapter 7). Prisoners destined for torture were also painted before their ordeals, probably because facing the fire was equivalent to facing the enemy in warfare. Men getting ready to play lacrosse painted themselves with "all colors" (Kinietz 1940: 234), and people painted before meeting important guests. Young men and women thinking about marriage went about with red faces produced not from shyness, but with paint instead (Blair 1911, II). In general, body painting was a means of heightening the importance of social or political events of many kinds. As more and more clothing was worn and bodies were covered up, painting was limited to the face alone, and, like tattooing, it became a mere remnant of what it had been earlier.

Body painting was only one of several kinds of painting, but very little has survived of any of the others. Skin clothing was once painted, perhaps in the same style as Cree or Naskapi long coats from more northern areas. Wisconsin women were described in 1709 as having skin clothing "painted very neatly with black, red, and yellow" (Kinietz 1940: 343) and were even seen "painting their dresses." Some elegant painted coats of the eighteenth or nineteenth century were made for traders, and they give hints as to the general style of earlier skin painting. The designs were mainly geometric, drawn or impressed on the skin and then filled in with colors (Coe 1977). Many of them looked like fine porcupine quillwork, at least at a distance. When cloth replaced skins, painting very quickly disappeared.

Many painted designs were ceremonial: bow emblems on canoes, symbols on paddles, and animals painted on sails during the trade period. They were meant to have an influence on what happened as well as act as decorations. The same can be said for painting on drums, grave posts, pipestems, religious scrolls, or sacred poles planted before wigwams. Grave posts, for example, were a means of recording a person's deeds in life (Blair 1911, II: 238); during the funeral ceremonies, those present struck the posts and recited war honors, marking them for each one claimed. Even painted buffalo robes were part of ceremonial life rather than being only decorated places to sit. Nicolas Perrot was seated on one, "as soft as silk," during a ceremony at a combined Miami-Mascouten village in 1668 (Blair 1911, I: 326).

Rock art is still another kind of Indian painting. Wisconsin is on the southern edge of the area around the Great Lakes where rock art occurred. Rock art consists of both supernatural and everyday subjects painted on flat surfaces, sometimes on cliffs or in caves. Many of the paintings look like the figures woven into fiber bags or drawn on the birchbark scrolls of the Midewiwin Society. Some of them may be hunting magic (Tanner 1830) or they may tie into vision quests. Painting (or even incising) on rocks may be very old, but dating them is not easy. Sometimes they contain clues to their age: if a horse appears in a painting, for example, it means a date after European contact; guns or European dress on figures would mean the same thing. Examples of authentic rock art are not rare in the Wisconsin area: an impressive group is located at Burnt Bluff on the Garden Peninsula of Michigan. They are on a limestone cliff overlooking Big Bay de Noc, only a short distance from the tip of Door County (Lugthart 1968). The paintings include human figures in shades of red and brown, and they seem to be part of a ceremony. The Gottschall rock shelter, another important rock art site, has a dramatic set of figures that probably dates from the Mississippian (Salzer 1987).

Ceremonial Equipment

Pipes

By historic times, the role of tobacco had expanded and was used on an everyday basis. Its role in ceremony was still important, but now both men and women used it even when no ritual was involved. Maybe the adoption of smoking by the French and mild trade tobacco played roles in spreading smoking among Indians.

The pipes used by Indians before they had European trade pipes had many prehistoric ancestors. One of them was a small pipe of catlinite, greenstone, or limestone found often on prehistoric Late Woodland or Oneota sites in Wisconsin. Catlinite, the red pipestone of Minnesota, was the most famous material for pipes, but other kinds of pipestone come from scattered deposits in Wisconsin. All of these pipestones were soft when dug out of the ground and could be easily ground or polished into pipes.

In the French period, before the coming of English clay pipes, catlinite or other stone pipes were made especially for the trade. These small reddish pipe bowls, often called "Micmac" pipes, were put on reed stems and used by French traders. As tobacco smoking spread, Micmac pipes were used by everyone, Europeans and Indians alike. Pipes were carried along with tobacco and fire-steels in tobacco pouches, small pucker-string bags of buckskin or the whole skin of an animal turned into a bag.

In addition to everyday smoking pipes, Indians also had calumets. These pipes were used on ceremonial or political occasions (see Chapter 6). Technically, the important part of a calumet is the long stem, made of wood, catlinite, or even metal. Wooden stems were often flat, but sometimes they were carved in spirals or elongated twists. The stems were hung with feathers and decorated with paint, beadwork, or quillwork. The quality of the decoration was very high; some of the finest surviving examples of quillwork and beadwork are on the stems of calumets. The bowls were usually made of catlinite, sometimes inlaid with lead, and shaped in a right angle elbow form. The bowls had to have large bore holes in order to attach the elaborate stems.

Records for the decorated calumet go back into the seventeenth century. Perrot was met in a large Wisconsin village by an old man with a calumet in his hand, "ornamented in its whole length with the heads of birds, flame-colored, and had in the middle a bunch of feathers colored bright red, which resembled a great fan" (Blair 1911, I: 325-326). So important were the stems that sometimes they were not even drilled and were carried in ceremonies without any intention of using them for smoking. The symbolic power of the calumet was so strong that people could travel safely through the countryside if they carried a pipestem with them.

Medicine bags

The post-contact Midewiwin Society of Algonquin speaking Indians and the Medicine Lodge of the Winnebago are known for medicine bags made of whole animal skins decorated with quillwork or beadwork. Medicine bags were an important part of Midewiwin or Medicine Lodge rituals (see Chapter 7), and they were prominent in the ceremonies, often as a means of ritually "shooting" participants and helping them in their restoration to life and health. They were made of an entire animal's skin with head, paws, and even the tail. Each animal was skinned whole through a cut in the chest. The skin was tanned, and then it was restored as much as possible to a lifelike form. In some cases, wooden whistles were put in the mouths of the bags to make animal sounds when the bags were squeezed (Hoffman 1896). Since medicine bags were not the only bags made of animal skins, they were set apart from ordinary bags by the presence of little bits of feather down in the animal's nose. Otter was preferred because of a special relationship between otters and the religious societies, but other animal skins were used as well: mink, beaver, weasel, bear paw, bear cub, badger, snake, and even owl.

Most medicine bags in museums are not very old, and there have been some changes in their decoration over the last 200 years. Early bags were ornamented very simply. A Chippewa bag of around 1800, for example, was made of a badger skin with bells and beads on the paws and long buckskin strips and little tinkling cones as a border all around the tail; a pair of eagle claws were perched on the head like horns (Coe 1976: 99). Other bags of about the same time look forward to what was to become standard treatment: very elaborate decoration only on the paws and tails. This began with pieces of decorated buckskin sewn on paws and the inner tail, sometimes with added bells and brass buttons. The earliest patterns on the buckskin were done in many colors of quillwork by women, who expressed their artistic feeling in many ways. Sometimes they would decorate only the tail or they would do only the forepaws and the tail, adding beads, bells, buttons, tinklers, and thimbles as trim. By the 1820s and 1830s, quillwork was still common, but by the end of the century, medicine bags were more and more alike with squares of beadwork attached to the paws and elaborate beaded strips, often done on a background of red flannel, on the tail. Beadwork designs varied with both floral and

Decorated Medicine Bags *Neville Public Museum* (485/219, 1074/1455)

geometric figures used. Over the years, a great deal of artistry has gone into fine medicine bags, often using prime furs and rare or rich materials in the trim (Landes 1968a).

Dream Dance drums

Of recent origin, the Drum or Dream Dance spread into the western lakes during the nineteenth century (see Chapter 7). The great drums that are the main focus of its rituals are sometimes called "Friendship Drums." They stress alliances between groups of peoples and the peace and friendship coming from the ritual. In theory, all the drums are related; they come from the original drum through the practice of one group's giving a drum to another, each new drum incorporating a small piece of the older drum.

The drums are very large, often over two feet in diameter and a foot in thickness (Vennum 1982), and their construction is variable. The basic framework was originally a large wooden washtub, but galvanized iron washtubs came into use as wooden ones were harder and harder to find. All recent drums are made from iron tubs. A large circular hole was cut in the bottom of the tub and thick moose, cow, or even horse skin drum heads fastened on each end. Inside the drum, a little bell was often put on a string across the top just under the head; when the head was struck, the bell jingled, adding another sound coming from the drum. When a drum is in use, it hangs from four curved sticks, much like shepherd's crooks turned outward.

The drums are decorated with a skirt of red flannel or velvet covering the outside. Narrow blue or yellow trim and a band of otter or other fur goes around the drum at the rim. Below the fur, a wide band of beadwork encircles the drum with four pocket-shaped beaded tabs suspended from it. The beaded tabs represent the intervals between the four directions and may be simple ovals or geometric forms. Feathers, ribbon streamers, and sometimes silver discs also may be used in the decoration (Densmore 1913). An important mark of Dream Dance drums is a broad yellow stripe painted down the middle of the upper head. Above the stripe, the head was painted blue; and below the stripe, it was painted red. These colors are thought to be symbolic of dark and light, cold and warm seasons (Vennum 1973). When not in use, the drums are kept in bags hanging from the rafters in the homes of the keepers.

Dream or Drum Dance Drum *Neville Public Museum* (151/173)

Water Drum: Menomini *Neville Public Museum* (866/599, 15/4510)

Other drums

Other drums were used in ceremonial life. The simple water drum, for example, was part of the Midewiwin Society rituals. These drums were made of a piece of log hollowed out by charring and scraping in much the same way as a dugout canoe was made. The head consisted of thick, untanned deerskin held in place by a hoop. A hole in the drum let water be put into it and the head wetted by turning the drum. Wetting the head from the inside produced a special tone, a vibrating voice that carried a long way (Densmore 1910). Log water drums were often decorated by carving Midewiwin symbols or figures around the body.

Different kinds of drums can be used for different things. A water drum, often made of a metal pot covered with a tightly drawn head, is used for the rituals of the Native American Church. A simple circular drum, as large as 20 inches in diameter and only a few inches thick, can be used whenever a drum is needed. This big drum, covered on one or both faces with thin skin heads, is a tambourine with little sticks fitted to the inside that vibrate when the drum is struck. The tambourine drum is used for War Dances, curing ceremonies, and even social dances. How old any of these drum types are is hard to measure. No drum parts have survived in archaeological sites. When historic records mention drums, they describe water drums made of clay pots with skin heads. These drums would simply disappear into the sherd counts of archaeologists as the clay pots were broken and their pieces scattered.

European Influence

European technology caused changes in material culture even before Nicolas Perrot gave away awls, glass beads, and other things to Indians in the seventeenth century. Many of the changes were so early that by the time information was recorded about Wisconsin Indians, differences in the way they looked and dressed and in the artifacts they used were of such long standing that they were already "traditional." Modern students of material culture often go to such sources as Skinner (1921) on Menomini material culture under the impression that his descriptions of nineteenth century life reflect ancient patterns of artifact use.

The new European technology that came with the French was a two-edged sword: it brought advantages, but it created dependence on undependable sources of supply. These sources could not be controlled or even counted on because of political problems between supplier nations: France, England, or the United States. The risks Indians took in relying on foreign sources for everyday tools had to be balanced against what could be done with these tools. The new technology liberated existing arts and crafts and allowed them to float free from the constraints of old materials. It permitted full expression of older patterns and, in some cases, even went beyond them to create new patterns of lasting value. But it put Indians at a permanent disadvantage because it made them dependent on someone else for many basic tools.

Many older craft forms changed. Styles of dress were retained in outline, but they were greatly enhanced. New materials, new means of decoration, and new tools used for making clothing altered old habits; in the hands of women, a revolution in equipment and material quickly occurred. New materials often slipped into the place of the old; for example, wool yarns from unravelling blankets replaced native plants for making fiber bags. These yarns, often combined with nettle or basswood strings, allowed more experimentation with color and form (Feest 1980). Metal tools made working catlinite much easier. In late prehistoric sites, catlinite beads, pipes, and pendants were present in small numbers, fitting in with the investment in time and labor needed for each one. By the eighteenth century, Indian craftsmen had iron drills and files, and the number of catlinite and other pipestone artifacts rapidly increased. In some historic archaeological sites in Wisconsin, pipestone scraps and things in all stages of manufacture show a great increase in catlinite working in Indian villages.

All during the historic period, material culture underwent dramatic change and growth. Not until the twentieth century did this growth slow down. Further change has now reduced the number of things made in the home, and Indians, like other Americans, make fewer of the objects they use every day. They have come to rely on standard industrial products.

Craft production

Some nineteenth century style artifacts are still made on an individual basis for special occasions or for sale as art objects to those who admire the old crafts. However, this is only the end of a long history of crafts made for trade, sale, or gift-giving on the part of Indians. Things made especially for trade or sale include birchbark canoes. They were sold at Michilimackinac for "200 to 300 livres each" by the Ottawa in the eighteenth century (Blair 1911, I: 282). Many of these canoes went to Europeans, but they were made for sale to other Indians in Wisconsin, especially to those living south of the Canadian Zone. Porcupine quills were exchanged with those who lived out of the normal range of porcupines. Quills moved between such northern peoples as Potawatomis and Ottawas and to more southern ones, such as the Miami (Kinietz 1940). Finished quillwork had an even greater distribution, and some of it was traded far out into the Plains. Beadwork moved from Wisconsin to North Dakota, Montana, and Idaho where fine Chippewa and Menomini pieces were traded to other Indians in exchange for horses. In the nineteenth century, buckskin clothing--moccasins, jackets, gloves--were regularly made for sale to traders (Barnouw 1954). Mats, decorated birchbark containers, and catlinite objects moved between traders and Indians as well as between one Indian group and another. In most of this trade, women were the major producers.

New arts and crafts

One industry that developed in the post-contact period was lead mining, which was carried on for well over a hundred years. Nicolas Perrot was one of the first Frenchmen to speak of lead-bearing lands and to assess the quality of the ore (Blair 1911, I). Indians were not working with lead then, and they did not mine or smelt it until the early eighteenth century. In 1710, the French took credit for teaching them the techniques and ruefully remarked that as a result, Indians no longer needed to come to the French for their supplies of lead (Kinietz 1940). By the end of the eighteenth century, Sauk, Fox, Winnebago, and Ioway were mining lead. By the early part of the nineteenth century, as much as a half million pounds of lead were processed by the Sauk and Fox alone.

The techniques for lead mining and smelting were very simple at first and probably built on whatever Indians knew of copper working and what they had learned about working iron. In general, the ore was taken out of the surface of the ground without any underground work. It was pried out with levers made of iron, often reworked gun barrels that look like the old antler levers from the copper mines on Isle Royale. Lead mining, however, required both smelting and casting. In the beginning, smelting was done by simply piling ore on fires out of which the melted lead flowed to form puddles on the ground. By the nineteenth century, other methods were used, including collecting the lead in molds by means of hoppers (Kay 1972). Initially, at least, mining and smelting were done by women and old men during midsummer when gardens did not need so much attention. As the volume grew and trapping for furs became less reliable, more and more of the work was done by men who used to spend their time as warriors and hunters. Lead mining was carried out mainly in southwestern Wisconsin, but references to lead mining include places as far east as Lake Koshkonong. Lead mining there has left remains at Crabapple Point, where lead globs, pieces of galena, lead residue, and smelting pits are signs of smelting and casting in an Indian village (Spector 1975).

Much more lead was made than could be used by the miners, and most of it moved into trade. The Winnebago were known for the great amounts of lead they traded with others. Many hunters, for example, stopped at Winnebago mines as a regular part of their hunting round (Kay 1972). Lead was used mainly as shot, but lead casting of such things as pipes and lead inlay on catlinite show that some of the possibilities in metal work were being tried out.

Silverworking spread widely during the late eighteenth and early nineteenth centuries. As long as the fur trade lasted and people could trade for silver ornaments, little silver working was attempted. With a decline in the fur trade, the silver ornament trade went downhill, too. Silver decorations had become an indispensable part of everyone's wardrobe, and people had to look for substitute sources: they began to make their own. Many groups in the Northeast worked silver (Ritzenthaler and Ritzenthaler 1970), but how widespread silverworking was in Wisconsin or when it began are not known. The Iroquois in New York started silverworking as early as the first part of the nineteenth century, and before long, smiths were so common that every Iroquois village was said to have at least one of them. Silversmiths were apparently not as common in Wisconsin, but one Menomini silversmith was working as late as 1920 (Skinner 1921) and some Winnebago silversmiths continue to work today.

The technology used in making silver ornaments was European in origin. The tool kits included homemade punches, hammers, pincers, soldering irons, compasses, and anvils. The basic technique was cold-hammering and cutting, using either silver coins that had been made into thin silver sheets or ready-made sheets of German silver. German silver is an alloy of nickel, copper, and zinc; and it became more widespread as silver coins became too valuable to use as a source for metal. Wisconsin silversmiths made many kinds of silver ornaments: brooches, bracelets, earrings, headbands, rings, bangles, hatbands. Most of the shapes and designs were the same ones that were popular during the Late Historic Period.

Summary

The material culture of Wisconsin Indians began in prehistory with some distinct local traditions, but after European trade arrived, many things were more uniform. Similar tools, styles of dress, and ornaments spread across the Northeast. What people used or wore became more similar as they all traded with the same European sources and as they interacted more with each other and shared ideas. New arts and crafts based on raw materials coming from Europe were not long in taking shape.

CHAPTER 6
Kinship and Political Organization

For Wisconsin Indians, the most important way people were organized was through kinship. A man or woman was a kinsman and family member, not a citizen or a voting member. The basic ties that bound people were marriage and descent, not legal residence. Many Indians included Europeans or Americans in this frame of reference by referring to government officials as "Father" or "Brother," depending on whether they felt their relationship was the equal one of brothers or the dependent one of sons to father.

Kinship, however, is much more than the names people are called. It is a network through which people can accomplish many useful things. For example, kinship systems often organized economic life. Women collected wild rice or fished or hoed corn with other women related to them as sisters, mothers, daughters, sisters-in-law, grandmothers, or daughters-in-law. Men hunted and fished with men who were members of their families. In making a living, the labor and experience of kinsmen might make the difference between surviving or not. A person can rely on kinsmen simply because they are kin, and people with large and powerful kinship groups had better chances in meeting basic needs.

Kinship also provided protection. In a world without state legal systems, a person was often only as safe as his kinsmen could make him. The knowledge that a man had a large and powerful group of relatives who would avenge him acted as a form of protection. On the other hand, each person was a kind of hostage for his own kin group: bad behavior by one kinsman might reflect back on his group as a whole and involve it in revenge killing or murder.

Kinship is a system of mutual rights and obligations and works best when relationships are face to face and can continue over time. Once the groups get large or scattered, it is harder to depend on kinship. The systems themselves often get larger but when they do, they weaken the obligation that members feel for each and every other member. The large kinship groups called "clans" are one result of increasing size, but even clans cannot always be as dependable as smaller, face to face kin groups. When kinship groups become very large, other forms of relationships develop to meet new needs. The political structure called "tribe" is an example. There are many ways "tribe" has been used, and most Wisconsin Indian groups have been called "tribes" in the past.

The social and political systems that made up the Indian world of the seventeenth century began to change when Europeans arrived. For the next two hundred years, community life altered in many ways, and it is not always possible to tell whether social life described in the nineteenth century was typical of any earlier periods. In some cases, nineteenth century records are all that exist, and they have to serve as guides to what was there before.

Winnebago Social Life

No one knows how the Winnebago were organized in their long ago past. The early records made by the French were not detailed enough to tell what kind of organization they had then or how day-to-day life was carried out. Most of what is known about the Winnebago comes from twentieth century memories of the nineteenth century (Radin 1923). At least some of this information can be pushed back in time: kinship systems, for example, change slowly, and some customs last longer than others. For the most part, the picture of Winnebago life that has survived reflects a very recent time.

A traveler visiting Winnebago villages in the early nineteenth century followed a route through the country between Lake Winnebago and the Rock River. At that time, villages consisted of tiny camps with perhaps one or two houses or large settlements with more than a dozen wigwams. The largest recorded village was one with 35 separate houses and a population of about 600. Throughout Winnebago territory a few very large villages plus many smaller outlying ones was the general pattern. The large villages served as centers where people could take refuge in case of trouble, come for news, set out on war parties, or meet in large groups. Sometimes these "grand villages" were located at strategic spots where defense was easier. Doty Island at the north end of Lake Winnebago is an example of such a place.

Villages were all very similar. They were located on water close to land suitable for gardens. People preferred to put their houses on sandy, well-drained soil in spots sheltered from the wind. Entering a village meant skirting or passing through fields of corn, beans, and squash and coming upon the large oval wigwams, roofed over with strips of birch bark and reed mats. Winnebago villages were not laid out in streets nor were there large town squares or lots owned by individuals. All the wigwams looked much the same, but some of them were special because of the standing of the people who lived there. According to some accounts, wigwams belonging to families of the Thunder and Bear clans usually were at the center of the village or at either end. The wigwam of the Thunder chief was regarded as a place of sanctuary, and an enemy would be safe if he took refuge there. Besides wigwams, villages had small lodges where women lived during menstruation and other buildings such as little bark houses for sweat baths and large ceremonial lodges.

The view of the world people had was from their membership in two groups: family and lineage. The family consisted of husband and wife with their unmarried children. Sometimes a man married a woman and then married her sister or niece, but in general, only one man and one woman lived as a married pair. The first marriage for each partner was arranged by the parents of the couple or, more likely, by the brother of the girl. Marriages took place without any religious ceremony, but an elaborate exchange of gifts took place between the families. The second kin group was a unit called a lineage. It consisted of a group of men and women related over several generations in the male line. A lineage usually had an older man who was its head, and it included his sons and daughters, the children of his sons, and the children of his sons' sons. It might also include the descendants of his brothers or male cousins. The line of descent ran through men, and children belonged to their father's lineage. A Winnebago, then, was a member of his or her own immediate family and could depend on a larger group, the lineage, in case of need.

Any one individual had ties to many lineages. The lineage of birth was first in importance. The lineage from which a person's mother came was also a special group; mother's people regarded her children as close kinsmen. Through marriage, people came to have ties to the lineages of their spouses, and as time passed, they were linked to other lineages through the marriages of brothers and sisters, children, and even grandchildren. The closeness anyone felt for kin ties acquired through marriage depended on circumstances, but overlapping relationships extended through the whole tribe and helped hold it together as one people. Each person also belonged to a clan. Clans are like very large lineages, many of whose members can no longer trace exactly how they are related to one another. A Winnebago village was likely to include lineages belonging to several clans.

Kinship

Within the family, each Winnebago child had a mother and father called by parent terms just as in other societies. The terms for brother and sister, however, were different. Birth order was very important, and there were four birth names for girls and four birth names for boys (Lurie 1971). These names were given in order as the children were born. If a family had four boys, they would be known in the family as first son, second son, third son, and fourth son. Any children born after the fourth would be given names that were diminutive of the third or fourth names. Thus all the children of any village would share in eight names, and any child called "first daughter" would know other girls called by the same name within their own families. Birth order names were not the only names children had, but in the family, they were very important.

Moving from the family to the lineage reflected a widening of the kinship world (Radin 1923). All of father's brothers were called "father." The term "father" is not equivalent to the English term but identifies all the adult males of father's generation in father's lineage. Father's sisters, the women called "aunt" by contemporary Americans, were all called by a term that stressed their membership in father's lineage. Throughout life, these women remained a close part of an individual's world.

The way the Winnebago referred to people called "cousins" in the American kinship system was more complicated. Cousins who were the children of a man called father were called "brother" and "sister." These cousins were also members of a person's own lineage; using "brother" and "sister" is one way of stressing this closeness. When these cousins had children of their own, a Winnebago man would call the children of his male cousins "sons" and "daughters"; they, too, belonged to his lineage. The children of female cousins he called "sister" were called something else since they belonged to their own fathers' lineages. The situation was reversed for women: they called the children of brothers by nephew and niece terms and the children of their sisters were their sons and daughters. The children of fathers' sisters were not members of a person's lineage, and they were called "niece" and "nephew." The children of a man's sisters were also called niece and nephew, meaning "the children of women who belong to my lineage." For women, the terms "niece" and "nephew" meant "children of men who belong to my lineage."

The lineage world for any Winnebago, then, consisted of men of father's generation who were all called "father" and the sisters of these men, the "father's sisters." The next generation of children included brothers and sisters, who were the children of the fathers, and nieces and nephews, who were the children of the fathers' sisters. The brothers and sisters were members of the lineage, the nieces and nephews were not. The same division occurred as a person grew older: the children of a man's brothers were his sons and daughters, and the children of all of his sisters were his nephews and nieces; the children of a woman's brothers were her nieces and nephews, and the children of her sisters were her sons and daughters.

Mother's lineage was also seen as a group of people with special ties to her children. For example, all of mother's sisters were called "mother" as well. "Mother" stood for "woman of my mother's lineage on her generation," and that might include several people. The children of all these mothers were called "brother" and "sister," and they belonged to a number of other lineages since they took membership from their fathers. Mother's lineage included men called by a term often translated as "mother's brother." Mother's brothers were very important; they were expected to give their sisters' children whatever was asked of them (Lurie 1978) or do whatever was needed without complaint. Mother's brothers were also available to discipline children when the need arose. Mothers' brothers' children were called "mother's brother" and "mother" also. These terms mean "male member of my mother's lineage" and "female member of my mother's lineage." The children of anyone called mother and mother's brother were called by the same names into other generations: the children of mother's brothers were called mother and mother's brother again while the children of mothers were brother and sister. All of mother's lineage, then, were called "mother" and "mother's brother." Any Winnebago might have mothers and mother's brothers who were small babies.

One category of kinsman whose role went beyond lineage ties is "grandparent." For Winnebago children, the parents of their mothers and fathers were grandparents, but as a title of courtesy, the term "grandparent" was extended to most old people. The Winnebago felt that between grandparents and grandchildren a warm relationship existed, an easier one than between parents and children. Grandparents often raised orphaned children and gave grandchildren a place of refuge when needed (Lurie 1971). As the term grandparent was a warm and loving one, so was the term "grandchild."

All these kinship terms and categories were not merely empty titles. Expectable behavior went along with them and gave people guidance as to what was polite and proper toward their kinsmen. In a world where kinship was so important, etiquette was something well-bred people knew and children were taught very early. For example, the Winnebago felt that it was not right for brothers and sisters to be too familiar. The proper attitude of brothers and sisters--including all the people called by those terms-- was very formal and respectful. Brothers were concerned with sisters' marriages and even made their choices for them. Ideally, girls had too much respect for their brothers to openly argue with them. Another very respectful relationship was that between mother-in-law and son-in-law; they spoke of each other using the grandparent/grandchild terms, but their mutual respect involved avoiding one another entirely. Conflict can hardly begin where people do not talk to each other. In contrast, proper behavior between people related to each other as brothers-in-law and sisters-in-law included joking and teasing. The Winnebago had standards of how "good" people behaved in public, and because the means of regulating behavior were informal, manners were depended on to a great extent.

Winnebago clans

Several related lineages made up a clan (Radin 1923). A person was born into the clan of his or her father and remained a clan member for life. Each clan had a name, origin story, organization, rituals, customs, and tribal duties; and some clans were more powerful and important than others, at least at certain times in Winnebago history. People took pride in what clan members did and had strong fellow feelings with other clansmen. Since the clans were usually large, no one knew exactly how every member was related to every other member. The members of the clan outside a person's own lineage were all called "brother" and "sister," and marriage to any one of them was not allowed. A person had to choose a mate from another clan.

In the early twentieth century, the Winnebago remembered twelve clans. They once may have had several more since clans can die out and disappear. The twelve clans remembered in modern times are Thunder, Warrior, Eagle, Pigeon, Bear, Wolf, Water Spirit, Deer, Elk, Buffalo, Fish, and Snake. Pigeon became extinct recently and, although no Pigeon people survive, the clan is still remembered. Almost all of the clans are named after animals, and in a general way, clan members felt a kind of relationship to the clan animal. In the twentieth century, Winnebagos did not think of living clan animals as the ancestors of their clans. Instead, they felt that long ago, before people lived as people and animals lived as animals, the spiritual beings who were those animals played a role in the original creation of the clans.

Clan organization revolved around lineages that owned heirlooms such as war bundles and war clubs. The holders of the bundles and other things inherited the right to have them and could not let them pass out of lineage ownership. During feasts in honor of these possessions and in regular yearly clan feasts, clan members came together and renewed their sense of identity. The gathering of the clans at those times helped to develop a strong clan feeling and a sense of difference from other people. Clan traditions and stories built a deep loyalty that made Winnebago people think first of their clan identity and only later of their membership in the Winnebago tribe.

The largest and most important of the clans in the nineteenth century was the Thunder clan. It was thought to have originated at Green Bay in the long ago past, and several versions have been told of the clan's origin story. One version began with Earthmaker resting in a void into which his thoughts created earth, water, plants, and winds. Earthmaker next brought into being four powerful guardians, the Thunders, whose job was to look after the earth. He next created four brothers, who were sent to earth with a tobacco plant and fire in order to live there. Earthmaker created animals for men to hunt in the forests and waterbirds for them to hunt along the shores. He even sent dogs for people to use and eat. These earliest Thunder clansmen were very powerful and wandered around the earth creating hills and valleys by banging on the ground with their clubs. The stories do not mention Thunder women or other women who might have become wives of the original Thunders. Nevertheless, the Thunder clan grew until it was thought to include almost a quarter of the tribe in the late nineteenth century (Radin 1923).

The duty of the Thunder clan was to preserve peace and settle disputes, and the Thunder chief was the main peacemaker. He was a man of age, wisdom, and good character; and he was always chosen from prominent Thunder lineages, perhaps those that owned war bundles. He was a peace chief, a person set aside from ordinary life and its problems. He did not go to war; and he could keep war parties from leaving the village if in his best judgment they should stay at home. He could not stand in the path of the warriors and stop them with force, but he could let them know what he thought. Men who ignored the opinion of the Thunder chief in matters of warfare went against the best judgment of the society. Besides, men who went to war in spite of the Thunder chief were responsible for any losses and could expect vengeance from any dead warriors' kinsmen.

The role of the Thunder chief as a peacemaker was very important within the tribe. It was his duty to prevent feuds from starting and tearing the tribe apart from the inside. Quarrels, disputes, and fights sometimes occurred, leading to injury or murder. In such cases, kinsmen had to avenge kinsmen, for only through a balanced expectation of revenge could everyone be protected. If this were allowed to happen, though, vengeance and counter-vengeance could lead to the destruction of tribal life as crosscutting kinship ties drew everyone into bloody dispute. The job of the Thunder chief was to act as a peacemaker, a mediator, and a smoother of tribal troubled waters. He might even try to ensure peace by offering himself as a sacrifice. He would insert skewers in his flesh, paint his body blue, and present himself to the kinsmen of a murdered man or woman in the hope that the sight of his suffering would cause them to forgive the murderer and let the matter rest.

The Bear clan was also important. Its origin myth is found in several forms, one of which brought the Bear clan from "across the ocean." In this tale, ten brothers came across the ocean to attend a clan meeting, probably at Green Bay. A Bear came from the water as a raven and assumed bear shape on the land. This great Bear became the spirit guardian of the bear clan and took his place in the gathering. From that point, there have always been Bear clan people.

Bear clan members were tribal sergeants-at-arms. During the year, Bear men kept order in villages or on hunts. They led on marches, placed sentries to protect villages, and had the right to punish those who disobeyed them. Bear men were in charge of prisoners of war and served as guards for people accused of crimes. Sometimes it was Bear men who delivered murderers into the hands of the victim's kin for revenge. Considering that Bears exercised authority within villages, the Bear chief, as controller of that authority, was a powerful person.

Other clans had special duties and rights within the tribe. The Wolf clan people, for example, were allied to the Bears and served as soldiers, helpers to Bear men in carrying out their duties. In smaller villages where only a few Bear clansmen were present, Wolf men helped out in defending and guarding the village. Members of the Buffalo clan were town criers and spread the news throughout the village. The Elk clan was associated with fire, and Elks had the responsibility of caring for fire when people were out hunting or on war parties. Members of the Water Spirit clan had a link to water and were concerned with crossing of streams and access to good drinking water.

Winnebago clans were joined into groups called "moieties." This word means "halves," and each clan belonged to one of the two sections. On one side were "those who were above"--Thunder, Eagle, Hawk, and Pigeon. On the other side were the rest of the clans, "those who were on earth." The two parts of Winnebago society did not have any strong moiety organization, but the division expressed itself in several ways. For one thing, the members of each half had to look for husbands or wives in the opposite half: a person who belonged to those who were above always had to marry someone belonging to those who were on earth. The separation of the society into halves really tied it tightly together by extending kinship ties over and over again between the two halves.

Each clan also had a "friend" clan. The friend clan of the Thunders was the Warrior clan; for the Eagle clan the associated clan was Pigeon, and for Bear, Wolf. The expectation one friend clan had of another was mutual aid. In general, members of friend clans buried each other's dead, avenged each other's wrongs, and showed each other hospitality. Members of friend clans respected each other and were ready to be of service whenever the need should arise.

Tribal organization

Winnebago tribal organization is poorly known. In fact, very little was recorded in the early centuries of contact just when great social changes altered whatever used to be there in the seventeenth century. For some things, there is no information at all, and the details of day to day operation are only suspected, not known from any witnesses. Further confusion was caused by British and American authorities who dealt with the Winnebago. They assumed there was a powerful political structure among most Indians and thought that strong leaders and lines of command were present everywhere.

Winnebago tribal organization rested on the individual loyalties of people to their lineage, clan, moiety, and friend clans. The interlocking of all these ties was the means through which the tribe was defined; it was expressed by overlapping relationships. Acknowledging relationships, however, is not enough to form a tribe. It worked as a unit only if it continued to be reinforced by frequent face-to-face meetings and a continuous flow of information from one related group to another. Councils, meetings among people of importance, spread information back and forth and acted to knit the tribe together. The Winnebago did nothing without talking things over in meetings and trying to see the outcome of whatever steps they were taking. This left time and opportunity for the men who spoke for their kinsmen to listen to them and hear their opinions while the council was being held. Sometimes, when a quick response was needed from the tribe as a whole, the Winnebago were at a disadvantage. They could not react as quickly as Europeans, whose decisions were reached by faraway governments and were not subject to discussion or change.

Winnebago villages all had chiefs and councils, formal or informal, depending upon the size of the community. The chiefs probably achieved their positions through a combination of being born in the right lineages and having the right kind of personality. It also helped to have a large group of kinsmen to support them. They were leaders and guides, but they were unable to impose their wills upon their fellow villagers except by persuasion and example. The greater their personal prestige, the greater their individual standing and ability to move people in directions they thought desirable. The influence of a great chief, however, died with him.

In considering matters that affected many people, councils of greater scope than village level were held. Large scale councils with representatives from all the clans met together formally in a council lodge, where each clan had its proper place and its chance to express its opinion. In a sense, these large councils were gatherings of kinsmen representing kinsmen when the matter at hand went beyond village boundaries and local concerns. They seem to have been called together when the need arose, and they relied on informal means for carrying out whatever was decided. And decisions were reached through consensus, not majority vote or formal legislation.

The most important political unit remained the village through much of the historic period. Whether formal Winnebago tribal structure was ever more complicated is unknown. Oral traditions mention a head chief over the whole tribe, someone who represented the Winnebago to outsiders and governed with authority within the tribe. What power a head chief might have had is unknown. Perhaps he was the clan chief of the Thunders; the chief of the largest and most important clan may have been regarded with respect by all the people by virtue of being head of that clan. The idea of a head chief may have come about after historic contact when chiefs were "made" by European or American governments. These chiefs were chosen and honored by outsiders and often had little standing with the tribe.

Warfare

The first time the Winnebago entered historic records, it was because of war, and the earliest detailed account of them was when they killed Ottawa envoys and later did the same to ambassadors from tribes of the Illinois. Their success in war made them the enemies of many surrounding people before the population reductions of the seventeenth century.

War was an individual affair. The tribe as a whole did not usually "declare" war, and men fought their own wars based on their need for revenge or desire for personal glory. A man recruited friends and relations to join him in his war party; and with so many ties to lineage, clan, moiety, and friend clan, one man could draw on a large pool of potential warriors. Villages that had not contributed any men at all to a particular war party might be pulled into the war if the relatives of enemies descended on them for revenge. The potential for warfare to get out of hand and involve everyone in revenge raids was behind the controls put on it by the political system. Thunder chiefs, "peace" chiefs, could stop war parties from going out by using their prestige and influence. They were backed up only by spiritual and ritual sanctions, but these informal means were supported by the tribe as a whole and could be very effective.

Winnebago warfare in the eighteenth century was directed at goals other than the usual ones of glory and revenge. Guns gave it a new dimension, and European traders used it for their own purposes. Winnebago warriors became involved in fighting European armies as well as other Indians, sometimes far from Wisconsin. Warfare was on a larger scale, although on the individual level the old goals of revenge and glory were still important. The persistence of older patterns of terrorism and torture in the large European wars led to a widespread conviction among non-Indian settlers in the Northeast that Indians were incapable of "civilization." This had an effect on the way Indians were regarded for many years afterwards.

Life cycle

Much of what is known about the lives of individuals comes from nineteenth or twentieth century sources (Radin 1923, Lurie 1971). They do not necessarily reflect life in the seventeenth or eighteenth centuries. but they are likely to provide at least some information on late eighteenth century practices that were remembered through time and flowed into the later years as part of the Winnebago tradition. Like kinship terms, the ordinary events of human life tend to be conservative, and the beliefs surrounding them change slowly.

Winnebago babies, like all children, were thought about long before they were born. Pregnancy is the foreshadowing of birth, and parents did what they could to make the process as safe as possible. The Winnebago mother-to-be was careful about what she did and what she ate. She tried to avoid snakes, dogs, cats, and other things that were thought to bring bad luck; and she was told not to sleep in the daytime since that was bad for the baby. Birth took place in a special house with the help of the mother's female relatives. By the twentieth century, a sister's house might be the chosen place to deliver babies (Lurie 1971). During the birth, the father had to be careful of what he did so that nothing bad would happen to the baby. He had to travel the whole time, and it was believed that this helped his wife in her delivery. Giving men special tasks during their wives' labor let them share in the birth. A man who faithfully kept on the move was doing his part in insuring the safe arrival of a new child.

A child was born into a clan through a mother who came from another clan. Even the women who attended the birth were from the mother's clan, helping to bring into the world a child of another clan. The women of the baby's clan, especially father's sisters, thanked them by giving gifts to the new mother and through her to members of her clan. In this way, the baby's clansmen celebrated the new addition to their clan and showed their appreciation for the clan whose daughter had made it all possible. They were also drawing attention to the baby's important relationship to its mother's clan.

Babies were given birth order names, but other names were added through time. Each child was given a formal clan name that often had meaning in clan origin tales. They were immediately recognizable as belonging to certain clans. For example, Thunder names included Walking-Thunder, He-Who-Shakes-the-Earth-with-Force, Thunder-Leader, He-Who-Has-Long-Wings. Clan names were given to babies at naming feasts or as part of feasts given for some other reason. Babies might also be given nicknames or adoptive names; and as Indians began to interact more and more with French or English speakers, they took first names and surnames. Today a Winnebago may have several names: a birth order name, a clan name, and an English name plus any nicknames earned along the way.

Winnebago parents expected children to become responsible adults through a process of formal persuasion and good example; spanking children or even scolding them was considered poor child-rearing practice. Parents preferred to frighten children with threats of "owls" or other things that might come to carry them away. Children were also encouraged to blacken their faces and fast in the forest to obtain a supernatural vision or dream, and naughty children were made to fast as a penalty. Hungry children soon learned that certain behavior was rewarded and other behavior was not. In many cases, a mother might call in her brother to speak to a child; his words had greater force than those of parents.

Children had to learn the techniques for living and how to handle tools and weapons. By watching parents, children learned how to do adult tasks themselves. They learned the jobs appropriate to their sex by being with adults who already had the necessary skills; mother's brothers often taught their nephews. There was a lot to learn: gathering, farming, hunting, making mats, preparing tools, preserving food, tanning hides, felling trees. Winnebago children had to become competent providers; anyone who could not perform adult tasks was not valued as a future husband or wife or as a useful member of the society.

As children reached puberty, more was expected of them. Boys fasted for long periods in the hope of receiving a supernatural blessing. This blessing was part of becoming a warrior, and it was necessary for a successful career in war. Boys blackened their faces with charcoal and went to a lonely spot where they wept, fasted, and prayed for spiritual guidance. Their misery made prospective guardian spirits pity them and be more willing to help in providing a blessing. Having a spirit helper gave confidence and self-possession to a young man on war parties that lasted throughout his life. By the late nineteenth century, being a warrior was no longer important, and parents who wanted spiritual experiences for their sons had more trouble persuading them to fast (Radin 1923). Girls were less often pressured into fasting, but they, too, were advised to try to receive a blessing of their own. A girl's blessing was not intended to be useful in war but was thought helpful in bringing her the best that Winnebago life had to offer: a good husband, healthy children, and a long life (Lurie 1971).

When girls began to menstruate, they were isolated from their families and told to pray and fast. Menstruating women were considered ritually unclean and had to keep apart from daily life during their monthly periods. For most, this meant staying by themselves in little wigwams and observing certain restrictions. They had to use special eating utensils and keep them only for that purpose. They were told not to scratch themselves with their fingers since that caused fever, aches, or pains; they were urged to avoid things endowed with supernatural power because their glance or touch could cause such power to be destroyed. Above all, they were supposed to avoid men so they would not cause spiritual injury to male power. Taboos such as these had wide distribution in North America, and there is as yet no agreement as to what function they served.

Marriageable girls were courted by young men, but in earlier times the choice of a mate was not left to personal preference. Marriage was vitally important in forging bonds between lineages and creating new subsistence groups, and it could not be left to chance. A girl's husband was chosen for her by her parents or by one of her brothers; and the selection had less to do with looks and personality than with prospects for success in economic life and "good" family background. Even as late as the twentieth century, some Winnebago girls continued to marry their brothers' choices and felt that brothers had the right to pick out future husbands for sisters even when the choice of a particular man was not to their liking (Lurie 1971).

As a social occasion, the marriage was arranged between the two families. The bride was dressed in her best, fine clothing prepared for her by her female relatives. She went to the wigwam of her new husband's parents, where she took off her wedding clothes and gave them to the groom's female kin. Those who received a part of the bride's clothing gave her back a gift of equal or greater value. In this exchange of gifts, the groom's family acknowledged the new marriage; and in a manner of speaking, blessed it by their acceptance of the new bride.

The newlyweds then returned to her parents' home where they lived for two years while the husband performed bride service for his parents-in-law. He provided meat, helped in fishing ,and generally made himself useful. During this time the new husband must have felt very much under the eyes of his wife's family and on his best behavior in order to assure them that he intended to be a good provider for their daughter. After bride service, the couple and any children they might have had during those two years moved back to the young man's family, often living in the same house with them. Now it was the turn of the wife to fit into the patrilineal family of her husband. Permanently living with the husband's family was not a rigid pattern, and couples were free to live with the wife's family as well as that of the husband.

In the "old days," marriages were often brittle and slight excuses might lead to divorce. Sometimes men were so jealous of the attentions of other men to their wives that they mutilated them by cutting off their noses. Women fearful of losing their husbands might recommend that a man take a second wife, often a sister or niece of the first wife.

For men, being a warrior was the most important part of their lives outside the wigwam. Not much has survived of details in the lives of Winnebago warriors, but if they were similar to the customs of people like the

Ioway (Skinner 1926), the status of "warrior" was very complicated. It involved highly organized warrior societies, war rituals, and systems of war honors. War was understandably a focus of ritual and other activities since it was a major source of personal anxiety. Warriors, in addition to winning honors and defeating their enemies, were likely to become casualties themselves. The formal organization and rituals connected with being a warrior helped men overcome their fears long enough to fight until they grew too old to participate.

A few men did not fit into the ordinary male roles and became berdaches instead, men who dressed as women (Lurie 1953). These men received a vision from the moon telling them to take up women's dress and women's work; and they were regarded as supernaturally special, able to achieve spiritual heights unattainable by ordinary people. Being a berdache may have been a kind of refuge for those unable to face the frightening role of warrior or it may have been a way to handle gender confusion or homosexuality. Another side to the role of berdache is an economic one. A berdache could do women's work "better than any woman," and wealth was a major consequence of adopting that way of life. At a time when goods produced by women were an important part of the economic system, a "woman" unburdened by child bearing was more productive than other women. The last known Winnebago berdaches lived in the early part of the twentieth century.

As Winnebago couples settled into marriage and child rearing, they began to take on important roles in ceremonial life and community affairs. As their own children matured and began to marry, Winnebago men became elders and their wives became matrons of the tribe. They were both keepers of custom and people of influence, depending on their own personal abilities and the size and extent of their kinship alliances. Some of them became chiefs and clan leaders; others were less influential, depending again on their personal circumstances. As people grew older, they were regarded with respect by the young, measured out not solely because of Winnebago regard for the elderly but also because as people aged, others thought their longevity might be owing to witchcraft. Witches might be dangerous to others and very easily offended.

Death was surrounded by ritual. The dead were buried simply, wrapped in fiber mats or later placed in coffins made of bark strips or wooden planks. Into the nineteenth century, objects owned or associated with the dead were buried with them. Early accounts say that some people were not buried at all but placed on scaffolds above the ground or in trees, but this custom died away early. The funeral for an important person included a procession to the grave site accompanied by drumming; and the graves were often marked by stakes painted with clan symbols. The etiquette of mourning included public expressions of grief by widows; they blackened their faces, wore rags, and wailed bitterly. A basic belief was that souls were recyclable and could come back through reincarnation. People who lived an upright life or died in battle were certain of reincarnation, and others could achieve it through joining religious societies and living according to their beliefs.

The Winnebago were at one time the major farming people of Wisconsin. In the earliest historic records, their many villages and large population represented a dominant fact of political and social life in the eastern part of the state. How they lived then is poorly known, but records of later years give at least a partial picture of what it was like to live within farming communities and depend on the land for domesticated crops. As farmers, they contrast with Indians of the Canadian Zone, whose social life reflects other answers to questions of survival.

Chippewa Social Life

Chippewa social life changed in the years after European contact; many new combinations emerged out of old elements. In general, there are three time periods that show different patterns in Chippewa political and social life. The first of these is immediately before the arrival of Europeans. The second is the period of French contact when they were heavily involved in trade as trappers and middlemen and were moving to replace the Santee Dakota in the lands west and south of Lake Superior. The third is the reservation period of the nineteenth century.

The most active period in the development of Chippewa social institutions was during the eighteenth century French fur trade. Much of what was internally complicated and more highly organized from a political point of view seems to have evolved then (Hickerson 1962). The kinds of social units identifiable included the family, the hunting band, and the village. All of these units were very independent, and not even villages were tied securely to other villages. Tribal organization or tribal chiefs that spoke for everyone were not present among the Chippewa.

The Chippewa family consisted of a household, the people who lived together in one or two wigwams. An example of this independent household was the family of Wawatam, Alexander Henry's adopted father. Wawatam's group, a patrilaterally extended family, consisted of several people: Wawatam, his wife, their unmarried children, and their married son and his family. Under certain circumstances, a similar family might include some other people--sons-in-law doing bride service or extra wives of some of the men. A Chippewa household in the forest would appear as a tiny settlement with a mat and bark-covered wigwam, supplies of firewood, family dogs, children, and the personal equipment of the family. The head of the family was the oldest active man, and probably the family camp would be known by his name. The camp in the woods had enough expertise and equipment to adapt to both the Canadian forest and the inland shores fisheries. Judging from Alexander Henry's description of Wawatam's family, the household was an efficient and independent economic unit. If it had to, it could manage on its own during the long winter months, and its independence increased its chances for survival if a natural catastrophe should hit one part of the food supply. The household, however, was not totally separate and apart. It belonged to a larger group, the hunting band.

Hunting bands were groups of about 20 households and a total population of around 100. Each group had a name, usually those of animals--Bear, Otter, Heron, Catfish--with an ancient connection to a supernatural forebearer. The bands held hunting rights over territories; and during the winter hunting season when people spread out in the forest, families went to the lands of their hunting band, not just anywhere in the woods. The hunting band chief in a way controlled any one family's access to game animals since he was the one who allotted sections of the hunting range to each household. Assigning hunting lands was a continuous process of re-adjusting hunters to resources, making more available to growing households, less to those with fewer members; and band chiefs had to do it without causing jealousy or seeming to be changing the way things had always been. Each household could depend on other band members in case of need, and sometimes men from the band joined together in a game drive or cooperative hunt.

The village was a more permanent place where the households of one or more hunting bands came together in the summer. Band members did not have to join a particular village but could go where they wanted. This ability to join in different villages was one reason why people could move so readily into new territory or gather in great numbers at places like Chequamegon. Hunting bands could move away from villages where they once spent their summers to form new ones, perhaps in new places. The hunting lands of the Santee Dakota were one of the areas penetrated by hunting bands pushing westward in this manner.

Summer villages were settlements with many different functions. People were concerned with seasonal food-getting: fishing, berrying, and hunting. Many of these activities could be done by single individuals or small groups, and village life made them easier only in the sense of socially sharing the work. Perhaps gathering bands into villages had less to do with economic cooperation than it did with war. A village was a safer place to leave women, children, and the elderly while men went off on raids, and a village with a big population could more easily raise war parties and supply warriors. At least some large villages became centers for summer settlement because trading houses were set up there during the French period.

Kinship organization

The kinship system (Landes 1969) was different from that of the Winnebago. In general, the categories of kinsmen were not extended beyond narrow limits. For example, a Chippewa had only one person he or she called by the term "father" and only one called "mother," quite different from the Winnebago custom of having terms that included brothers and sisters of parents' siblings as well as parents themselves. In addition, the Chippewa did not have lineage organization that divided the world into groups of mother's people and groups of father's people.

In the Chippewa view, a person's father's brothers were called by a term that is close to the English term "uncle" and father's sisters were called by a term similar to "aunt." In each case, the term meant relatives who were siblings of someone's *father*. The brothers and sisters of a person's mother were called by terms that indicated that they were related through the mother. This division into mother's and father's siblings was made less important by calling the spouses of these people by the terms proper to the other side. Thus the wife of a man who was a father's brother was called by the same term as a sister of a person's mother, and the husband of a mother's sister was called by the same term as a father's brother. This usage is one of several reasons for thinking that at one time the Southwestern Chippewa used to marry their cross-cousins (Hickerson 1962).

Another clue to the long ago presence of cross-cousin marriage is the terminology used for cousins. Like the Winnebago, the Chippewa system identified two kinds of cousins, cross and parallel. Parallel cousins, the children of a person's mother's sisters or of a father's brothers, were called by the same terms as siblings. Marriage with them was out of the question, just as marriage with biological siblings was prohibited. Cross-cousins, the children of father's sisters or of mother's brothers, were set apart and called by other terms. Chippewa marriage rules as far as is known in the historic period have forbidden marriage with cross-cousins, but most of the other groups who have similar cousin terms, allow it. Many of these people consider cross-cousin marriage highly desirable, whether they are always able to manage it or not. Cross-cousin marriage was common among other Chippewa people north and east of the Wisconsin Chippewa.

Cross-cousin marriage was important when people lived in hunting bands. When the hunting band was the only important group over and above the family, cross-cousin marriage would have been one way for a hunting band to have had long term cooperative ties with other bands. This would have been especially useful when the number of hunting bands was small, and each one was of importance to its few neighbors. Required cross-cousin marriage would ensure that the bands continued to be related to each other generation after generation, and dependable long term ties could be maintained. As people moved into the complex new arrangements of the fur trade period, cross-cousin marriage became less useful. It limited the options available through marriage and required people to marry over and over again into the same groups. In the trade period, breadth of marriage ties was more important as the hunting bands began to move into new lands and meet new people. Intermarriage was still the most important means of establishing friendly relationships with other people; and, because cross-cousin marriage was so restrictive, it was no longer adaptive. It had become a liability and eventually was forbidden.

Often first marriages were arranged by fathers or brothers, the initiative being taken by the groom's family. A desirable spouse ought to be from a "good" family and be hard-working, well-off, and, in brides, modest as well.

A man might marry more than one wife, if he could manage it, and sometimes the second wife was the sister of the first one. Having more than one wife was hard for people in the Canadian Zone, where supporting even one wife and her children and her other relatives could be a burden. For the Southwestern Chippewa, however, alternative food sources--fish and wild rice in particular-- made an extra wife, an extra pair of hands, of benefit in any household. The work of a second wife in helping to process furs was a powerful incentive to polygyny during the fur trade era. By the time kinship information was collected in any detail for the Chippewa, the idea of more than one wife had fallen into disfavor, and women were said to dislike sharing a husband with even one other wife (Landes 1969).

When a man married, he became a son-in-law and worked for his father-in-law in much the same way young men among the Winnebago worked for their parents-in-law. His major obligation was as a provider of meat and furs. Chippewa men treated their wives' parents with great respect; they were not supposed to speak to them or even to look at them. The same respectful behavior was expected of a wife for her parents-in-law. She showed her respect for them by speaking only when necessary to her mother-in-law and not at all to her father-in-law (Landes 1969). After a few years, the couple might move back to the home territory of the groom's parents, but Chippewa residence patterns after marriage were flexible, letting the couple settle where they thought their best advantages lay.

Marriage created a wider network that included brothers and sisters-in-law. Like the Winnebago, the Chippewa treated these relationships as outside the usual respectful feelings that existed between relatives. Joking, teasing, and outrageous behavior were expected between people related to each other as sisters or brothers-in-law. People were also expected to joke with their cross-cousins on both sides, suggesting that those cousins were potential marriage partners. The patterns of respect and joking generally created bonds among kinsmen and helped to sidestep potential trouble between people whose day to day activities might involve them in competition.

The Chippewa practiced both sororate and levirate in the past, probably even before the early French period. Both sororate and levirate are second marriages, undertaken at the death of a spouse. In a sororate marriage, a man married the sister of his deceased wife; and in the levirate, a woman married the brother of her

dead husband. In either case, the children were provided
for, widows and widowers comforted, and family ties continued. Of course, if there was no suitable person to step
into the shoes of the deceased spouse, neither sororate nor
levirate could take place. In Chippewa society, parallel
cousins were also brothers and sisters, and more possible
candidates for second marriages were therefore available.

Chippewa clans

Chippewa people all belonged to clans, which may
represent a development out of the older hunting bands.
The pre-contact Chippewa lived in small localized groups,
several of which were linked by descent and each of
which was a separate hunting band. As the Chippewa
expanded westward along the south shore of Lake
Superior, these groups kept their ties with one another by
the use of a name that descended through the male line.
Since all those using it were considered to be related and a
person's affiliation could not be changed through marriage
or personal choice, through time the membership groups
became more and more like clans. In a way, the hunting
bands became clans, but not in any one-to-one development. The whole process was more of a gathering together
of related independent groups rather than a simple descent
of each band into its own clan. The kind of names that
Chippewa clans had closely resembled the old hunting
band names. A partial list includes Caribou, Moose, Duck,
Loon, Lynx, Bear, Eagle, Marten, Muskrat, Crane,
Sturgeon, Catfish, Mink, Otter, and Kingfisher.

People who belonged to the same clan considered
that they shared the same totem animal. In practice, this
did not involve a feeling of descent from, or a spiritual
kinship with, the totem. At least in modern times, some
Chippewa said each totem was "only a name" and nothing
more (Landes 1969). It is hard to know what the totems
meant in the past; John Tanner, a member of mixed
Ottawa and Ojibwa groups, treated his totem affiliation
very casually except when he used it to establish some sort
of tie with strangers (Tanner 1830).

Chippewa clans played an important role in
regulating marriage. No one could marry into his or her
own clan and had to look for a mate in another clan. The
feelings against marrying within one's own clan seem to
have been powerful, and they have survived into recent
times (Landes 1969). All the members of an individual's
own clan were called "brother" and "sister," except for the
members of one's own immediate family.

Comparing Chippewa clans to the clans of the Winnebago reveals some striking differences. Chippewa clans had none of the suggestions of an earlier ranked society characteristic of Winnebago clans nor did they have functioning clan organizations. There were no powerful clan possessions, no really strong clan leaders, no important roles for the clans in everyday village life, and no origin tales to explain how the clans came to be. It is as if the Chippewa clans were in the process of developing as people began to play larger roles in the affairs of the north country. Perhaps the pressures of warfare made larger organization useful, and Chippewa clan structure was one of the first complex organizations to come into being.

Leadership and political organization

During the eighteenth century, the summer village was the most important setting for Chippewa life, and in some cases it became a year-round population center (Hickerson 1962). In some places, this was possible as rice beds, corn fields, and fishing stations provided enough food to support the population while men went out to hunt, sometimes in the dangerous lands also claimed by the Santee. The pattern of winter dispersal into hunting bands in their own hunting territories was still important, but large permanent settlements introduced a new trend toward more stable community life. The village, whether the usual temporary summer form or the more permanent year-round settlement, was independent and without lasting ties to other villages. It operated on its own without consulting or depending on others.

Internal village structure was not tightly organized. The residents were members of one or more hunting bands that had come together year after year, perhaps because they were neighbors or because they were kin to each other. During the summer, when the village was in existence, it included people with separate interests who were brought together as a convenience. In case of problems arising, the population could break into smaller parts; hunting bands or sections of them could leave villages where they felt uncomfortable. Sometimes the village people came to blows and split apart as a result of real quarrels, and sometimes villages quietly separated as populations grew too large for available resources and small segments broke away.

Village organization consisted of chiefs and councils. Several kinds of chiefs have been mentioned over the years within villages: war chiefs, village chiefs, hereditary chiefs, clan chiefs, talking chiefs, and chiefs appointed by outside governments (Smith 1973). Village chiefs were "men of stature" with authority coming from their personal abilities and accomplishments. When a man was outstanding as an individual, people were more likely to follow him since he had already demonstrated his abilities and personal wisdom. Even when a chief was a man of renown and entitled to a respectful hearing, decisions affecting the whole village were discussed in village councils. Among the Chippewa, the councils were often simply gatherings of all the older men, and sometimes older women, of the village. They represented the opinions of everyone else, but not in any formal way.

Villages contained both military and civil chiefs, but the civil chiefs usually had greater influence and prestige. Heredity was involved in the selection of a civil chief, probably based on the importance of the clan or hunting band from which the chief was chosen. Clans were not ranked, but because of size, personal standing of the members, and other factors, some clans were generally more respected. Chiefs from those clans were more likely to have enough personal following to become important chiefs within their villages.

Villages were independent, and few things brought them together in joint activities. Clan membership from one village to another helped to bring people together, and intermarriage provided still other links. The most powerful factor that brought villages into occasionally larger groups was war and the diplomacy that surrounded it. In the eighteenth and early nineteenth centuries, the Chippewa were replacing the Santee in their hunting lands south and west of Lake Superior, and warfare was increasingly important. People unable to defend themselves in those lands had better not hunt there at all. Often winter hunting bands went into the forests armed for war as well as the hunt, and they lived in "forts" protected by palisades and armed men. Under those circumstances, enough warriors often had to be recruited from more than one village.

Chippewa warfare was like most historic Indian warfare described for the Northeast. The underlying causes were often control over new lands or resources, but the motives for individuals were usually glory and revenge. Any man could propose a war party; and if he had a record of success, he was sure to attract men who wanted to add to their own reputation and younger men who had yet to establish one. In the seventeenth and eighteenth centuries, the right of any successful warrior to lead a war party for his own goals was held in check by the advice of older and wiser heads, but in the early nineteenth century, warriors began to exert real political force within villages. Their independent raids and counterraids led villages into situations where they would rather not have been and made diplomacy, peace-keeping, and relations with traders and European officials more difficult.

War meant hardship and risk for everyone. It sometimes involved long journeys into unfamiliar lands with no safe refuges in case of accident or injury. Enemies were pursued with stealth and surprise, and individual exploits were prized. Allies were uncertain and could not be depended upon; even the members of the war party itself were not a sure thing until the very moment of battle. John Tanner was a member of a large war party against the Santee Dakota in the early nineteenth century; the group began with over 1400 men, but by the time the enemy was found, the warriors had dwindled down to a single man, who finally had to abandon his attack without the Santee even knowing that he was there (Tanner 1830). Failure in war meant death, torture or enslavement, the disgrace of having been held prisoner by one's enemies. Women, children, and old people were frequent victims of war, suffering the same fate as the warriors and enduring the same hardships but without any of the glory. A general pattern was to kill the men and women and then sell the children to the traders (Quaife 1922). Warfare exacted a continuing price from all the western Great Lakes people, and it was made even worse when equipped with guns and iron weapons.

Managing peaceful relations between groups of people and even between men meeting by chance in the woods was difficult and gave rise to some special devices. One of these was the display and exchange of shell wampum beads. They were woven into belts or collars that validated peaceful interaction between different groups. An emissary from one group brought a proposal to another group and made his points by displaying wampum belts; if the belts were accepted, the exchange stood as an agreement between the two. Belts were kept as lasting signs of harmony, and they could be brought out to remind people of their agreements should anyone forget to honor them. Europeans very early understood the high regard Indian people had for wampum and began making the beads in small factories in the east; many of the shell wampum beads in museums or from archaeological sites come from these sources.

The Calumet Ceremony was an even more elaborate means for establishing ties of peace and friendship. Many early French explorers were met with this ceremony as they moved into Wisconsin. Radisson witnessed a Calumet Ceremony given by the Santee for the Chippewa in 1662 (Adams 1961), and many others spoke of it: Allouez, Marquette, and Perrot. John Long noted in the eighteenth century that "the savages hold it in such estimation that a violation of any treaty where it has been introduced would . . . be attended with the greatest misfortune" (Quaife 1922: 62). The ceremony was centered upon a sacred pipe, and the rituals built close ties between those who sang the calumet and those who were the guests. Often the ceremony became a spiritual adoption in which kinship ties were created between unrelated groups through the ritual adoption of a single person. In Wisconsin, the Calumet Ceremony was present among all Indians from the Chippewa in the north to the Miami in the south.

The ceremony that Radisson observed on the south shore of Lake Superior took place some time in the early spring of 1662 (Adams 1961). He and his companions were an important focus of the ritual, and through them the French back in Quebec were also part of what went on. The first stage consisted of eight Santee ambassadors bringing gifts of food and new skin clothing, which they then put on the Frenchmen and probably also on the main Chippewa leaders. Following this gift, the Santee wept over their hosts, a typical Santee expression, and the whole group smoked calumets in order, blowing smoke over the possessions of the French and throwing tobacco on the fire. The next day they smoked the calumet again, and Radisson has left a description of the pipe: "of red stone, as big as a fist and as long as a hand; the small reed as long as five foot in breadth . . ." (Adams 1961: 134). The typical fan of eagle feathers was attached to this seventeenth century calumet along with the feathers of ducks and other brightly colored birds. Radisson in a dramatic gesture, substituted iron projectile points for the feather fan and laid a long iron blade along the pipestem. His message was clear to the Santee: friendly relations with the French were the only means to obtain trade goods.

As part of the ceremony, Radisson and Groseilleurs followed the example of the Santee and threw tobacco on the fire. They had previously prepared gunpowder for the purpose, and the explosions almost disrupted the ceremony, scattering participants left and right. Afterwards, "there was nothing but feasting for eight days." A further stage in the ceremony took place later when a procession of young men arrived from the Santee to announce the coming of "elders of their village," presumably to carry out the alliance prepared earlier. When the elders arrived with "incredible pomp," they were gorgeously apparelled in feathers, paint, and porcupine quillwork; they carried their calumets and sat down to rest in a specially prepared lodge. The Santee leaders spoke at length and then presented gifts to their hosts: beaver skins and buffalo robes. Feasting, smoking the calumets, and singing followed; and the next day gifts were given back to the Santee, and an alliance against the Cree was arranged.

Stripped of its ritual, the Calumet Ceremony was an effective means of creating political alliances in a politically uncertain world, and it also became a means for establishing trade relations. In historic descriptions of the Calumet Ceremony, the pump of economic exchange was primed at every opportunity. Gifts were given to stimulate reciprocity, and, since the ceremony often lasted for days, the quantity of goods offered and received could be considerable. Perhaps one reason for its eventual decline was a growing understanding of European trade and an acceptance of new ideas of economic exchange. No ceremony at all was necessary for participating in that kind of trade.

Larger scale organization

The Chippewa represent people with the same language and culture who lived in independent bands. Through time, as the lands south and west of Lake Superior opened, the hunting bands began to separate as segments moved to where they thought their best chances at trade, hunting or fishing might be. In the large gatherings at the Sault or at Chequamegon, the Chippewa began to change their ideas about hunting bands; the bands went from localized groups to non-localized clans and sometimes wound up living within several villages. The villages became politically more important than they had been.

Many forces acted on the various groups of Chippewa to develop more complex kinds of political organizations. Outside influences occurred as spokesmen were expected to be able to speak for large groups of people. The United States government, for example, appointed chiefs whom they tried to treat as having wide authority. These "paper" chiefs often had no standing within the villages, but when they were given privileges from the outside, what they said or did had an effect there. During the nineteenth century period of land cessions, negotiating treaties made speaking for larger groups a necessity and some level of unity desirable. Annuity payments also had an effect of strengthening community feeling if not of fostering the development of larger institutions. Integration of the Chippewa was also supported by warfare. Recruiting men from many villages for war aided the development of almost tribal consciousness, and in the nineteenth century when war ended, other things took their place. One of the most powerful of these was the Midewiwin Society, a religious organization that crossed community lines (see Chapter 7).

Life cycle

Data about child rearing practices (Hilger 1951) among the Chippewa comes from early twentieth century recollections of past practices. Powerful beliefs existed about the effects on unborn children of something done or not done by mothers in the months before birth. Many of these ideas came about as an after-the-fact means of explaining unusual events at birth. Women were told to avoid certain animals to keep their babies from looking like those animals when they were born. Seeing a lizard, for example, might produce a child with lizard-like arms or legs; eating porcupine could make a child clumsy or club-footed, and rabbits caused bulging eyes. Even plants could do bad things: eating berries, for example, was thought to cause birthmarks. The uncertainty and fears that all expectant parents feel found expression in restrictions on behavior and diet for both mother and father. Observing them made parents confident; and if a child was born with something odd about it, an explanation was there, readymade.

Chippewa babies were sometimes swaddled, wrapped tightly around with deerskin or rabbit fur blankets so that they were as immobile as if they were on cradleboards. The swaddled baby was like a caterpillar in a cocoon, a neatly wrapped little bundle that could be put where a mother wanted it. Swaddled babies were often put in hammocks, first made of deerskin and basswood string

(Hilger 1951) and later of blankets and ropes. Little hammocks were good places to swing babies and encourage them to sleep through the gentle swinging motion. The practice of swaddling may go back a long way, but it may be a modern custom, made possible by long strips of cotton cloth (Densmore 1979).

While babies were still small, their ears were pierced; and in earlier times, their noses might be pierced as well. This was done for the sake of beauty, not for ritual reasons. Sometimes, more than one hole might be made in the ears, and tiny pieces of metal or bone inserted. Through time, the Chippewa gave up the custom of wearing nose rings, but in early paintings and descriptions, they often were shown with large nose rings hanging below the lips.

More important than ear piercing was providing babies with names. Children were first called by nicknames and continued to be known by those names throughout life. More important was the formal name given shortly after birth by a person chosen as a "namer," someone who had received the power to name children in a dream and might bestow power on the child. The namer gave the child a name during a special occasion when guests joined the family for a feast, and the baby was the center of attention. The name given at this time was private, and the baby was not called by it. Throughout life, this formal name was kept secret and was not told to strangers. The reticence about names had to do with the blessing that came with the name; the blessing might be lost if the name became too public. Other names were given to Chippewa children as they grew older, and in modern times they, like the Winnebago, have English names as well.

Chippewa children were encouraged to fast when they were very young in order to obtain a blessing for their future lives. Very small children of sometimes five or six were sent out with faces blackened to ask for a blessing from a supernatural being. Parents might have been told in dreams to send their children out or they might interpret the children's dreams to mean that now was the time for a fast to begin. Children often fasted for several days, perched in trees where they had made platforms (Hilger 1951). Fasting was successful if a spirit helper came or the child learned how to use a talent given by a guardian spirit. People felt that smaller children were more likely to contact the supernatural: they were "innocent" and could receive communications from spirits.

Once children had passed puberty, they were expected to have less of a chance for successful contact with the supernatural world. From then on, no further regular fasting was necessary, only on special occasions.

Child-rearing was permissive with emphasis on precept, example, and encouragement of efforts to reach adulthood. European observers who noticed children in the first years after contact often found their behavior intolerable; it seemed uncontrolled, mischievous, and very hard to endure with Christian fortitude. By contrast with European standards, it probably was, but permissive child-rearing practices worked well in a world where choices were few, the road to adulthood clearly laid out, and the whole society supportive of every step on the way.

If spanking or physical punishment was not acceptable, there were other techniques used to control children. Most of these involved frightening children into better behavior by threatening them with an evil source that came from outside the home community. The owl was summoned to carry away naughty children, and the sound of an owl in the night made Chippewa children more sober, restrained, and obedient. More dramatic than threats of the owl were visits of the "frightener," a man wearing a mask with a long nose, dressed in ragged clothing, and carrying a cane (Densmore 1979). He came to scare children into obedience, not to carry any of them away. In the evening, his visits sent children running for their beds, leaving the village in peace.

When girls reached puberty, they lived for the time of their menstruation in small wigwams. While isolated in these little shelters, they fasted and worked at sewing or beadwork in the belief that idleness then might predict a life of idleness in the future. Contact with menstruating women was thought to be dangerous to men, and there was also some danger to the economic well-being of the group if menstruating girls gathered or touched first fruits in season. They could ruin the entire wild rice crop by carelessly handling some of it. After puberty, girls were kept under the watchful eyes of mothers or other female relatives, and their lives as children came to an end.

In choosing husbands or wives for their children, Chippewa parents were concerned that both young people contribute practical expertise and knowledge of everyday skills to the economic partnership that constituted marriage. During childhood, parents paid special attention to what children were learning; if they were scolded at any time, it was for failing to measure up in the skills that adults should have. The future of a girl rested upon her reputation for industry and modesty, a reputation that should attract people of good family whose son was a good hunter. In most cases, prospective bride and groom did not know each other, and the arrangements were made by their parents. Some of the women who have described these marriages to anthropologists in the twentieth century spoke of having been forced into marriage, made to marry against their wishes (Hilger 1951). In the past, however, parents who did not carefully arrange the marriages of their children were inviting disaster for them.

There was not a religious marriage ceremony. Marriage consisted of the groom's being accepted into the home of the girl's parents. No elaborate exchange of gifts was made between the families although gifts from the groom to the bride's family were common. Sometimes gifts took the form of clothing for the new bride or household equipment for the new family. The important thing was the public acceptance of the relationship by the kinsmen of both bride and groom and a recognition of the groom as a son-in-law.

Marriage could end in divorce, and in the early twentieth century, at least, Chippewa marriages seem to have been brittle (Landes 1969). Some older people thought that long ago, marriage ended only with the death of one spouse, but they may have been idealizing the past. Divorce was easy and took place when the couple ceased living together as man and wife. Either spouse might decide to pack up and move back to the parents' wigwam or into the wigwam of a new mate. A common reason for divorce was lack of children; and a childless woman was regarded as very unfortunate.

Those who died were thought of as going on a journey. The funeral included speeches, the burning of fires at the graves, and providing clothing or food necessary for a long trip. Small burial houses were built over some graves where shelves held offerings of food, which might be taken and eaten by relatives or even strangers at need. Grave markers with totem symbols were often placed in the ground with the totem drawn upside down to indicate death.

Widows blackened their faces, wore ragged clothing, let their hair hang long and uncombed, and mourned for a whole year. During that time, they carried "spirit bundles" around with them. These bundles were made with a lock of the dead person's hair wrapped in a birchbark container, and they were closely identified with the deceased. In the year of mourning, a widow wrapped and re-wrapped her husband's spirit bundle in whatever she had of beauty and value (Densmore 1979). Beadwork she had made, fine clothing she had prepared, blankets she had acquired--all were added to the little bundle, which by the end of the year was a much bigger bundle. When mourning was over, the dead husband's kinsmen held a feast in which the spirit bundle was taken apart and everything was given away. The widow then received gifts in return and was declared free to marry again. Husbands carried spirit bundles for their dead wives, too, but because men did not make beadwork or clothing, their bundles were always smaller.

Chippewa political and social organization represents the life of hunters and gatherers in Wisconsin, people of the Canadian Zone. It changed during the historic period, always in the direction of greater complexity of institutions and greater integration of what was previously a more scattered and independent existence. Through time the Chippewa and Winnebago have come to resemble each other: the one developed new kinds of structures and the other lost some of the complexity reflected in the prehistory of the southern half of the sate. In neither case is it possible to fully reconstruct what was there when Europeans arrived.

Social Life of Other Wisconsin Peoples

Other native and immigrant groups varied in how their kinship systems, political structures, and economic relationships worked. Details from the Early Historic period are often poorly known and have to be reconstructed from historic sources and what was remembered in later years. Much has been lost, but at least a general outline has emerged; the reliability of details can always be questioned.

The Santee Dakota were hunters and gatherers who lived in independent villages well into the nineteenth century (Landes 1968b). The villages were the major units of organization, and people regarded themselves as villagers, not members of a tribe. All the people of a village were kinsmen and hunted together as a permanent group, probably because bison hunting was more efficiently done in organized groups. The villages acted independently, sometimes even quarreling with and fighting other Santee villages. When they acted together, the circumstances almost always had to do with war. Single villages might carry on their own war, helped by kinsmen in other villages, but larger wars often involved common offense and defense under the leadership of well-known chiefs. In most instances, war chiefs held authority only as long as the crisis lasted and were not permanent "tribal" chiefs.

Menomini settlement in the early days also involved villages, divided into two groups, Bear settlements and Thunder settlements (Keesing 1939). People belonged to clans and perhaps also to hunting bands although details of the organization have not survived (Hoffman 1898). The kinship system seems to have been like that of the Chippewa and included both the deeply respectful behavior toward parents-in-law and a joking relationship between such kinsmen as brothers or sisters-in-law. Much of what became Menomini tribal structure developed in the nineteenth century, for in the French period, authority rested in individuals of personal merit and extended only as far as their reputations reached.

Fox, Sauk, Potawatomi, and Kickapoo shared some features of social life with the native people of Wisconsin and brought other customs with them. The Potawatomi lived in villages when they "removed" to Wisconsin, frequently in small ones and sometimes in larger ones such as their famous fort at Mechingan on Lake Michigan. Villages included representatives of several clans and lineages very like those of the Winnebago. The Potawatomi seem to have been more formally organized than other Wisconsin people; and, through time, they retained a cohesiveness that was more like Winnebago village life than Chippewa or Santee patterns. Fox, Sauk, and Kickapoo were similar to the Potawatomi in the nineteenth century, at least, and perhaps earlier as well.

The political and social patterns of Wisconsin Indian societies were not all the same nor were they unchanging. At one level they were concerned with operating two different ways of life: hunting and gathering with marginal gardening in the northern Canadian Zone and mixed farming, hunting, and gathering in the southern zones. In addition, they had to handle what happened as societies interacted with each other and as the circumstances of European contact caused basic economic and political changes.

CHAPTER 7
Religion and Religious Life

From the very beginning, Europeans who came to New France were interested in religion and kept records of what they saw. Specific information from Wisconsin, however, is scarce, and many things were described in passing or not at all. As a result, it is difficult to know when something represents an older pattern or when it came about through contact with new ideas brought by the Europeans themselves.

As a whole, people used religion to manage many of the problems of everyday life. Hunting often required more than human skill since even an expert hunter sometimes could not find any game. Fishing also needed protection from things that went wrong: people fell unexpectedly through the ice, nets tore, and canoes were wrecked. The behavior of plants was less often a problem, but supernatural things might affect them, too. Menstruating girls, for example, were warned away from picking wild crops unless they had supernatural help. Religion was useful in attempting to cure the sick. Wisconsin Indians had pragmatic knowledge of plant cures and first aid, but people had to rely on supernatural healing when they had no practical cures. As a result, most religious rituals had something to do with curing. The greatest need for disease control was probably after European contact brought epidemics of smallpox and measles to Wisconsin (Dobyns 1983).

Social life was tied into religion in many ways. Religion encouraged good behavior, not through an ethical code held up as a guide but through fear of sorcery practiced by powerful people against the less powerful. Rituals helped to build tribal feelings by joining people from more than one village in a common ritual that expressed the concerns of large groups. In some cases, rituals supported societies in trouble and revitalized those that had faced natural or physical disasters. Religion helped make people less afraid to go to war and more confident of success. It even justified and inspired warfare through dreams that told men they would return covered with personal glory.

The supernatural world

Indians regarded the supernatural world as filled with power that could be gathered like any other resource if the proper techniques were known. Everyone had to have some of this power, perhaps a modest share for an everyday life or perhaps an extraordinary amount for those whose lives were extraordinary. Power was distributed unevenly, controlled sometimes by supernatural beings and sometimes existing in places and things quite apart from the spirits. Medicine bundles, for example, were effective because they stored supernatural power; clan bundles and war bundles were similar, holding power to support the clan or the men going to war. It was not always known what objects contained power, and people relied on guidance from dreams in identifying them.

The search for power took many forms and was central to a variety of religious experiences. Obtaining personal power was the goal of puberty and other fasts. Girls in their menstrual huts and boys fasting and praying in the forest were power seekers, hoping for contact with a being that could give them power. People could even inherit power if they became custodians of something already filled with power. An individual's power increased or became more easily used as he or she got older; the aged might use their enhanced power for revenge or even to answer back imagined slights.

Dreams were the major sources of power, and proper dream interpretation was very important. Both dreaming and dream-telling were encouraged from earliest childhood. Children were asked about their dreams by adults, and a dream life was regarded as worthwhile, approved of and discussed by the adult world. So much attention sharpened the abilities of people to remember dreams and stimulated the dreamers' imaginations. The content of dreams was enriched by hearing about other peoples' dreams and by internalizing the symbols that were used to interpret them. Not all dreams were equally important, and sometimes a dream had to be tested before it could be understood or the power brought by it could be used by the dreamer. Sometimes the only way this could be done was through experience when a survivor of war or accident could look back on a dream and see its meaning in hindsight.

In order to remind themselves of their dreams, people recorded important dreams in symbols whose meaning was known only to the dreamer. Dream signs could be worked on clothing, woven in bags, or carried in medicine bundles. They might even be painted or drawn; many of the historic rock paintings in the Upper Great Lakes area look as if they contain symbols derived from dream experiences. Dream signs might be openly displayed, but the true inner meaning of each one could be learned only from the dreamer, who might or might not explain it. Sometimes power received in dreams would be lost if the dream were discussed with others. In some cases, dreamers could tell their dream experiences in detail. At times, especially powerful dreams could be described and their power given to others for a fee, and sometimes powerful dreams could be revealed only at great risk to the dreamer.

Dreaming as a means to power was open to everyone although some people remembered dreams more easily and interpreted them better. Those who were more sensitive in this regard often became religious specialists and advised others on the meaning of their dreams. Ordinary people who used their dream power in everyday life might not be believed when they spoke of their own dream revelations. People made judgments as to whose dreams were true and on what occasions their dreams could be relied on. For example, John Tanner's Indian mother regularly used dreams to predict where hunters could find game, and she was just as often ridiculed and her dreams rejected as she was accepted and her advice followed (Tanner 1830). Even dreams, so individual and so private, had to be filtered through a cultural screen before they were regarded as true religious experiences.

Because dreams were so important in religious life, they were continuous sources for new ideas. A man might shape some of his behavior or the way he dressed or the way he went to war by what he experienced in dreams. Even those who lied about dreams of power have had their personal lives changed by the reactions of others to their false dreams. Crashing Thunder, for example, came to believe that he was "holy" when his faked dream experience benefited a relative about to give birth (Radin 1963). Dream messages, dream signs, and guidance through dream-received visions were powerful influences on everyone.

Dreams were thought to come from spirits called by the Algonquin word "manito" (also spelled manido or manitou). Dreaming was the point where the world of the manitos came together with the everyday world of people. Manitos were guardians, protectors, or controllers of something in nature. They might be spirits who looked after animals: bison, bear, deer, fish, and other creatures. Manitos also represented small plants, especially those having medicinal value, as well as useful trees such as birch and basswood. Even berries picked in the summer had their own special manitos. They also stood for the earth, sun, moon, and other features of the sky, and in some instances for things that could not be easily seen: seasons, directions, light, or the winds. Even conditions of existence such as poverty, life, motherhood, or even cannibalism might appear as manitos. The number and variety of manitos was limited only by human spiritual experiences, and in general, all of nature was filled with them.

Manitos could directly influence human affairs. Men and women needed blessings from them in order to succeed, and much of spiritual life was spent in seeking those blessings. Through time, the way people approached manitos and the way manitos treated people gradually changed. At least one authority (Radin 1923) thought that in earlier times, perhaps as far back as the prehistoric period, the relationship between manitos, the blessings they controlled, and human beings was a simple mechanical one. A person made his or her offering, and the manitos had no choice but to do as they were asked. As time passed, the manitos began to be more and more selective about granting requests and more particular about what people had to do to receive a blessing. Eventually, the manitos consciously chose to give blessings only to those they thought worthy.

The world of the manitos, like the world of the Indians, was generally egalitarian. Some manitos were more powerful than others just as some people are more capable and gifted than others, but they were not ranked with different levels of power and authority leading to one supreme being. In the early accounts of religious life in Wisconsin, some European observers were so bothered by the absence of a "higher power" that they became convinced "that almost all the Savages in general have no notion of a God, and that they are not able to comprehend the most ordinary arguments on the subject" (cited in Hoffman 1981: 152). Father Allouez remarked that the Ottawas had no supreme being, only manitos (Kinietz 1940), and as late as 1702, Deliette recorded the same impression of belief in manitos, not in a hierarchy of gods.

Through time, however, Indians began to speak more and more of a Great Spirit, the Kitchi Manito of so many accounts. Whether or not the Great Spirit was present before European contact is unknown, and the records made in the seventeenth century are equivocal. They can be interpreted both as supporting the existence at that time of a Great Spirit and also as showing that the Great Spirit was a reinterpretation of Indian concepts in Christian terms. Allouez, who found no supreme being among the Ottawa, nevertheless thought the Fox, Illinois, and other "southern" tribes had a "great and excellent genius, master of all the rest, who made Heaven and Earth" (Kinietz 1940: 211). In this case, Allouez may have been mistaken; many Europeans learned that Indians had a "creator" and leaped to the conclusion that the Indian creator was the same thing as the Christian creator. In addition, once they learned about the manito of "life," they thought it was a superior being, the master of all Indian lives, the "Almighty."

It is very difficult to know where the truth lies in the matter of the Great Spirit before missionary teaching and the exposure of Indians to Christian concepts (Vecsey 1983). In general, they were willing to listen to new religious teachings just as they listened to new dream experiences and followed the teachings of new prophets. They listened to and weighed what Europeans told them and tried to interpret it within the framework of their own religious understanding. In the face of European scorn for their beliefs, they may have built upon any similarities to the Christian God until the Great Spirit emerged as an approximate equivalent. The appearance of a Great Spirit, "one who ruleth over all," among people whose entire cultural system was so egalitarian seems unlikely, but the evidence one way or another is not conclusive.

Through the historic period, the Great Spirit changed. He became human in form, the chief or controller of all other manitos. The power other manitos gave to people came to be regarded as his gift, and he emerged as the final source of all power in the same way that Christians regarded blessings through the saints as coming from their own "Higher Power." In the very early nineteenth century, the Great Spirit came to individuals in dreams, offering them revelations and direct contact (Tanner 1830). Later he became unapproachable and needed intermediaries to communicate with people. Religious specialists interpreted his will, and he became more and more a reflection of the Christian religious world around him. In time-honored fashion, Kitchi Manito adapted Indians to Christianity and made it easier for them to use whatever in the Christian tradition suited their needs.

Among the many manitos of skies, earth, air, and water, a number stand out as more important. Perrot thought in his day that the principal ones were the Great Hare, the Sun, and the "devils" as well as Michipissy or Missipissi, the spirit of the water (Blair 1911, I). In the early accounts by Father Allouez and Father André of the people around Green Bay, no one manito was singled out as more important than any of the others, but the Sun, Thunder, and the Water Spirit were mentioned more often. By the time nineteenth century memories were being recorded, Thunderbirds, Sun, Moon, Water-Spirit, the Morning Star, and Earth had become outstanding and approached the status of human-like gods. The Thunderbirds, often spoken of as Thunderers, were thought to cause thunder and appeared as great birds with lightning flashing from their eyes. They became more and more popular through time and played important roles in origin tales and stories about the early days of the clans. Both the Sun and Morning Star were once closely connected with war, but the Thunderbirds took over that function from them both. The Moon among some groups was especially important as a source of blessings for women. Earth, Grandmother Nakomis in some versions, began as a far-from-benevolent old woman and changed into the kindly and protective figure of later time. The Water-Spirit, described by the Jesuits as the Indians' "Neptune," was an important figure, perhaps because of fishing and water travel. People saw the Water-Spirit as an Underwater or Underground Panther, a being whose horned figure is on fiber bags and appears in rock paintings. It was a powerful creature, one capable of great mischief as well as great benefit if it was approached in the right way. The Underwater Panther could provide good weather on voyages made by canoe on the lakes if the proper offerings were made, but it was also thought to cause people to drown, sometimes totally without warning.

The best known of all the Algonquin supernatural beings is the culture hero known as Nanabozho (also spelled Ma'nabush, Wenebojo, Nanabush, and Manabozho). In English, he is called the Great Hare or the White Rabbit, and he is a Trickster, much like Coyote in western North America or Loki of Norse mythology. Tricksters have a mixed mission: they are often messengers of hope who bring people fire, knowledge, tools, or special sources of food, but they can be mischievous, foolish, and harmful (Radin 1973). Sometimes, like Nanabozho, they serve as creators of the world and the people in it. Perrot recorded a creation story in which the Great Hare and the muskrat saved all the other animals. In this version, all the animals were on a raft in an endless sea, and the Great Hare said he would create earth for them to live on if only one of the animals would swim down and bring back a bit of soil from the bottom to serve as a starter. Both beaver and otter failed to bring back anything, but the muskrat brought up a single grain of sand from which the Great Hare created the earth. Nanabozho went on to become an important intermediary between people and the Great Spirit. In his remarks in the seventeenth century, Perrot listed the Great Hare as the most popular of all the manitos, and he thought that people "revere and adore him as the creator of the world" (Blair 1911, I: 48). Counterbalancing this position is the picture of Nanabozho as that "nephew of us all," a privileged and special kind of kinsman.

Nanabozho has a great number of stories told about him and the things he did. His main home was at Michilimackinac, but he traveled about having adventures in which he bettered human life and also did many foolish and ridiculous things. Nanabozho tales were meant not only to instruct but also to entertain, as in the following extract from the travels of Ma'nabush (Hoffman 1896: 164):

> He . . . after a while saw a Mink crossing the path which he was following. The Mink had a long tail, to which were attached many small bells of shell which jingled at every step. Ma'nabush said to the Mink, 'My brother, you have a long tail with many ornaments on it; would you object to telling me where you got those beautiful shells, and if I might get some likewise?' 'No, Ma'nabush,' said the Mink, 'I do not object to telling you where I got my bells, and I will show you how you may obtain some. I cut these from my body, from the back of my buttocks.'
>
> Ma'nabush then asked the Mink to take a knife and cut some from his body that he also might ornament a tail and hang it to his back. The Mink, in compliance with the request of Ma'nabush, cut away a number of slices of flesh from his buttocks and, handing the pieces to Ma'nabush, the latter tied them to a tail of buckskin and fastened them to his back; but every time Ma'nabush attempted to

walk it hurt him, because the exertion caused the cut flesh to move. Ma'nabush went along slowly for a short distance, when happening to look back at his trailing tail, he saw that the Mink had cut away so much flesh that his entrails were dragging along the ground. Gathering his entrails together, he threw them up into the air so that they fell upon a tree; then he said, 'Now, you remain there and become food for the people.' The vines are still found clinging to the trees, and people even now cut them to pieces and boil them to eat, for they are very good.

Good and evil were not clearly separated. Nanabozho could be a benefactor and at the same time a cause of mischief. The two sides of the Winnebago supernatural being known as Disease-Giver were similar: one side of his body gave out life and success, the other death and failure. There was no group of good beings on one side battling with bad ones on the other. Even the Underwater Panther, a very dangerous spirit, could be persuaded to give some of his power for human benefit. Much of the information on the existence of good versus evil in the early historic records is very ambiguous, but a plain statement by a Menomini man to Father André may show that aligning the universe in a dualistic pattern with people supporting the "good" was not of any interest then; "we care very little whether it be the devil or God who gives us food. We dream sometimes of one Thing, sometimes of another; and whatever may appear to us in our sleep, we believe that is the manitou in whose honor the feast must be given, for he gives us food; he makes us successful in fishing, hunting, and all our undertakings" (Thwaites 1896-1901, vol. 56: 283). Later, good manitos and bad ones battled with each other, and people were often caught in the middle, attacked by evil forces and protected by good ones. The model for this development was very probably Christian teaching, which singled out good and evil in a way that changed the personalities of manitos and interpreted their roles in new and different ways.

Supernatural experts: shamans

When French missionaries began their work in Wisconsin, they found shamans, supernatural experts, already working among all tribal groups. Their knowledge and rituals were generally similar, but their skills varied. Each shaman received his supernatural call in a dream or vision through his own special manito. These manitos were often of the most powerful and impressive types, and an invitation to become a shaman could be a frightening and negative experience. If a man resisted the call, he might suffer misfortune as a result. If he heeded it, his life as a shaman was very difficult; only the strongest and most dedicated men could persist in dealing with the supernatural world. The power given by the manitos often matured with age. A young man might receive a message from a great manito that he was to become a shaman, but he would not do so until he was more mature, perhaps even past the age of being a hunter, warrior, and father. As shamans aged and their knowledge ripened, they might inspire fear as well as confidence; in some instances their personalities blended with the unseen world, and they became manitos themselves (Landes 1968a).

What a shaman did depended upon the needs of his neighbors or of those who came to ask his help. Sometimes shamans predicted the future or found out the causes of events in the here and now. A man or woman with an illness might ask a shaman to find out what caused the disease. In this case, the shaman asked his manito to be an informer, a source of knowledge that could trace something to its source. Shamans were paid for their services in food or raw materials and, in the trade period, European goods as well. A successful shaman might become a rich man, but wealth could become a problem if people became envious. They might think the shaman caused illness in order to get a large fee to make the disease go away.

Shamans' techniques included many different kinds of things. They often received messages from their manitos in a little hut or enclosure from which anyone could hear the conversation (Hoffman 1896). The manitos' distinct voices could be heard by anxious people outside, and sometimes the shaman struggled with his spirits, causing the enclosure to shake and the shaman to exhaust himself trying to control them. A common practice was curing with sucking tubes. The shaman used spiritual means to find whatever had caused an illness and then drew it out through long tubes. The things that came out of the tubes might be little bits of shell, feathers, stones, or strings. Shamans also used sweat-bathing, a custom that has much in common with the sauna of Scandinavia. Sweat-baths were made in a small circular wigwam with a central firepit. Water poured on heated rocks produced steam to surround the people inside with its beneficial warmth. Sweat-baths were taken by the shamans themselves before speaking to their manitos or before they began to cure or seek new visions. A sweat-bath was also prescribed for the sick, for those starting out on a difficult journey, for mothers after childbirth, or for returning warriors. Sweat-bathing was a persistent and important means of purification for everyone as well as a means of learning sacred lore.

Among Algonquin peoples, other supernatural experts had more ambiguous roles. Called "wabenos" by some, these were the people who used power for questionable or even evil reasons. Part of the work of a wabeno might be benevolent or even neutral, using magic to ensure success in love or hunting, for example. Some magic, though, was intrinsically evil, used for vengeance, to cause disease, or even to kill people. Wabenos were feared; and in time of trouble, they might be handy scapegoats on which to blame misfortune. In some cases, they might be killed themselves, if someone were brave enough to try.

Wabenos often became wicked through visions from powerful manitos, which in modern times have come to be regarded as evil spirits. In earlier days, wabenos may have been blessed by spirits powerful for good or evil, and why they came down on the evil side is less clear-cut. Wabenos had their own peculiar powers. For one thing, they were skin-changers, thought to be able to take on the forms of animals at will. A common shape for wabenos to assume was the bear, so human-like in its ability to stand upright and walk like a man (Salzer 1972). Wabenos also became fox-like creatures that shot fire from their mouths each time they spoke (Hoffman 1896). Another thing a wabeno could do was put his hands into boiling maple syrup. John Tanner described wabeno fire-handlers in the early nineteenth century taking up hot coals with their hands or in their mouths, feats Tanner thought possible only after the use of a yarrow-based plant mixture to protect the skin. In Tanner's time, wabenos were "fashionable" among the Chippewa, but he said that older and wiser heads dismissed them as dangerous and even false (Tanner 1830).

Besides wabenos and ordinary shamans, a group of herbalists acted to heal the sick using plants and teas made from plants. Many different plants were used; and while some seem to have mainly a magical reason behind their use, others have real ability to reduce symptoms, if not actually cure a given condition. For example, white pine bark is a specific remedy for coughs and is still sometimes used as an ingredient in cough syrups. Bearberry, a low evergreen shrub of the Canadian Zone, is a recognized home remedy for urinary disorders; its leaves, boiled and made into a tea, are antiseptic and diuretic. Other helpful plant remedies include boneset, violets, mints, and jewel-weed.

The main religious specialists in more recent times have belonged to the Midewiwin Society. These people combine the traits of the older shamans with those of the wabenos. In the twentieth century, Mide shamans have been regarded as both evil and good, a blending of older ideas about shamans and a reflection of the difficult conditions of modern life (Landes 1968a).

Community rituals

Much of religion was individual, shaped and inspired by one person's dreams or visions, but there were community aspects of it as well. Feasting, for example, was often for religious purposes. Early Christian missionaries quickly noted the religious quality of many feasts and were puzzled about which to encourage as harmless social gatherings and which they had to denounce as "unlawful." Manitos were given many feasts during which they were offered food and asked to remember their promises. Some of the feasts were "eat-all" feasts in which guests had to finish all the food in honor of the manito, and some were feasts after which the leftovers were carried home by the guests. Feasts served many ends: honoring the manito, giving the host a reputation for generosity, and sharing food. During the feast, the host sang and in the presence of the assembled company, prayed and danced solemnly, following the instructions of his dream. Many of the feasts featured dog meat, which had a special sacrificial connotation. Manito feasts were carried on with formal etiquette; strangers were made welcome, invited to attend, and offered the best of what was there (Blair 1911, I).

War feasts were also inspired by dreams. Prayers for safe return alternated with a kind of psychological driving in which the host and his guests used rhythmic chanting and audience response in chorus to move towards greater and greater enthusiasm. The climax was reached when people took up hot coals to throw on spectators, imitating what they hoped to do to their enemies. Each warrior sang his own war song and danced in his own style. With the firelight at night catching the colors of quillwork, feathers, and paint, a war feast was an impressive way to begin a campaign.

Ritual followed the warriors to battle. They sometimes camped at night in an oblong space with an imagined door facing in the enemies' direction; they slept with the most experienced man nearest the enemy, the least experienced farthest away, and they all tried to sleep facing home. It was bad luck for warriors to step over weapons left on the ground or people sleeping there. Warriors should not sit on the bare ground or walk on beaten paths; their drinking cups must be used in a certain way, drinking out of one side on the outward journey, the other side on the way back. Enemies were found by the war leader, who detected them through prayer and song (Tanner 1830). Young men on their first war party had restrictions on their behavior resembling girls' puberty observances: they used scratching sticks, wore head coverings, fasted, blackened their faces, and ate from special dishes. The ceremony surrounding war was important because war leaders had few other means of keeping their groups together.

Another community ritual was the Feast of the Dead, observed by Perrot in Wisconsin among Ottawa, Fox, and others and by Radisson (Adams 1961) among the Chippewa south of Lake Superior. People from miles around were invited to attend a ritual that ensured status in the afterlife for the souls of the dead. Elsewhere in North America, a major part of the ceremony was the reburial in one grave of all the people who had died since the last Feast, but this part was omitted in Wisconsin. Radisson remarked that people saved the bones of the dead and exchanged them, not put them in a common pit. The Feast was held once a year, and those who had been guests took turns at being hosts for days of dancing, feasting, and gift-giving. Ceremonial gift-giving involved large quantities of clothing, trade goods, and "all that they possess" (Blair 1911, I: 88), apparently reducing the hosts to poverty.

Many other things were going on under the surface during a Feast of the Dead. For one thing, alliances were created as hosts invited people who could be of use to them in trade or warfare (Hickerson 1960). In addition, the giveaways of possessions were not what they seemed: each gift a host gave to a guest had to be returned in the form of a gift of equal or greater value at the next Feast of the Dead. It was trade in installments. Each host gave as much as he could to encourage next year's hosts to make an even better return. The hosts' prestige rested upon their generosity and willingness to compete in the gift exchange. The Feast of the Dead meant that people had to gather together things to give away during the whole year in which they were to be hosts. The Feast did not survive the seventeenth century in Wisconsin as more direct means of trade became universal and yearly giveaways of increased quantities of goods became harder to manage.

Prophetic movements

Several prophets were recorded in Wisconsin during the historic period, and some of them had lasting effects. One of the earliest was the Shawnee Prophet, Tenskwatawa. He was a brother of Tecumseh, who tried in the early nineteenth century to unite the Eastern tribes and create an independent Indian state. Tecumseh's vision was sweeping and his goals were revolutionary as far as Indian political life was concerned. He visited Wisconsin in 1810 or 1811, trying to persuade people to join him in war against the Americans. As a result of his visit, many Winnebago and other Wisconsin Indians fought in the War of 1812 on the side of the British.

The Shawnee Prophet's message supported Tecumseh, providing spiritual backing for his political movement. The Prophet had a vision during which he received new rules for Indian life, ones that rejected European goods and condemned European ways. Indians were told to return to native dress and to live as warriors did in the past, by hunting rather than farming and raising cattle. Men were to have only one wife, and each spouse was to strictly observe what was proper for that sex. Prayers were to be said morning and evening, and anyone hearing the Prophet's word and not following it was to be killed (Blair 1911, II). The Shawnee Prophet was a charismatic leader: when he spoke, people listened, and their own hopes and fears were echoed in his warnings and promises. The message of the Shawnee Prophet was heard by many Wisconsin people. It came indirectly and was garbled in the telling, but its impact was real. John Tanner, then living to the northwest of Lake Superior, reported the arrival of the Shawnee Prophet's messenger, who simply appeared without any prior announcement. He told people to follow the Prophet's instructions: they were not to let their fires go out; men were not to strike women and children; drinking, lying, and stealing were all prohibited; and no one was to go to war. If people had to light fires, they had to go back to rubbing one stick against another. Medicine bundles were all to be destroyed, and dogs were to be killed. Tanner said that people received the message with "great humility" and fear and tried to obey the Prophet in spite of the hardship of doing without hunting dogs and a means of making fires, but gradually they abandoned the new rules and finally rejected them entirely.

After the Shawnee Prophet's message faded, a number of revelations from the Great Spirit came to the Indians of John Tanner's area (1830). People told others of messages they had received in dreams, but very few of these had any effect and none approached the impact of the Shawnee Prophet. Religious life was in a state of renewal, but only people whose advice was useful acquired any following. In a religious world where dreams were a source of inspiration, the coming of prophets was much like mutations in germ cells: only the ones that had some survival value stood a chance of becoming part of the cultural gene pool.

Winnebago Religion

By the nineteenth century, the themes that were important in Winnebago religion included power and the search for individual power. Power could be obtained during puberty fasts when boys tried to get a personal spirit whose blessings could be a help in future life. Sometimes boys received visions or dreams from the spiritual beings who had once blessed their fathers, and sometimes different ones appeared to them. These spirits became permanent guardians, always there to be called on in personal crises. A spirit could be persuaded to become a personal guardian through fasting, concentration, and offerings: tobacco, deerskins, or even dogs.

Winnebago spirits included Sun, Moon, Earth, Morningstar, Thunders, and Water-Spirit; others were Earthmaker and Disease-Giver. Earthmaker, as his name implies, was a creator, and he became the Winnebago version of the Great Spirit. Earthmaker almost never appeared to people as a source for blessings, and his major role seems to have been the source for other spirits' power, at least in recent versions of the tales. Earthmaker does not appear at all in some of the oldest accounts, and his development can be traced through time as the stories enlarged to include him (Radin 1945).

Disease-Giver was a Winnebago supernatural without parallels elsewhere in Wisconsin, a being in a human shape who gave out death with one half of his body and life with the other. He is not a figure of any importance in Winnebago myths, and he plays no role in origin tales or stories about the early lives of the spirits. His emergence as an important figure may be explained as a result of the terrible impact of European diseases (Dobyns 1984). In the early years, epidemic diseases went in waves as susceptible people were affected by the thousands. Curing disease and explaining why it had come became a major focus of dream visions. Disease-Giver, both a source of evil and a means of curing it, may have had his origins then.

The Winnebago also had several culture heroes: Hare, Trickster, the Twins, Red Horn, and Turtle. The formally designated Trickster (Radin 1973) was man-like, dressed in a raccoon skin blanket and carrying a birchbark box with his extremely long penis inside. Trickster was a classic combination of the foolish creature, who makes mistakes even when warned of the consequences, and the culture hero, who may also be a creator or spiritual guide. Hare was originally not as important as he was elsewhere in Wisconsin. When he appeared in early Winnebago tales, they were like those told about Nanabozho, even to his living with his far-from-kindly old grandmother, the Earth. Later Hare was regarded as a deliverer and became equated with Christ among some peyotists of modern times.

The Winnebago universe was complicated and filled with things seen and unseen. It had four layers, each with its inhabitants and purpose, arranged as islands surrounded by seas (Radin 1973). The top layer was occupied by Earthmaker, aloof and unapproachable. The second layer was the home of Trickster, who was the chief being there, and the third world was presided over by Turtle. The bottom world was "this world," the human world, and Hare and sometimes a Water-Spirit were its main figures.

Death was treated as part of the nature of things, a consequence of old age and a move to another kind of existence. In the twentieth century, some people expressed a belief in reincarnation, an idea that may be much older (Radin 1923). Soul re-cycling was one of the benefits of belonging to religious organizations such as the Medicine Lodge, but it was open to others as well. Those who had lived an upright life or were killed in battle might expect reincarnation as well.

Warfare involved ritual. War blessings were sought from spirits, sometimes from those whose connection with war is not obvious. For example, the Thunders, Disease-Giver, Sun, and Morningstar were guardians who blessed the warrior, but even Grandmother Earth and Grandmother Moon were asked to favor men with "war and life." Warfare was idealized in tales and treated as a mystic journey that could end in reincarnation for a warrior killed along the way. Even the berdache, who turned from war to another way of life, was sanctified in his path by a vision or repeated dream that told him to abandon war and take up women's dress and women's work.

Regular ceremonies were held by clans and religious societies. Clan rituals, the clan feasts, were given by prominent clan members who served as hosts once a year. Each clan had a special time for its feast: spring for Bird clans, fall for Snakes, and early winter for Bears. Clan feasts honored the clan animal, but it also brought life and health, good fortune and blessings. The feasts conferred a general good on those who gave them as well as those who attended. Even more grand than clan feasts were the ceremonies of the religious societies. In the nineteenth and early twentieth centuries, four societies were remembered: Night Spirits, Grizzly Bears, Buffalo, and Ghosts. All the people who had received power from one of these beings joined together for a long and elaborate ceremony. In extra large wigwams, hosts recited stories of their blessings, made speeches, danced, and sang, joined by their friends and kinsmen. Each ritual was formally organized with alternate speeches and music, dance, and pantomime.

An important emphasis was also placed on war bundle feasts, the great Winter Feasts of the Winnebago. War bundles came into being through dreams received by warriors, who then prepared the bundles and later passed them on to their descendants. The bundles eventually were associated with clans and became part of clan rituals as well. When a feast was held, the power of the bundles was renewed, ensuring success in warfare for all clan members. The songs and stories that went with the bundles as well as what was in each one varied from one clan to another.

War bundle feasts included several separate rituals. A description of one held in the late nineteenth century begins with the holder of the bundle sending out invitations and arranging for a deer hunt to supply food for guests (Radin 1928). The host and other important men then purified themselves in sweat lodges in anticipation of the ritual. When all the guests had arrived, a feast in honor of Earthmaker or the Thunders was held in a large wigwam especially prepared for the occasion. The host formally gave gifts of deerskins to the guests; and prayers, singing, dancing, and the music of flutes, drums, and rattles followed. People made offerings of tobacco, and a feast followed. Then the great wigwam was cleaned and fresh kettles of meat put on the fires to cook. Finally, the Night Spirits, beings powerful in war, were honored by more singing, praying, dancing, and feasting. As an appropriate signal at the end, a strong-voiced man sounded the war whoop four times, and the company broke up as each person danced out of the wigwam (Radin 1923).

Over time, Winnebago ceremonial life has included feasts linked to clans, war bundle feasts, and those associated with religious societies. Other special observances were the Scalp Dance, a ceremony giving thanks for success in war, and the major religious movements, the Medicine Society and the Native American Church. In addition, many Winnebago have been members of Christian churches since at least the nineteenth century.

Chippewa Religion

The Chippewa shared many religious ideas with other Wisconsin Indians. They understood spiritual power and the importance of obtaining power for survival in a hard land. Nature was alive with spirits that controlled power and would share it with people who asked in the right way. Dreams, visions, and rituals were means of reaching these spirits; and some people were more adept at it than others. Many of the rituals were aimed at making a living or curing the sick, and many were part of a common Wisconsin heritage: Calumet Ceremony, Feast of the Dead, bear ceremonialism, and feasts concerned with war and the vision quest. In years of war with the Santee, Chippewa war rituals were more frequent and intense; and by the nineteenth century, warrior societies had emerged (Hickerson 1962). They were the focus of ritual surrounding warfare and had their own sacred equipment, costumes, and religious customs.

In the historic period, the Midewiwin or Grand Medicine Society became the most important Chippewa religious organization. It consisted of groups of religious experts who knew how to cure the sick and how to injure their enemies through supernatural means. They combined the abilities of shamans, herbalists, and even wabenos; and their special knowledge was a body of lore handed down to members from one generation to the next. In this respect, the Midewiwin Society had both priests and a priestly tradition, and few people could ever claim to know it all.

To understand what the Midewiwin Society meant is to ask when it started and how it changed through time. The first mention of the Midewiwin is not until the early eighteenth century. At that time a French official at Detroit said that old men dance the "medelinne" among the Ottawa there (Kinietz 1940: 270). Other early descriptions included comments that the rituals were special curing ceremonies held in long wigwams. The main part of the ceremony was thought to be the public part when many people came to witness the power of the priests. One of the dramatic events of these occasions was when the priests showed their power over life and death by ceremonially killing people and then bringing them back to life. Even in these early accounts, the priests used otter skin medicine bags, the most familiar of all the Grand Medicine ritual equipment well into the twentieth century (see Chapter 5). Since these early descriptions, much more complete and detailed records have been made of Midewiwin rites. Some of these came from priests who wanted to have the correct rituals recorded before they were forgotten (Hoffman 1891); others were learned from priests, correctly, through the payment of the proper fees (Landes 1968).

The major goal of the Midewiwin was to cure the sick and ensure the well-being of all members. This was phrased as "life and health," and it included hunting success and well-being in a material sense as well as a spiritual one; "health" meant cures for specific illnesses as well as general appeals for a longer life. In some versions, members were told to stay away from liquor, avoid lying, and not to steal (Densmore 1979). Public teachings called for "neighborliness, forbearance, concern for the sick, respect for all, paternalism, honesty," and honor to all the manitos (Landes 1968a: 42-43). In many ways, these concerns fit comfortably with the goals of older religious beliefs; the Midewiwin Society had its roots in the past and grew out of what had existed before.

Midewiwin was a group religion that did not need to be informed by an individual dream or vision; personal contact with a manito was not necessary. Special experiences of the members were not expected to add to or reinterpret the lore kept by the priests (Hilger 1951). However, powerful Mide priests, either alone or in discussions with others, were able to change the content of the rites; and from year to year and place to place, the ceremonies varied (Landes 1968a). Individual ideas about power, manitos, and individual access to the spirit world were not replaced or forbidden; they were enhanced as many people acted together and pooled their spiritual energy. People could still cure through their own dreams of manito blessings, but difficult cases or desperate situations could be handled by bringing the Midewiwin community together.

Midewiwin was secret, and a person could become a member only after instruction from people who were already members. The stages of membership were arranged in a pyramid with most people at the bottom levels and fewer and fewer in the top ones. In the twentieth century, eight successive grades were open; no one skipped a grade but had to move through them one after another. The first four grades were lesser ones and were called "Earth" while the other four of increasingly higher power were called "Sky." Most people entered the society at the lowest Earth level and never went any higher. Earth grades were for ordinary people, and the higher grades, because they contained concentrated spiritual power, were too dangerous for most people. Only the very ill or dying were initiated into the top steps where powerful priests held the lore of the Sky grades.

Even at the lowest levels, fees had to be paid to be admitted. The fees needed to move up increased through time, and people sometimes had to save for years and often borrow from kinsmen to accumulate them. Eventually Midewiwin became more and more a society for those who were already well off. The fees paid the officials who served at initiations, and as they became larger, more people wanted to participate in order to share them. In the eighteenth century, fees included fine furs, buckskins, and blankets; by the twentieth century, they could be cloth, blankets, tobacco, fresh and cooked food, wild rice, skins or hides, horses, pails, and dishes (Hilger 1951).

People had to have a reason to join Midewiwin. Someone who was very ill, especially with a long and severe illness, was a good candidate. People who had dreams telling them to become members did so to avoid misfortune in the future. Some people joined at the request of their families; children might be singled out as future members as early as their naming ceremonies. Some people joined for reasons of their own: a desire for greater status or even in order to share in the fees. The "Ghost Midewiwin" could be said for a deceased member or it could initiate a dead person into the society with someone serving as a proxy during the rites.

In the case of a man or woman who wanted to be cured, the first step was to find the right Mide priest to carry out the ritual. Priests of high grade were few in number, and the proper choice had to be made. Two other priests--called Bowman and Steersman--were asked to be assistants. These men had to have a staff of helpers to carry out the complicated ritual. The helpers had to be trained officers, people who had learned the ritual through paying a fee to those who already knew what to do. Women could serve as assistants, but they were not supposed to do any of the public singing or dancing and had to appoint a proxy if their office called for them to do either one. Since all the officers shared in the fees, the chief priest seldom had a problem in finding someone willing to serve. Once the staff was assembled, the curing ceremony began. It consisted of seven or eight days of private ritual and another day of public ceremony. The private sessions took place by day or night: Midewiwin lore was taught to the initiate then. For a lower Earth grade cure, the bare outlines were taught; and at advanced levels, more and more was given to the initiates. Often the lore consisted of moral or ethical teaching with emphasis on a simple, upright way of life. In addition, the initiate was taught how to use herbal medicines and given a few herbal cures to keep in a medicine bag (Densmore 1979). The secret curing sessions were the heart of the Midewiwin, and the greatest good for the patient was accomplished then through the skills of the presiding priest, who used both shamanistic and herbal techniques.

People initiated into Midewiwin could wear special face paint proper to the grade they had attained. Designs consisted of stripes, dots, and circles in a variety of colors--blue, red, white, black, green (Hoffman 1891). The paints were worn during rituals by those entitled to do so, and after death, the designs were painted on the faces of the dead. Midewiwin members thus faced the afterlife wearing visible signs of their proper grades.

The public ritual was held in a long wigwam, sometimes open to the sky, and featured songs, speeches, music, and dance. The climax of the public ritual was the shooting of shells from the medicine bags, the ritual killing and then revival of those who had been shot by the shells. The shells (called "megis") were small and white, often cowrie shells brought in by trade. They were kept in medicine bags where they stood for the manito called Shell, and they were expressions of his power. At the proper moment, each Midewiwin member held up his bag and shot at others with the shells flying magically through the air to their targets. Individuals struck by the shells were supposed to collapse and then be revived, illustrating the power of the shells for "life." The major target for the shell shooting was the person being initiated; afterwards he or she would be able to shoot shells using a medicine bag that was newly activated by the transfer of power from the priests to the initiate. After receiving this power, the new member danced and shot at others who in their turn, after being revived, would shoot other members of the society. It was proper to shoot initiated members, but those who were not members could not stand the power of the shells and might be seriously hurt. Stray shells shot by careless Midewiwin members were thought to be dangerous in a spiritual sense if they hit bystanders, and real consequences such as illness or death might follow (Barnouw 1960).

Reciting the Midewiwin origin tale was the most important part of the rite for the priests. For a low grade initiation, only parts of the story were told, but by the time a person reached higher grades, he or she heard it all. The origin myth was of great interest to the Mide priests, and they thought carefully about its structure and ultimate meaning. When important priests sat down together, they discussed and even debated the interpretation of the origin story. They criticized the way the rites were carried out and the way the story was told by other priests. In this way they kept a check on innovation and helped to keep the ritual from changing.

In spite of their care, however, even the important, central origin tale exists in several versions. One story begins with a man named Cut-Foot, who received the origin tale after eight years of manito dreams. The manitos told him of a time when people were covered with a protective shell-like coating like fingernails. Nanabozho, thinking that people would soon crowd the land, brought death by destroying the coating and making sure there would always be room for new people. Shell, a powerful manito, was sorry for people who now had to suffer from disease and death, and he sent Bear to ask the Great Spirit if anything could be done. Between them, they worked out the Midewiwin ritual and sent Bear to bring it to earth to comfort humanity (Landes 1968a). A second version of the origin tale excuses Nanabozho from causing illness and death and gives him the role of bringing Midewiwin. In this tale, Nanabozho's helper is not Bear but Otter, whose skin plays such an important part in the ritual (Hoffman 1891). Still other versions omit the Great Spirit entirely and introduce a "Grand medicine spirit," a teacher of the spiritual and material means to a long and healthy life (Densmore 1979). This manito had the form of an old man who taught other old men herbal cures and powerful remedies for illness.

The priests and their assistants stood for the manitos who were responsible for success. In the lower grades, only a few manitos were needed, and only a few assistants represented them. In the higher grades, many manitos were summoned with more assistants needed. The manitos in the origin tales were the ones that came to the Midewiwin rites; and they were represented by the chief priest and his officers, with the lesser manitos personified by assistants. A powerful priest could be at the same time himself and the manito he represented, a fusion of power that could accomplish great things if kept under control.

Midewiwin belief rests on abstract principles of good and evil. The origin myths emphasize the struggle between good manitos on the one hand and evil ones on the other. For Midewiwin members, there were such things as evil manitos (Hoffman 1891) who tried to prevent people from succeeding in the initiation. They lurked around the wigwam and tried to stop the "good" being done inside. The Great Spirit in one version of the origin myth was an image of that good, an ultimate source from which good things derive. Shell in one tale and Nanabozho in another stood as kindly, well-disposed spirits, who sought to bestow blessings on human beings as a matter of course, because they were virtuous themselves.

The long origin myths, the songs each priest had to know, and the many steps in the ritual placed a great premium on memory, and Midewiwin priests knew that memory could only do so much without help. They made records to serve as their own private means of recall. They drew pictures on pieces of birchbark by engraving lines with a sharp point and then rubbing dry paint into the lines. The figures drawn were their own symbols and their own means of recording the plan of the ceremony, at what points songs were to be sung, and what everyone was supposed to do. These scrolls jogged the memory of one person and were not writing that could be read by anyone. The scrolls could be of use to someone else only if the original priest went over them explaining the symbols he had used.

Over time some of the symbols came to be understood by many people, but the scrolls themselves were records kept by individuals and could be truly understood only by them.

Mide priests have held an ambivalent position. They were men of power capable of great good, but because they went farther into the mysteries of the supernatural, they were often feared as well. The Sky grades of the Midewiwin were thought to involve teaching sorcery as well as healing, and the same man who could cure through his power might cause disease if he were insulted or offended by less powerful people. Because they were feared, priests could push people into joining the society and paying the fees that benefitted the priests and their kinsmen.

In the early nineteenth century, the Chippewa began to think of Midewiwin as a "national" society and take pride in it. Some of its symbolism came to be interpreted as standing for all the people who called themselves Chippewa. The Midewiwin shells, for example, were considered to have come out of the lakes settled on by the Chippewa and reached into every village (Warren 1984). The megis itself was identified with by all Chippewa.

Widespread Religious Movements

Midewiwin

Midewiwin was practiced by most Algonquin-speaking people. The Menomini version, for example, is well known, at least in its late nineteenth century form (Hoffman 1896, Skinner 1921). Menomini rites were much like those of the Chippewa, even down to some fine details, and it seems likely that Midewiwin came to the Menomini directly from Chippewa sources, probably during the same period when it was spreading through Chippewa villages. Chippewa influence on the Menomini Midewiwin is clearest in the parts of the ritual where the Chippewa language was used and in the respect given Chippewa experts. People in doubt about some part of the ceremony always felt that Chippewa priests should be consulted since they held the "real" Midewiwin lore. In origin tales, Menomini priests described Nanabozho (Ma'nabush) as bringing the rites to mankind: Nanabozho had been sent to the earth by the Great Spirit to perform good deeds to benefit his human "uncles." He created animals for them to hunt, gave them herbal cures, and taught them many useful things. Afterwards he went to live at Mackinaw where his "uncles" continued to visit him. The Menomini version of the Midewiwin origin tale thus became part of the longer story of the travels of Ma'nabush, which was considerably earlier.

Winnebago Medicine Society rituals were recorded in the twentieth century (Radin 1945). Originally they were influenced by Chippewa ideas, but how they entered Winnebago life is unknown. The rites might have come to the Winnebago indirectly through the Fox or Ioway or both. In any event, the Winnebago reinterpreted what they heard to suit their own needs, and the Winnebago Medicine Society has its own distinctive character. For one thing, the origin myth begins with the formation of the world by Earthmaker and a poetic account of the creation of all creatures, human and non-human alike. From there it moves into the introduction of death and the sorrow of Hare that his human "uncles and aunts" should have to die. Hare intercedes with Earthmaker, leading to the gift of Medicine to humans. Winnebago rituals included many of the same elements as the Chippewa rites, but the organization was different. There were five separate Medicine Society bands, each one with its own staff of leaders and assistants. At an initiation, one of the bands served as host to the others and performed most of the ritual as its candidate was received into membership. During the rites, the other bands had their own roles to play, myths to tell, and their share of the fees. The strict system of grades found among the Chippewa and Menomini is not reported for the Winnebago although people moved into larger roles in the Medicine Society rites through payment of fees in a similar way (Radin 1963).

Drum Dance

The Drum or Dream Dance (Barrett 1911) developed in the last part of the nineteenth century when conditions for many Indians were very difficult. In the west, the way of life of the horse nomads was ending, and warfare among Indians and between Indians and soldiers took a dreadful toll of young men on both sides as well as people in camps and villages. Several religious movements spread on the Plains, some of them imports (such as the Ghost Dance) and others home-grown. One of the latter was the Grass Dance, a ceremony that began in an Omaha warrior society and later emerged as a religious movement. The Grass Dance moved from tribe to tribe, and by 1860, it had reached the Santee. Significantly, the Grass Dance featured a large drum that accompanied the dancing.

The Drum Dance developed from the Grass Dance through the vision of a Santee Dakota prophet, Wananikwe (Tailfeather Woman). She was a young girl in one version and a respected mother of adult children in another. Her people were caught in war; and in order to save her life, she lay hidden in a lake among the rushes or under lily pads for many days and nights. During this time of trial, she had a vision in which she was taught songs and a ritual to end war by a manito, sometimes specifically the Great Spirit. The center of her vision was a large Drum whose voice was protective and whose message was peace. Wananikwe told her vision to others, and in some accounts, brought the Drum Dance east to the Chippewa herself. The transfer of the Drum Dance from the Santee to the Chippewa involved the oldest war in Wananikwe's memory, between her people and their ancient Chippewa enemies. The Drum Dance was meant to settle that war for all time.

The Chippewa received the Drum Dance not only because it had a message of worth but also because the Midewiwin Society by then had acquired a bad name. The wealth exchange that was a major feature of the ritual had led to larger and larger fees accumulating in the hands of Mide priests and their kinsmen. Fear of sorcery from Midewiwin priests also gave the society a bad name, and the Drum Dance was a welcome replacement. For a long time the adherents of the Drum Dance and the members of the Midewiwin Society went their separate ways.

Wananikwe told Drum Dance members to share her message with others. The Drums were supposed to move from group to group; and since the Drum Dance spread in recent times, there is a documented history of its movement. The members themselves have traced its path from one place to another in recent years (Vennum 1982). In Wisconsin, it moved to the Menomini and Potawatomi between 1875 and 1880 and then went south to the Winnebago, who rejected it, and to the Fox; the Kickapoo, who by this time were far away, never received it at all. Once a group had a Drum and were carrying on the ceremony, other Drums could still come to them; there is no single Drum for each people but several, depending on people's interest and their ability to carry on the ceremony. Furthermore, a Drum was supposed to stay only a few years in one place before being given to someone else.

The Drums are not just musical instruments to play with singing or dancing. They are powerful objects, similar to medicine bundles in that they are far more than they seem to be on the surface. Each Drum contains power that can bestow blessings as well as cause harm (Slotkin 1957). Since it is so powerful, it is treated with great care, kept carefully and stored in a place of honor when not in use. The Drums have distinct personalities, voices, and costumes; and Drum members feel toward them the way they might be expected to behave towards a manito who has come to live with them. The Drums are given offerings, often of tobacco, and they have their own pipes, which have to be smoked in their honor (Densmore 1913). When people come or go, they formally greet the Drum or take leave of it. And people are supposed to behave with dignity in its presence, observing proper decorum and good manners.

The coming of a Drum to any community often begins with a dream telling a man that he should become a Drum caretaker. Then someone who already has a Drum is asked if he will give it away to form a new Drum group. Moving the Drum to another home involves a presentation ceremony through which a new Drum Dance society is established. The society is organized around the keeper of the Drum, who must devote both time and attention to the Drum's well-being. In his home, he will smoke its pipe (Barrett 1911), offer it tobacco, and leave a light burning beside it if he has to leave the house. People may come to pay their respects to the Drum, and the keeper has to be hospitable, generous, and wealthy enough to entertain all comers. In addition to the keeper, about 30 people, usually kinsmen, "belong" to the Drum and serve as its wider community. They act as officers of the ceremonies and assistants to the keeper. Membership in this group is for life; and when someone dies, the vacancy has to be filled by appointment or sometimes by vote of the membership.

The Drum society is predominantly an organization for men in spite of the prophet Wananikwe. Women, however, may belong to a Ladies Drum Society, a group of women who prepare food and blankets for dances and serve as assistants. The women have a leader, often the wife of the keeper, and they frequently carry on a dance of their own after the main Drum Dance ceremonies, using a special secular drum.

The main activities of the Drum Dance are dances held over several days, out of doors in fine weather, in dance halls or other buildings when the weather is bad.

The main features of the dances are sessions of powerful, rhythmic drumming and singing. The Drum's voice communicates with the Great Spirit or whatever manitos have given power to the Drum (Slotkin 1957). In addition to drumming and singing, people dance, chant, give speeches, smoke pipes, and give away gifts (Hoffman 1891). The commonest offering is tobacco, laid out on blankets which are later given away. People enjoy the dances but they are religious occasions when the origin myth of the Drum is recited and everyone is urged to think about bettering their lives. After the formal ceremony is over, secular dancing is held, often using the Drum itself for music.

The Drum Dance was a means of adjusting Wisconsin Indians to life within a modern state where most of the people were no longer Indians. The new culture had different values and ways of life than the ones that had guided Indians in the past, and the Drum Dance eased the transition. It spoke of peace, of accommodation, of obeying laws. For some tribes, the Drum Dance became even more, a means of expressing tribal identity and retaining Indianness in the face of so much that had changed.

Christianity

Wisconsin Indians have been exposed to Christian teaching since the 1640s, and Christian ideas and beliefs have had a profound influence. Much of the Christian teaching was an active effort to persuade Indians to give up older beliefs and adopt new ones. Christian missionaries thought their beliefs were superior to those of Indians, and their preaching was unrelenting. Few Indians could escape the information provided by Christians, even if they were deep in the forests and far from the missions.

The earliest information Indians heard about Christianity came from people like Perrot, who lost no time in explaining the French reliance upon one great spirit instead of many manitos. Perrot was taken for a manito when he appeared among some Potawatomi near Green Bay, but he rejected the honor and began to discuss the nature of Christianity in terms he thought his listeners might understand (Blair 1911, I). In speeches to the Menomini at about the same time, Perrot linked together the possessions of the French, specifically iron tools and guns, with their belief in the French God. The reasonable conclusion of all this was if the Indians accepted French religion, material benefit must follow. This expectation accounted for some of the earnestness of Indian questions about French religious practices but not for all of it.

Indians were intellectually stimulated by new ideas that could be harmonized with some of their own beliefs. Many things the French did could be understood in Indian terms. For example, the French evidently accepted the idea of supernatural power. Their religious symbols, equipment, chapels, and ceremonies were charged with power; and Frenchmen behaved in ways that showed that they respected powerful things. They certainly knew that there were consequences from careless use of power and great benefits that could come to those who used it wisely. The French religious experts did not seem very different from the local shamans. Both fasted and prayed, attempted to help the sick and comfort the dying, and placed reliance upon visions and direct communication with spirits. French priests were even more understandable because they were, like local shamans, sources of evil as well as good. When a French priest baptized someone and that person died, evidently as a result, people drew the obvious conclusion: baptism caused illness or death.

French priests often reinforced their similarities with local shamans. For example, Father Allouez impressed upon some Fox that the cross was a magical sign that could accomplish wonderful things in its own right. He told Fox warriors of the miraculous appearance of the cross to the Emperor Constantine and led Indian warriors to believe that all they had to do was bear a cross on their shields and, like Constantine, they would win their war. They went on a raid with their shields marked with a cross, and their success in that raid was thought to have come from power in the cross (Thwaites 1896-1902: vol. 56). Even more interesting was Father Andre's dispute with a Menomini chief in which he tried to minimize dreaming as a guide to human life. He suggested that the Menomini man dream of iron and merchandise, of hatchets, and see how far dreaming would go as a means of getting those things. The French, as he pointed out, did not use dreams but possessed them anyway; Father Andre's opponent was left with a perception that French religion was so powerful that it produced goods without dreaming, not that material objects were made in ordinary ways back in France. In time, Indians realized that it was not religion that controlled access to trade, and some of them came to believe that European religions were of no practical use at all (Kinzie 1975).

Parallelisms between Indian and French beliefs led to a free exchange with missionaries and a consideration of their claims. Indian religions were open-ended, stimulated by individual dreams and visions, and ready to consider new ideas. The insistence of Christian priests on their own views meant that Indians heard over and over again the tenets of a faith that was different from, but not completely foreign to, their own. They were influenced by Christian belief even when they did not become practicing Christians themselves.

A direct source of such influence was intermarriage between French men and Indian women. Indian wives learned from their husbands about Christian beliefs and attitudes expressed in French homes. In the case of fur traders, there was probably never any formal attempt to convert women to Christianity, but the customs of religious life were bound to affect wives, especially when observing holidays or feast days gave them an enhanced position in their social world. When children were born, Indian women may have felt it proper to follow the religious practices of husbands for sons, in particular, and a major break with the past occurred. In the case of well-to-do traders, children might be sent to Quebec or to Europe to be educated. Returning children were a force for religious change after having practiced Christianity or observed it while living abroad in French families. An example is one of the children of the prominent Winnebago family of Decorah, who is thought to have introduced the concept of Earthmaker into the Medicine Society after coming back from a long stay in France (Radin 1945).

The small number of Christian converts was discouraging to French priests in the early years, but they always had some adherents. These Christian Indians were important in bringing Christian ideas into the rest of the community. They were intellectual bridges that may help explain the growing prominence of the Great Spirit, the identification of Hare with Christ, and the emergence of a division between good and evil spirits.

French religious orders withdrew from Wisconsin in the eighteenth century, but they left behind many ideas, symbols, and practices. Another wave of mainly Protestant missionaries came in the nineteenth century. They represented many denominations and brought many new ideas into the Wisconsin territory. Mrs. Kinzie mourned the absence of a clergyman to lead services at Ft. Winnebago, but at nearby Green Bay, missionaries were already active in opening schools for Indian children and, through them, reaching the adults.

Eastern Indians who moved to Wisconsin in the early nineteenth century came as Christians. The Oneida arrived as an already organized congregation of Episcopalians; they had been officially Christian for a long time and no longer followed older Iroquois ceremonies. The Stockbridge and Brothertown people were also Christians, some of them originally part of the "praying Indians" of seventeenth-century New England. These newcomers were models and sources of information for Indians already in Wisconsin (Marsh 1900).

Native American Church

The Native American Church, also called the Peyote Religion or the Peyote Way, is the latest Indian religious movement to reach Wisconsin. It began in the nineteenth century among some of the southern Plains people, probably Kiowa and Comanche, and it moved rapidly from one tribe to another through an active missionary program. The Winnebago, for example, received it from Oklahoma through the missionary John Rave, who brought it to them by 1895. The Menomini learned about it from a Potawatomi missionary, and the Chippewa learned about it from the Winnebago. The Native American Church was different from other Indian religions: it was a replacement rather than an addition. It dismissed Midewiwin, the use of medicine, and the older "ways." It was a break with the past except in the matter of power; members still sought power, although not within the older frameworks.

The central feature of the ritual is the use of peyote. Peyote is a small cactus plant whose dried buttons are eaten as part of the service and at other times as well. These have a hallucinogenic effect for many people, resulting in visions. They may be visions of spirits: the Christian God (explicitly the same thing as the Great Spirit), Jesus, the Holy Ghost, the Peyote Spirit, Waterbird, and spirits who appear as angels. Peyote is the means for communicating with them, a surer way to a vision than fasting and a more reliable way to receive power. Peyote is said to let people concentrate their thoughts and examine their lives in a way that promotes self-discipline. Peyotists define sin and think it important that people confess and resolve to sin no more. Peyote has replaced the medicine bundle; it is powerful in itself and can be used to cure the sick: "peyote is good for all ills, spiritual as well as bodily" (Slotkin 1956: 76).

The major ritual is an all-night service that combines drumming, speeches, feasting, and smoking. It is held in a house or in a Plains style tipi set up in the yard of the giver of the rite. Saturday night is the proper time so that people will have Sunday as a day of rest before returning to the workaday life of Monday morning. The service is led by a man who knows the ritual, assisted by several others. Each service has to be sponsored by someone who will provide a place, feed all the participants, and pay the leader's fees. The ceremony is usually held for someone's benefit, but everyone derives spiritual benefit from just being there.

Inside the tipi, people sit on cedar branches around a fire on the floor. The fire is near an altar, a crescent-shaped pile of sand on which has been placed the "chief" peyote and sometimes a Bible. When people come in and sat down, the sponsor explains why the ceremony is being held; and then the service begins. Peyote is passed around and eaten, as much or as little as each person wants. Drumming and singing help induce the visions or revelations that are sought through prayer and concentration. The meeting ends at dawn when refreshments are brought in and special blessed food is served. Most of the following day, people share meals and the religious experiences they had during the night (Spindler and Spindler 1971).

The Peyote Way is an Indian religion made up of things that have come from elsewhere. It is heavily influenced by Christianity: the central spiritual being is the Christian God with Jesus and sometimes even the Holy Ghost accompanying him. Indians understand these beings not only through reading the Bible but also through using peyote to help interpret it. Peyote is the Indian way of Christian revelation; it delivers knowledge directly. In addition, the Peyote Way helps people adapt to the non-Indian religious world around them. It is "another form of Christianity" (Slotkin 1956) and reduces the conflict between Indian and non-Indian religions by accepting the Christian spirits and following Christian ethical principles. Many of the converts to the Peyote Way have been members of other churches but felt uncomfortable in them and more at home in this Indian form of Christianity. For these people, the Peyote Way is a means of making use of religious principles they had accepted as Christians, but it allows them to remain "Indian."

Summary

Wisconsin Indian religions form a complicated tangle within which the oldest known root probably reaches well back into prehistory. This ancient framework set the conditions for the emergence of all the others. With themes of power, visions and dreams as means of reaching the holders of power, and the lifelong dialogue carried on with guardian spirits, it was not a simple system of thought. On that living trunk were grafted such things as Midewiwin, Christian beliefs about the spirit world, the Drum Dance, and the more foreign Peyote Way. Modern beliefs may include several of these at the same time.

CHAPTER 8
The Fur Trade

Furs were among the earliest things traded by Indians to Europeans. Records go back to fishermen bartering for them off Newfoundland years before any settlements were made on the North American mainland. Furs continued to be a valuable resource that had a market well into the twentieth century. At first, Europeans acquired furs in a kind of hit-or-miss fashion, but as trade was formally organized and the supply more reliable, fur trading became a successful business. For a lucky few, it earned fortunes, but for most people, it was only a means of keeping financially afloat from year to year, sometimes only from hand to mouth. Indians did not make fortunes in European terms, but the trade changed patterns of wealth and wealth distribution among them, too.

Over the years, the demand for furs in Europe went up and down, affecting the prices paid to traders and what Indians received for them back at the trading house. Governments tried to control prices by manipulating the supply, usually without considering the effects on traders or on Indians. As a result, the trade went from years of glut when prices fell to periods when trading for furs was forbidden by the government and then back again to times when furs were harvested by the thousands. In a good year, the number of furs shipped from New World ports was immense, especially considering the way they were obtained and moved. In 1735, for example, nearly 100,000 skins of the best quality went through Quebec (Thwaites 1906). Every one of them began as an animal skin trapped by an Indian hunter, processed by his wife, and carried to a trader. From there, the furs went in bundles on human backs or in canoes out of the wilderness and finally into the hands of exporters and shippers. The weather, the miles of travel on land and water, and the luck of the trail made moving the furs a risky business, even in the best of times (Wheeler, Kenyon, Woolworth, and Birk 1975).

Trade from the European point of view can be reconstructed from records kept by governments and trading companies, and some of this information helps in understanding how the trade affected Indian life. In general, the picture that emerges points to the fur trade as a major and continuing agent of change, as important as the ravages of European diseases and the warfare that came with European settlement. Changes caused by the fur trade were both technological and social, and they happened quickly, during a much shorter time span than any of the major changes that had occurred in the past.

One of the most impressive changes in Indian life linked Indian economic activities to the world market. It was only in a peripheral way, but Indians came to be affected by things and events in faraway places that touched their own economic well-being. The laws of supply and demand had an impact on them, but they knew as little of those laws or of the events that triggered them as modern people know of the workings of international finance. Their independence was diminished as they became part of a larger economic world.

Early Patterns of Trade

The European fur trade built on patterns of behavior that existed in Wisconsin for a long time. As early as the Paleo-Indian period, people collected skins for making clothing, processing them as they were needed. The animals sought then may not have been furbearers such as beaver, except when furs were needed to trim or decorate the more supple skins of caribou or deer. Through time, furs were gathered for use by the people who hunted them and perhaps also for trade to others. The skins of furbearing animals were likely to have been part of prehistoric trade between Wisconsin and Hopewell or Mississippian people to the south. Regular and persistent harvesting of furbearers for such purposes, however, does not mean that fur trapping of the pattern that dominated the European period was simply a familiar activity of prehistoric life that was only expanded when Europeans arrived.

Gathering furs in large numbers for the European trade meant a difference in the way people regarded animals and hunted them. It meant changing from an occasional catch of beaver for food or fur to a single-minded pursuit of those animals mainly for their skins. It meant moving from an attitude of hunting animals as an end in themselves for food or fur to hunting them for their skins as a means to an end. The change from one attitude to the other happened almost overnight: it did not take long for Indians to realize the importance of beaver skins to the early French traders, and they began to give the traders

beaver skins as gifts in the hope that the French would re-
ciprocate with things from European factories. Radisson
and Groseilliers kept their eyes fixed on beaver skins
when they came into Wisconsin in the seventeenth century,
and Radisson in his memoirs (Adams 1961) dwelled lovingly on every appearance of "castors' skins" worn by Indians
as robes or given to the French as gifts. His pleasure in
beaver skins and his delight in accumulating them were an
object lesson for all those he met along the way.

The French notion of trade as a straightforward
exchange of one thing for another of equal value was a
new idea. Indian trade originally operated in a different
context, and the major way that goods moved from one
person to another was through reciprocal gift-giving
(Sahlins 1972). A gift always had to be returned, but it did
not have to be right at that movement nor did it have to
be something of equal value. Giving gifts was a means of
establishing friendly ties with people, of reinforcing
relations that already existed, and supporting social life in
general. What was given away at one point would come
back to the giver at some time in the future as people
reciprocated the gifts originally given to them.

It is an error, however, to assume that the movement
of gifts from one person to another and back again was
simply an expression of altruism. People usually knew
what to expect when they gave things to someone else and
tried to maximize their own interests by giving gifts to
those from whom they expected something special in
return. When the "something special" was a raw material
or a finished product rarely found in the giver's own land,
an exchange took place that was of real economic importance. It used no money, though, and had no general
standard by which equivalence could be measured. When
gift-giving like this occurred on a large scale, perhaps
when people of one village met people in another, the
quantities of goods that could be exchanged might be enormous. Such occasions as the Feast of the Dead or the Calumet Ceremony were times when elaborate gift exchanges
were expected on all sides between hosts and guests
(Blakeslee 1981; Hickerson 1963).

Early explorers and missionaries quickly learned that
a pattern of gift-giving dominated social relations (Blair
1911). Gifts were given and received on all formal
occasions to build alliances and establish social ties. The
French themselves began to use gift-giving to create
loyalties among Indians and to bind them to French
sources for trade. French understanding and use of gift

exchange accounted for the closeness that some Indians felt for the French; it was hard for them to give up the partnerships that had been established through years of gift-exchange going all the way back to Perrot and Allouez.

A subtle thread running through gift exchange was the matter of personal prestige. Enhanced prestige went to the giver of gifts and made people eager to be givers. Important people gave the most and were expected to do so; as they gave things away, their prestige increased still further. Europeans, who scattered gifts in the early years of the trade, built a backlog of goodwill. They were able to give gifts in great abundance in the days when a single axe was a rare object and glass beads were greatly appreciated. Later, as people became more familiar with such things, traders were forced to pay a higher price in goods for the prestige they once enjoyed so cheaply.

The importance of reciprocal gift-giving as a means of moving goods among Indians is clear from their reactions to explorers and missionaries in the French period (Wright 1967). Yet it leaves some questions unanswered. For example, if gift-giving were the principal means of exchanging goods, how did it operate over long distances? The prehistoric trade that carried shell, copper, and other things from one place to another shows that effective long distance trade is very old: what was the role of people in between the place of origin of something and its final disposition somewhere else? In Wisconsin, not much information survives from the earliest years of contact, but trade goods clearly moved faster than Frenchmen. Long before they saw their first French faces, Indians had at least some European goods. The long distance trade routes were working well during the archaeologists' "protohistoric period."

How this long distance trade operated among Indians in prehistory can be understood from what is known about historic people such as the Seneca (Wallace 1970). A major part of Seneca trade rested on formal friendships between men of standing. These men, heads of lineages or chiefs, inherited the direction in which they could give and receive trade, and they often inherited trading partners as well. Such rights remained in the hands of important men, and in theory, no one else was supposed to join in. It was a daring and brave thing to do, to carry gifts of goods in a direction held by someone else, but anyone caught trying to build a trading partnership of his own could be safely robbed of his goods should he be caught. The framework of the trade involved each partner's traveling to visit the other and formally exchanging gifts. The visits were often full of ceremony (see Radisson's experiences in Adams 1961) and included speeches, feasting, and marriages as well as giving and receiving gifts. Skillful trading depended on the intangibles of friendship, hospitality, family honor, and the self-image of each partner. There was no public bargaining, haggling over prices or expressing disappointment over gifts that might be smaller than expected. The good manners of trading partnerships helped to keep the trade going, but the whole thing would not work if either partner did not meet the other's expectations over time. Trading partnerships lasted only as long as both sides felt that the exchanges were worthwhile.

Trade goods were not the only reason why people continued their trading partnerships from one year to the next. Trade was also a means of building military alliances in an uncertain world. Villages needed allies in war, and trading partners were obvious choices. When alliances became an overriding consideration, men were willing to give their partners some things that they themselves considered rare or knew were scarce in the lands of their partners. In this way trade goods could travel many miles from one trading partner to another and the participants supported alliances, to some extent to assure themselves of a continued supply of a valued resource.

Lineage heads or chiefs who controlled trade in a certain direction enlisted others to support their rights. Followers received some of the "profits" of trade as the main controllers gave gifts in turn to villages they thought might help them. Such redistribution of trade goods was encouraged by the high status accorded to generous men and the correspondingly low opinion people had of misers or hoarders of any kind. Whole groups of Indians regarded themselves as the proper agents for trade with groups of people up the river or down the lakes or somewhere whose direction they regarded as their own. "Middleman" status was understood and all its advantages fully appreciated well before European trade became a local institution. During the years of the fur trade, Indians worked to get and to keep middleman positions with regard to anyone in the interior who wanted French trade goods (Innis 1973).

The European fur trade eventually broke open the system of trading partnerships because the French did not really understand what lay behind them nor did they abide by the rules of the game. They acted as trade "raiders" by going around middlemen and bypassing people who thought they had the right to trade goods in specific directions. With the French example in front of them, fewer and fewer young men honored the inherited trading ties of their elders, and the chance to carry goods to far off places was more and more tempting. Those who had rights over certain trading directions needed to protect their positions and in turn gathered followings of warriors who were attached to leaders through gifts. The more followers a chief had, the more likely he was to need to participate more intensively in trade in order to reward his people. In this way, small and powerful groups could be developed in the interests of trading and supporting others in trade.

Gift-giving as a means of exchange continued to affect the way Indians operated in spite of the changes brought by Europeans. They expected gifts as part of their interaction with Europeans (Blair 1911), and through the years, they interpreted many of the actions of Europeans in terms of gift exchange. The presents of the French, the British gifts, and even the annuity payments of the Americans provided continuity with the past in spite of growing Indian participation in a money economy.

Europeans in the Trade

Many Europeans deliberately or unconsciously used trade to do other things besides exchanging furs for trade goods. Some of their goals were long term ones intended to last for years and were the result of policy decisions taken in Europe or in places like Quebec (Norton 1974). Others were more spur-of-the-moment decisions based on problems that needed action then and there. Most of the things Europeans wanted to accomplish were not seen clearly by their Indian clients, but they affected Indian life profoundly.

One major part of the fur trade was its use as an arm of national policy for the governments of France, Spain, England, and the United States. During times of international tension among these countries, trade was used to compete for control in North America, far from European homelands. National rivalries were often reflected in competition among the fur traders themselves. Traders acted as government agents, enlisting Indians on one side or another in wars that were fought over European national interests. The well-known example of the French and Indian War (see Chapter 3) is only one of several occasions when trade and warfare went hand in hand. The traders joined in wars themselves; they moved with Indian allies against their common enemies and became soldiers as well as traders. They raised troops and personally led them into battle (Kellogg 1935). The role of traders in war and their efforts to push Indians to fight each other or Europeans lasted century after century no matter what European government was involved.

In the early years of exploration, it was often the traders who had the first on-the-ground contact with Indians in the interior: where others might hesitate to go, the traders moved in. They were very effective in bringing distant people into direct contact with Europeans. Fur traders, for example, persuaded the Santee to send envoys from beyond Lake Superior all the way to Montreal to meet Frontenac (Wedel 1974), and it was the promise of trade that took Duluth into the western end of Lake Superior in the seventeenth century (Kellogg 1925). Explorations by fur traders were not always official. They sometimes went into the interior without government blessings and met with Indians on their own. Many of these men have left no records of their activities; they were either illiterate or they did not want the authorities back home to know what they were up to. Their presence in an area, however, could be used as a means of staking a claim by one government against claims by other nations. Formal ceremonies for taking possession of lands--such as those held in Wisconsin--were staged by traders as well as government officials.

Trade goods were used as a direct means of maintaining alliances with Indians. Traders were told to give gifts, special prices, and special privileges to people who would promise to support the home government of that trader. At times, traders used their gifts and special prices to keep Indians away from their European rivals. Indians soon learned to manipulate the traders to their own advantage; they attached themselves to whoever gave the most, as a French source ruefully observed in 1715 (Thwaites 1902). Indians began to judge prices and the quality of trade goods as they moved from an exchange economy based on reciprocal gift-giving to one based on a standard of value. They appreciated high quality and compared British to French goods and put their alliances where the prices were the lowest and the trade items the best.

Missionaries were an integral part of both French and Spanish trade. Sometimes missionaries gathered furs themselves and were active traders; sometimes they opposed trade and trade policies. Missionaries moved with the trade as it went west, often in an official capacity. For example, Ft. Beauharnois, the Sioux post on the Mississippi River, was built in 1727 to supply trade goods to the Santee, to keep the Fox in check by a military presence, and--as a distant third--to further religion (Thwaites 1906). When trading companies were formed, the presence of missionaries was often plainly stated in the contracts, and chapels for religious services were built into trading posts (Birk and Poseley 1978). Missionary work was so intertwined with the fur trade in the French period that Indians had every reason to think that the goals of each were the same.

Trading houses and traders played an important role in determining where Indian villages were located in the historic period. Europeans made deliberate efforts to move whole groups of people from one place to another to make trade easier or to shift military balances in their favor by moving villages. In 1704, for example, French authorities tried to persuade all of the Santee to move south to the mouth of the Des Moines or the Missouri, many miles from their lands at the western end of Lake Superior (Wedel 1974). The British frequently tried to draw Indians from all over to a few centrally located places where trade could be more easily controlled. Indians themselves moved in order to take advantage of trade sources. Historic records are full of references to groups of people turning up at places such as Chequamegon (see Chapter 3) or "removing" to the Mississippi or traveling great distances in order to be near a trading post (Thwaites 1896-1901: 58). Even some of the Cree came down from Hudson Bay to be near trade at the Sault (Adams 1961). In a sense, traders and sources for trade were magnets for Indians; they shifted their settlements at least partly to take advantage of trade. Trading houses were like any other important natural resource in the environment, and Indians either went to them to harvest what they needed or tried to develop social ties with people close enough to exploit the trade source directly.

From the European point of view, trade was a powerful means of maintaining alliances, manipulating the relationships between one people and another, and fostering whatever national goals were important at the time. From the perspective of many hundreds of years later, it appears that trade was the only means that Europeans could have used to exert influence on the outcome of events in the Northeast. Indians, in what they thought were their best interests, were rapidly tied to the trade, and it offered a direct means of applying leverage in their affairs. Sometimes it worked and sometimes it did not, but it always exerted pressure on Indian life.

French Trade Period

The year by year history of the French trade is well documented in official records that summarize the comings and goings of traders and the troublesome regulations that were supposed to govern them (Kellogg 1925; Thwaites 1902, 1906). Official and unofficial accounts follow the reactions of Indians less directly, but they provide many revealing pictures of what went on in the first years of the trade.

As early as the time of Champlain in Quebec, French observers were aware of the widely ranging trade activities that took Indians into the western lakes. Some Ottawa men had trading partners in that direction, possibly as far away as Wisconsin. What moved over this trade route initially were mats woven by women and furs, for which the exchanged items included paints and "other rubbish" (Kinietz 1940). At this point--1615 or thereabouts--trade was still in the hands of Indians and almost certainly operated by means of reciprocal gift exchanges by formal trading partners. As time passed, European objects became part of the movement of goods, filling in exactly as any other trade item. Because European things were still so rare, their appearance far in the interior must have given the Ottawa traders a notch up on the prestige scale and encouraged them to share what they were getting from the French. In the time-honored fashion of traders, however, they saved their worn-out kettles, cast-off knives, and blunted awls for their faraway trading partners, trusting that no one was informed enough to notice (Blair 1911: I). Indians in Wisconsin were receiving French trade goods through other Indians and were not exposed to the French at all.

No one knows how many French traders began to try to reach the western lakes country on their own, joining in the long distance trade for furs. Before the collapse of the Huron (see Chapter 3), their number was limited as the personal dangers outweighed the potential profits. When the once vigilant Hurons fled from their homes in Ontario, they left the route open to all comers or, at least, those willing to risk being caught by the Iroquois. By 1658, Radisson and Groseilliers were in Wisconsin on their way to the Mississippi River, and they met with Potawatomis as well as Mascoutens. In each case, the Frenchmen presented gifts and in so doing were understood to be offering trading partnerships. The expectation of receiving French trade goods well into the future probably accounts for the celebration, mirth, and general good cheer given the occasion by the Indian hosts. Radisson and Groseilliers dealt with the Indians within a commercial framework of "swapping" one thing of value for another, but they understood the importance of gift-giving and continued to press gifts on their hosts as long as the trade goods held out. The expected reciprocity produced "a good store of skins" as well as the goodwill of those who joined in the exchange. As Radisson and Groseilliers moved around in Wisconsin, they became aware that Indian groups tried to get exclusive rights to French trade. Trading partnerships and the pomp and ceremony of ritual exchange did not stand in the way of Indian attempts to corner both markets and the sources of goods.

From the point of view of the Indians, Radisson and Groseilliers and the nameless others that came after them in the seventeenth century were still operating within a native trade framework. They acted as daring men who had circumvented the older ideas about rights to trade in certain directions. Perhaps the unusual things they were carrying made people less forward in asserting their rights and more inclined to try more subtle ways to control trade.

Until about 1680, French trade in Wisconsin followed the same pattern: carried by a few men whose presence was not often sanctioned by the government and was not part of some larger trading company. Illegal traders, "coureurs de bois," did not set up permanent trading houses, but they probably operated on the basis of trading partnerships, in some cases sealed by marriage to Indian women. Their expeditions after furs were campaigns to carry goods to specific Indians, and points of rendezvous had to be set up. Since most of the traders seem to have used the south shore of Lake Superior for this purpose, an increasing number of Indians gathered at places such as Chequamegon, looking for a chance to participate.

More regulation of the trade brought new kinds of traders to Wisconsin. One of these was LaSalle, who had received official permission to trade west of Lake Michigan. On the strength of his "patent" to trade, LaSalle sent a group of 15 men into the west to act as his agents in collecting furs before he arrived himself to carry them away. Six of these men refused to go any farther west than Michilimackinac, but the rest went to winter-over among the Indians, both at Sault Ste. Marie and among the Potawatomis on Rock Island in Wisconsin. It was toward this island to join his men that LaSalle set sail in the *Griffon*, the first sailing ship on any of the Great Lakes (see Chapter 3).

The men that LaSalle had sent ahead of him had already gathered furs, which they brought to Rock Island to await his coming (R. Mason 1974). None of these men ever wrote his memoirs so exactly how they obtained the furs, what they gave for them, and in what context the exchange occurred is not known. By this time, however, commercialization of the trade was well under way and the old concepts of trading partnerships may have been replaced by more straightforward bargaining. LaSalle's men may have fanned out and gathered furs as individuals or perhaps they stayed put on Rock Island, drawing people with furs to them. They were certainly at home in the Potawatomi village by the time LaSalle came to get his furs, but when LaSalle and his party turned south, they went along as part of the expedition.

How those few traders lived on Rock Island has been partly revealed through archaeological excavation of their winter quarters there (R. Mason 1986). They had two buildings kept separate from the rest of the Potawatomi village by a small stockaded enclosure made of cedar posts jammed into the sandy soil and sometimes held in place by chunks of limestone. At least one of their buildings had a chimney and probably served as living quarters. It was built of cedar planks stuck upright into a narrow footing trench, nothing at all like the log cabins that one day would come to mean frontier architecture to most people. The other building may have been a kind of warehouse since it did not have a chimney, and less debris was found around it. Between the buildings was a large firepit made of dry-laid limestone slabs, just what Europeans might make for outdoor cooking. This little settlement on Rock Island was not elaborate, but it was the kind of thing to be expected as trading houses became the rule across Wisconsin. The day of the traders with packs on their backs was not over yet, but the day of the permanent trading houses had begun.

What the local Potawatomi Indians thought of all this is not known, but they welcomed the traders, and they welcomed LaSalle when he came to check into what his agents had accomplished. The description of his landing on Rock Island and the reception of the *Griffon's* passengers indicates that the people were glad to see the newcomers and were more than hospitable. In their enthusiasm, they loaded LaSalle on a blanket and paraded him around the village, a mark of high regard and far more than one might expect of people simply greeting a new French face. Perhaps they saw in LaSalle a promise of enhanced status in trade and a more central role for themselves as middlemen.

LaSalle was later involved in building a trading "fort" in Wisconsin, intended less as a place where people came to trade than a place to store furs. LaSalle claimed to have built this fort on the Wisconsin River (Kellogg 1925) at Prairie du Chien. Whether or not he actually did has never been discovered, but from this time on, the pattern for the Indian trade became one of trading forts and houses in many parts of Wisconsin.

Nicolas Perrot built a number of them in late seventeenth century Wisconsin, especially along the Mississippi River (Kellogg 1925). The first of these, Ft. St. Nicholas, was put up near Prairie du Chien and a second at Trempealeau. A third, Ft. St. Antoine, was built near Lake Pepin, and it was there that Perrot took possession of the surrounding country for the crown of France. Ft. St. Antoine was in use for a very short time and was abandoned at the beginning of King William's War in 1689, when the interior west of the lakes was abandoned by the French. By 1693, they returned and began to build trading houses or forts in both the Green Bay area and along the upper part of the Mississippi River. They temporarily left again after 1696 as the political situation changed once more.

What these forts and trading houses meant to the Indians included both the tangibles of trade goods and the intangibles of increasing pressure on their lives as French influence grew. The major intended function of the settlement was as a storage place for goods, warehouses for the convenience of the traders. But with the coming of Perrot, they had official status as well. Soldiers were stationed at some of them, giving Indians a close view of French warriors as well as priests and traders. The soldiers were supposed to help keep the peace between Indian groups, often between the Santee and everyone else. Over time, the trading houses became neutral ground and came to have authority in balancing the claims of one Indian group against another. The French spoke as "elder brothers" and took on the role of moral leadership in speaking for war or peace, and Indians used their services as political go-betweens.

The trading houses were also places of refuge, safe houses where people could find shelter (Thwaites 1902). Much like the lodge of the Winnebago Thunder Chief, trading houses were havens where single men or whole parties received protection once they were within the walls. This shelter, of course, was only for the friends of France, and it became one more reason for an alliance with the French. Once a man left the trading house, he was fair game for his enemies, but an effective umbrella of French protection now reached into the wilderness where the number of French soldiers might be really too small to prevent the Indians from doing as they pleased. Trading houses were sometimes sacked and burned by Indians and even abandoned in fear by the soldiers supposed to protect them, but their influence grew and the *idea* of their being places of authority spread.

Trading houses built on the old patterns of redistribution of wealth by being the places for gift-giving, sometimes on a massive scale. Perrot, for example, gave gifts to make peace with people, to get help in war, each time he spoke in council, to cover accidents, in cases of natural catastrophe or death, to welcome visitors, and to say a proper farewell (Blair 1911). In social life, the kettles, tobacco, guns, blankets, and other things were a sort of social oil, lubricating relationships in both directions. The trading houses were places of gift-giving, and Indians continued to think of them in this way long after the French period when other governments tried to give up the custom as a needless expense.

Another important role that some trading houses filled was in education. The many things that went on at trading houses gave them the potential for spreading technical information among Indians. Trading houses sometimes had blacksmith shops or men trained in metal-working; Indians often specifically asked for them (Hennepin 1966). By bringing guns and other tools to be repaired or refitted, Indians learned about iron-working, and through observation they became familiar enough with the techniques to move into metalworking themselves. By the nineteenth century, their experience spanned several hundred years of metalworking all the way from cutting and cold-hammering to smelting and casting (see Chapter 5).

The only French trading center for which there is a surviving floor plan is Ft. Beauharnois, on the Mississippi River near Lake Pepin (Birk and Poseley 1978). A drawing of this fort has been found as well as a description of the land where it was built. Of a more military character than any of Perrot's "forts," it probably reflected the growing importance of French military power as a result of the Fox Wars. Ft. Beauharnois was rectangular with each 100 foot long wall built of stakes, twelve feet in height. Inside were a guardhouse, a warehouse, trading houses, a house for the "comendant," a chapel with an attached priest's house, and a powder magazine, well away from the other buildings. The walls took only four days to put up, and the whole thing was finished within a month. The site was poorly chosen since it flooded in the spring, forcing the French to camp outside on higher ground (Thwaites 1906). This first Sioux Post was abandoned shortly after it was built, but its floor plan shows what the priorities were in the early French settlements in the western lakes country.

Indians continued to react to places such as Ft. Beauharnois as centers of influence, but the seventeenth and eighteenth century accounts do not show exactly how Indians as individuals were connected to them. In the early years, Perrot and other trader/officials did not have Indian wives and avoided entangling themselves in kinship relationships. Other Frenchmen were probably more willing to make use of local social organizations; the "coureurs de bois" lived with the Indians, in some cases hunted with them, and married among them. As they became regular traders, many of these patterns persisted. How many Frenchmen there were in Wisconsin is hard to estimate. In 1680, a general king's amnesty for illegal traders who "came in" out of the woods brought 600 from the western lakes area. If only half of these were from Wisconsin or even only a third, a really substantial French presence can be inferred.

Growth of trading centers

In the eighteenth century, a number of places became centers where trade was a settled business. In the north, Chequamegon served as a trading rendezvous within reach of the whole south shore of Lake Superior and the lands to the south and west. It had once sheltered Radisson and by 1665 was home to refugees from Huronia. Allouez built the mission of St. Esprit at about the same time and set up housekeeping with traders for neighbors. All the French left Chequamegon after the Santee forced the refugees back toward Mackinac, but by 1679 Duluth was there to restore an active French presence once more. By 1693 a large trading house with a military garrison was built on Madeline Island, and it remained an important center for French trade until the end of the French regime in Canada (Hickerson 1962).

Along the Mississippi River, the trade operated from trading forts built and abandoned and then rebuilt again by Perrot, Le Sueur, and others. Certain sites were used over and over again: perhaps the geography of the river made some places easy to locate, even for newcomers. Perhaps some of them had been Indian villages in the past and were already cleared and open. The area around Lake Pepin is one of these. Year after year it was a usual location for French trading houses, and it remained important as long as the French were in Wisconsin. Prairie du Chien was another of these critical places in Wisconsin. Fur traders and Indians both used it for gatherings, and except for a twenty-year abandonment during the Fox Wars (see Chapter 3), Prairie du Chien grew to become the most important trade center in the west (Oerichbauer 1976). Eventually Indians came to live there permanently, first with the French and later with British and Americans. As a place where cultural interchange occurred, Prairie du Chien has to be ranked at the top of the list among all the trading centers. A third historic location on the Mississippi was the land near Trempealeau. It was first used for a French fort in 1685 when Perrot wintered there on one of his many journeys into the west, and a second fort may have been built there in the eighteenth century. As time passed, though, it lost its importance to Prairie du Chien.

In the eastern part of the state, the mouth of the Lower Fox became another center for trade and for permanent settlement by both Indians and Europeans. It was a natural spot right at the eastern end of the Fox-Wisconsin river road, and it received all the traffic going in either direction. The earliest European settlements at "La Baye" were by missionaries and a few traders, but by 1717, a fort with a military commander was built there. Some of the importance of Green Bay at this time was owing to the Fox Wars and the fact that La Baye was a reasonably safe place to be. Bitter enmity with the Fox and all their allies meant that settlements beyond Green Bay were exposed and open to attack.

Expansion of the centers at Prairie du Chien and Green Bay created a new kind of European settlement in Wisconsin. It included both Indians and Europeans living in a common area in what were "mixed" villages. Not much is known about how people interacted with each other or how they carried on their day-to-day activities.

The Europeans were for the most part living like the Indians, and their relationships must have been close, at least in terms of proximity. At times there was trouble, but Indians profited from the location, especially when they were able to marry their daughters to traders. Such marriages required gift exchanges and committed the new husbands to their wives' relatives, but they were not often considered binding by the French. Indian women had more liberal ideas about divorce and could choose new husbands if and when their French traders left and never came back. A lasting legacy of these marriages was the number of children born and what many of those children came to be. French traders, if they were well off and settled for life on the frontier, might send their children to school in Quebec or even to France. The children abandoned by their fathers and left to live in their mothers' groups often rose to positions of high standing, perhaps because it was thought that they retained kinship rights among their fathers' people. This was the beginning of what later became a distinct population of people with mixed French-Indian heritage, the Métis. In the early French period, Métis often served as links between the two communities, especially if they were fluent in both languages. Many became permanent parts of the French community; the famous Wisconsin families of Langlade and Grignon both had ties to mixed French and Indian ancestors.

The effects of trade on Indian life

The fur trade was not an immediate disaster for individual Indians. As a way of life it promised more than it could ultimately deliver, but for people joining the trade for the first time, long term expectations were not important. Few people were able to look ahead, and neither French nor Indians knew at the time where the fur trade might lead them. The trade changed Indian life, but under the French regime it changed life in a way that most participants would probably have judged to be beneficial.

The most obvious changes that occurred in Indian life had to do with the substitution of European trade goods for homemade Indian artifacts. European goods were regarded as remarkable, and at first some Indians thought that they might have a supernatural origin. Indian interest and pleasure in all the new things is evident in their reactions as they received them as gifts or as payment for furs received. The novelty of what the French brought was a continuing stimulus to thought, experiment, and whole new ideas (see Chapter 5). In the seventeenth century, Indians were ready to go any distance, undergo any hardship, and try any subterfuge to keep a hold on a reliable source for trade. The French appetite for furs, things that Indians took freely from nature, must have seemed peculiar since Frenchmen were willing to give so much for the ordinary and everyday furs that anyone could obtain so easily.

As time passed and trade goods became commonplace, Indians were more shrewd in their dealing with the traders. Once they had a basic European tool kit, they did not need as much, except in the way of replacement of worn-out or lost tools and weapons or worn-out clothing. They learned to fix or re-make many things, reducing further what they needed from traders. Hardware and weapons would always move in the trade, but the softer, more consumable goods were what brought Indians back year after year. "Supplies," things that were eaten or drunk or worn or expended, became the heart of the Indian trade.

The perception of their own needs was limited as much by practical considerations as by cultural preference. Indians could carry only so much around or wear only so much or give away only so much. Fur traders had no ready-made consumer culture that endlessly demanded new things and consumed them as a way of life. Indians were not willing to gather furs for trade over and above what they thought was enough to supply themselves. They were willing to work hard for whatever they thought necessary; but work for its own sake or for some imagined future benefit was a foreign concept. This put traders in the position of sometimes having to persuade Indians to go out and hunt, and it was sometimes very difficult. Indians did not respond to French notions of what volume of furs was needed nor did they worry about traders' margins of profit. Some of the pushing of liquor on the part of traders was because it was addictive and could be consumed on the spot; a market for liquor intensified hunting for furs.

The early years of the trade were years of great culture change, but Indian life did not grind to a halt or deteriorate or become disorganized as a result. The French period was still a time when European settlement was limited and Indian cultures continued to operate under their own steam. In some ways, the French period was one of cultural fluorescence: people were exposed to many new ideas and materials. The mixed Indian villages of the trade period brought people together from great distances, and common dialects such as Ottawa or Southern Ojibwa made cultural sharing easier. In spite of future problems, much of value came out of the stimulating exchanges of the time.

One of the breaks with the past that resulted from the trade was the way people hunted. When Europeans first arrived, hunting was a means of getting food and clothing. Beavers were caught and, if their pelts were not needed, roasted whole over fires, fur and all. Beaver was often eaten by Indians, the fatty tail being a special delicacy. The great advantage of beaver meat as food for Europeans was for pious Frenchmen; religious authorities back in France had classified it as a fish, and it was therefore proper food for fast days. When Indians needed beaver for fur robes, they waited for fall or winter when the pelts were in their best condition. Early hunting techniques were simple in concept, more difficult in execution (Shorger 1965). Beaver were caught in winter by cutting a hole in the ice of a beaver pond, baiting it, and putting in a net. When the beaver came to take the bait, it was caught in the net and could be clubbed to death. While effective for hunting a single beaver every so often, this technique requires long patient waiting until the beaver shows up at an ice hole. Before the formation of winter ice and deep winter snow, beaver were trapped by deadfalls as they moved from one part of their range to another. A technique reported by Father Hennepin (1880) involved breaking beaver dams, letting the water drain, and then catching the beaver in nets in the shallow water. Whole colonies of beavers could be caught in this way, but in the period before the fur trade, there was little incentive for putting so much into hunting beaver.

After European contact, hunters turned tools received through trade back into a means to get the only currency of any use in the trade--beaver pelts. Guns could be used on beaver although the shot left holes in the skins, and dead beaver might sink in water and be lost. Beaver were also speared with barbed iron points attached to lines that let them be hauled in afterwards.

In the early days, iron traps were not used (Schorger 1965), but by 1750, traps had become the main hunting technique. Traps could be made on the spot by blacksmiths at trading houses or by the Indians themselves; they were often baited with beaver castoreum, an oily yellow secretion from beaver glands, or with a mixture of spices--cloves, nutmeg, cinnamon, or ginger--thought to be equally attractive to the beaver. The use of castoreum and other lures was a technique learned from Europeans, and it apparently worked well.

Beaver pelts generally were not used by Europeans for clothing. The French wanted the furs for the hairs, which had tiny scales along the shaft of each hair. These scales allowed the hairs to interlock, thus making them the perfect raw material for felt, which was then made into hats. Beaver felt hats were the most desirable headgear in Europe for centuries: warm, waterproof, and durable. At first, felt was made only of beaver hairs, but as time passed and beavers became more scarce, the hairs were mixed with other things--mainly wool--to make the felt for hats. Once the hairs were stripped off, the beaver skins were made into glue.

During the French period, the skins that came into the hands of the traders were graded and different prices paid for different qualities (Schorger 1965). The very best were "fat" winter beaver with rich undercoats and long guard hairs. Many of these started out as robes worn by Indians; the friction with human skin, often coated with bear grease, added suppleness to furs that had been scraped and rubbed by Indian women. Furs that had not been worn so long or treated so well to begin with were known as "half-fat" winter beaver and were good ones, even if not as well greased as the "fat" ones. "Summer fat" furs were not desirable because of thin undercoats and long guard hairs, but traders were forced to take them anyway. They felt that to refuse *any* beaver was a mistake and might discourage hunters or persuade them to take their skins somewhere else. Another category of pelt was "soft" beaver, well-prepared but not worn, only slightly slick and lightly greased. "Soft" skins were highly valued by traders and contrasted with the "dry" winter beaver, badly prepared and "thick." Very fine furs were sent to Russia, where they were made into clothing rather than being turned into felt.

Hunting beaver to sell the skins affected where and when Indians chose to hunt. Prices paid for winter beaver pushed them to hunt in the coldest months of the year, and traders urged them to go out then. Long winter hunts that took people away from winter villages became the rule in the eighteenth century, and they in turn affected the time and duration of hunting for food. The basic cycle of food-getting, however, was not broken into in any major way. Women were probably more pressured by the new tasks of processing large numbers of skins, but fish runs were still being met, wild rice gathered, and the corn raised in spite of the long winter hunts.

Once everyone became a professional hunter or processor of beaver, it did not take long to deplete the supply. Beavers were easy to find and with new tools, easy to kill in large numbers. As the number of beavers became smaller and smaller, hunters had to go greater distances to find them. The search for fur-bearers is one of the major factors that pulled so many Wisconsin people west and northwest, and it was a powerful reason why the French originally stretched themselves beyond Mackinac and into Wisconsin. In Perrot's and LaSalle's day, many beaver were being caught in Wisconsin, but even LaSalle began to grumble about smaller than expected catches of beaver. It did not take long to put enough stress on the beaver population to push it past the point of recovery in many places. By 1700, beaver were very scarce at Mackinac and by the end of the eighteenth century, much of eastern Wisconsin was hunted out (Thwaites 1906). Indians had to move after the beaver, leaving their home villages to trap far away, often in someone else's territory.

The animals hunted during the seventeenth and eighteenth centuries were mainly beaver, but others were taken for their furs, too (Kay 1979). The fine furs of martens and the hides of bison moved east where they became coats or robes. Through time muskrat, raccoon, deer, bear, and otter were added to the list. Efforts at conservation of beaver or any other wildlife were very few. Neither Indians nor Europeans put limits on catches or thought in terms of careful harvesting of a renewable resource. It would have been unusual to find such attitudes at a time when the land was endless and the numbers of animals so apparently limitless. Indians understood when an area was "hunted out" that it had to lie fallow until the animals returned, but for them it meant simply moving elsewhere. "Elsewhere" was always there, filled with new supplies.

Many other things were traded to the French, some of them the products of old hunting and gathering techniques and some that they developed themselves (see Chapter 5). Raw materials such as catlinite or lead moved to the traders and often went back again to Indians in another form. Some of the things given to traders were used by them and not passed into the commercial trading networks. Indians were often expected to feed traders; and supplies of meat, fish, corn, and wild rice went to the trading houses where they were consumed by traders. Often things made by Indians and traded to Europeans are not mentioned directly in the sources. For example, Hennepin and LaSalle camped in shelters covered with Indian mats, mentioned only when one once caught fire and the mats burned (Hennepin 1966). The mats must have come from Indian sources either as gifts or through trade.

As Indians became more familiar with what came through trade, their tool kits were changed in a one-to-one replacement (Quimby 1966). European tools enhanced what they had been doing: hunting and gathering and horticulture were made easier through the use of iron tools, but both hunting and gathering and horticulture continued on as before (Fitting 1976). Women's daily habits changed as they could more easily prepare clothing from cloth, chop wood with iron axes, buy twine for nets, and cook in sturdy kettles. Modern people looking back on the Indian past often regret the way old things were abandoned; but Indians voted with their purses and adopted European trade articles as fast as they could. Their own perception was that what they were getting was better than what they already had.

As long as each side in the trade got what it wanted, the fur trade was mutually beneficial. However, much depended on honest dealing on the part of traders and on their resisting the temptation to make the most of their time in the forests. French records are full of bitter complaints on the part of authorities about the traders (Thwaites 1902). Many of them were men whose behavior and moral character were not acceptable by the standards of the time, and they caused trouble by attempting to cheat Indian customers, keep them in debt, and make brandy an indispensable item in trade. Illegal traders, the "coureurs de bois," were often held up as the standard for bad behavior among the Indians, but they clearly held no monopoly on such dubious practices.

Brandy as part of the trade was a disaster for Indian society, and was recognized by the French themselves as at times making orderly life impossible. It was introduced into trade very early and moved quickly into prominence. Hennepin, as early as 1680, remarked that water was the usual drink of Indians until they had contact with the French. At that point brandy became a passion. Indians drank to become intoxicated, not merely to enjoy an afternoon or evening of fellowship mellowed by drink. The quantities consumed by them--even if it was watered down by the traders--were enormous, and the consequences of drinking to excess were very harmful. People often gave up their furs for drink, letting traders carry off the profits of a whole winter's hunt for almost nothing. People sometimes injured or killed one another during bouts of drinking; behavior that would mean vengeance and feud under ordinary circumstances was excused on the grounds that brandy was involved. Sometimes men were killed by other men hired as killers when drunk in order to avoid the vengeance of relatives.

Why Indians became so addicted to this worst part of the French experience has not been fully explained. In the early years of contact, Indians had the example of drunken fur traders or soldiers before them, men carrying their problems into the interior. But bad example by itself is not enough to explain the single-minded pursuit of liquor by Indians. Part of it might have been the way traders pushed it, a consumable, wasteful resource in the trade. Some people have thought that Indians had a special biological weakness for strong drink while others have suggested that the conditions of their lives had become so bad that alcohol was an escape. While alcoholism can be an escape from a difficult life, the early years of the fur trade were not a time of great hardship or depression for Indians in Wisconsin. They were years of discovery, self-confident assertion, and control over their own subsistence activities. The Indians were not helpless in the face of adversity.

One possible explanation for the attractiveness of brandy is involved with religion. Indian religious experience was an individual matter, shaped and formed by tradition, but rooted in a single person's contact with the supernatural. Contact took the form of a dream or vision brought about by fasting, praying, and lonely vigils in the forest: dreams and visions were at the heart of religious life and came about through pain and suffering. Using brandy was another way of having an other-worldly experience, enhanced and improved by the effects of alcohol. Men and women could enjoy a continuous revelation, almost at will as long as brandy was available. Religious experience could be shared by everyone.

The new worlds of European technology and religious experience were joined to a sober and realistic understanding that life had become bound to them. Indians themselves felt that they could no longer do without European trade, and when they had to make do with less than adequate supplies, they could suffer real hardship. Their understanding of their new dependence explains the lengths they were willing to go to get hold of a reliable trade source and to keep it. Self-interest helps to account for some of the tolerance Indians showed toward impossible traders and their interest in tapping other national sources for trade. Once they found out that the French were not the only traders in the world, they had knowledge that gave them more power in dealing with them.

Even while the French dominated Wisconsin, Indians were establishing contacts with traders from other nations. The British were probing French weaknesses and offered their cheaper goods to Indians whenever they had the chance. French officials in Quebec tried one technique after another trying to keep the trade in their hands (Thwaites 1902). The long water routes and the complicated system of Indian alliances, resident traders, and procurement systems could not be shielded from the British. Choice Wisconsin furs and a large number of Indian consumers were temptations for British traders and a challenge to their ingenuity, and they could not be kept out. They came into Wisconsin from the east, bypassing the long water routes of the north, and slipping in south of the Great Lakes (Norton 1974). Indians found the British to be less particular about the skins, and the French grades no longer figured in establishing prices. Above all, the British had almost unlimited supplies of rum. It came from the West Indies as part of the molasses-sugar trade that kept many colonial merchants in business, and it became a mainstay of the British fur trade.

In summary, the trade that came into Wisconsin in the hands of Radisson and Groseilliers quickly became an established part of life for the Indians who lived there. The most obvious changes were in the material equipment for everyday living, which overnight went from a stone-bone-clay-hide basis to an assemblage right from the factories of Europe. In accepting so many new things, Indians used them in their own ways, often flamboyant variations on what Europeans might consider proper. These basic changes in the tool kit went along with large shifts in hunting patterns as Indians became professional fur hunters rather than subsistence hunters. Hunting for food was still carried on and for the most part was compatible with gathering beaver for the trade. The shifts in location needed for beaver hunting once the supply was exhausted in any one area could still accommodate the fishing, gathering, and large game hunting that had to be done.

The changes in social life were more subtle on the surface but as deep and as marked as what happened to material culture. For one thing, economic life as part of the larger social scene made a leap from the kinship-based system of exchange to one where the values were those of the market place. The old means of trading through gift-exchange where the important outward purpose was social ties, not economic ones, began to be replaced: Indians did not shift from one to the other all at once, but as time passed, the older patterns gave way to an understanding of trade in European terms.

Political life underwent many changes. In some cases the power of chiefs was strengthened, and in others the older power structure was weakened. The French with their soldiers were a new factor that was bound to affect the relationships groups had with each other. The role the French assumed as peacemakers and their leverage as controllers of the sources of European goods made French opinions important in the decisions Indians made. French officials wanted to deal with people who were agreeable to them, and they rewarded some individuals more than others. They came to regard men of their own choosing as "chiefs," and in this way they interfered with the older routes to achieving chiefly standing. The fur trade itself was an important factor in intensifying warfare as people competed over hunting lands; with war, the power of warriors and war leaders grew, changing political life within groups as well as outside. Political life, while still under Indian control, was not the same as it had been before the coming of the fur trade.

The effect of the trade on individual lives is harder to assess. On one hand was the convenience of all those new things, but on the other was more warfare, unsettled conditions, and economic dependence. Indians at the time do not seem to have been depressed or disorganized, probably because the value of trade outweighed what Indians could see of the problems that came along with it.

British Trade Period

After the French and Indian War, British traders moved into the old French Northwest. The first ones were illegal, coming on the wings of the British victory on the Plains of Abraham in 1760, and they arrived even before military government was set up there. They were a lawless, unscrupulous, disreputable group of men; and their actions were denounced by the British government (Kellogg 1935). Their behavior was at least partly responsible for the shape the British trade took in Wisconsin.

When the military arrived, steps were taken to tie the trade to military posts in order to control and regulate it. Each trader was assigned to a specific military post and subject to its commanding officer (Thwaites 1902). The traders were under military discipline, strong action in those days and something that might be expected to keep them in line. The most important military post as far as the trade was concerned was at Ft. Michilimackinac, and most of the old centers in Wisconsin were, at least in theory, no longer in business. Green Bay was supposed to be the center of the Wisconsin trade, but owing to disputes over local rights to trade there, no military post was established. In the first years of British rule in Wisconsin, legal trade could not be carried on there at all.

Tight control over traders meant that Indians had to go to the nearest legal post to cash in their furs. For Wisconsin people, this meant making a journey from the Mississippi Valley or the northern lakes country all the way to Ft. Michilimackinac. Bringing people to the trading posts from a huge hinterland was very different from the older French pattern of trading houses throughout the interior, and Indians were not eager to change their habits. It was a hardship and an inconvenience; and British officials and agents had to persuade and pressure Indians to come.

Even at the beginning, Indians did not care much for the British or their methods of trade. For one thing, the British were insensitive to the social side of the trade; they were not as interested in using personal and family ties in trading. Their whole approach was to distance themselves from what had been the older patterns. They did not at first think much of giving gifts to their clients, a change that appeared to be unfriendly or even hostile to the Indians. In general, Indians found the British to be stingy and close-fisted, unwilling to show the generosity that people of importance exhibited in the Indian social world. Even the use of credit was cut off, a policy that would not let Indian families get the supplies they needed to produce a steady and dependable source of furs.

The closest personal account of Indian life during the early British period is Alexander Henry's description of Wawatam's yearly round. By this time, Indian life revolved around trade. Wawatam's activities as reported by Henry are not aimed at feeding his family and living off what nature provided but at producing commodities that could be carried to Ft. Michilimackinac and sold. The labor of production took place in the woods and the workers were Wawatam's family, but the frame of reference had become a commercial one. Henry takes for granted the whole operation and does not even comment on the fact that the older pattern of production for use is gone. Wawatam scheduled his life around the yearly trip to the Straits, where he dealt with the British traders. Since his home grounds were in Michigan, he was closer than Indians in Wisconsin; moving his produce to market was, however, a long and difficult process (see Chapter 4).

The British tried to persuade other Indians to make the long journey to Michilimackinac. In 1766, Jonathan Carver made an expedition up the Mississippi River in order to set up good relations between Indian and British traders back at the Straits (Parker 1976). Carver's journal offers insights into how the different national groups were competing over the Indian trade. When he reached the Santee north of Lake Pepin, he repeatedly warned them of the wickedness of the French and tried to use liquor to smooth his way. At Prairie du Chien, he matched the French in gift-giving and tried to make allies for his government. Carver's journal is a window into British anxieties as they took over the fur trade in their new territories and their uncertainty as to what policies to follow. He points out that everyone understood that Indians held the key to any profits coming from the trade: as long as the British, Spanish, and French were competing for their furs, Indians were in a strategic position and their decisions were important.

What finally forced changes in British policy was that Indians actively sought other, closer markets. By the middle of the eighteenth century, the west bank of the Mississippi River was in Spanish hands, and St. Louis had become a major Spanish outpost. Spanish traders took over the fur trade along the Mississippi; and by 1767, they were as far north as Prairie du Chien (Gilman 1974). The Mississippi River was also an open highway to French settlements in Louisiana, and French traders continued to come north into Wisconsin. French and Spanish traders began to take a lion's share of beaver pelts from the rich lands west of the Mississippi and from dissatisfied Indians in Wisconsin (Thwaites 1906).

Eventually the British had to relax their rules and throw the trade open, letting independent traders go into Indian territory. In 1767, a fleet of sixty trade canoes left Mackinac bound for Green Bay and points beyond. French and Spanish trade was almost lost in the ensuing flood of British traders and goods, and the threat from these other nations lessened. The Spanish continued to send boats up the Mississippi to confiscate furs they thought might have come from land under Spanish influence (Draper 1888), and they continued to give generous gifts to Indians who would come to St. Louis to receive them. In 1769, for example, many Wisconsin Indians were among those listed as being in St. Louis to receive gifts of trade goods and food from Spanish sources (Thwaites 1906). The pressure on their customers from the Spanish and the French angered the British and was one reason why traders from these European nations fought with each other and, using their Indian allies, increased the level of warfare in the region.

The pattern of trade in Wisconsin turned again to small trading houses set up in the interior, sometimes in the same places occupied by the French houses in earlier times. Traders often had staffs of "clerks," who went out from the main trading houses to winter in especially strategic positions (Gates 1965). These agents rendezvoused in the spring at Prairie du Chien or Green Bay, where they counted their take, celebrated their success, and made ready for the long trip back to Ft. Michilimackinac. Colorful and exciting, the trade fairs drew Indians from all over to camp for days or weeks and meet with each other as well as with traders.

As in earlier times, the fur trade was an important part of official government action in Wisconsin. British fur traders were used as a means for the government to communicate with Indians and let them know what government policies had been decided. Traders were also expected to establish and support alliances with Indians on behalf of their government, and sometimes they served in extremely sensitive diplomatic positions. For example, the fur trader Peter Pond, operating out of a base on the Minnesota River, was a major mediator between the Santee Dakota and the Chippewa; and he tried to bring about peace between them (Hickerson 1970). The peace arranged by Pond at the cost of "six large belts of wampum" (Gates 1933: 48) was only a temporary break in the long Santee-Chippewa war, but the fact that it was negotiated by a trader indicates the reliance placed on some of the traders by the British.

Towards the end of the eighteenth century, the British government was trying to decide what its long range policies in the Northwest should be. For a long time, a debate centered on whether or not to forcibly evict all people of French nationality, leaving only the British to deal with Indians in Wisconsin. In the end, the French were allowed to stay, partly because an evacuation was not feasible and partly because French manpower was needed to help in the trade: many "British" traders were actually French throughout the British period. Another problem faced by British policymakers was deciding what kind of civil government should be extended into Wisconsin. The fur trade had become "civil" in the sense that there were civilian boards of trade that licensed traders and a civilian commissary who was the representative of a civilian superintendent for Indian affairs (Kellogg 1935). But what kind of government should be set up was not decided. British policy appeared headed for a decision that Indians and traders were the people who should live in Wisconsin, not European settlers in villages or towns. This "Indians only" vision never reached any official stage because the American Revolutionary War began, and new directions had to be taken.

The fur trade itself seems hardly to have been affected by the war. It intensified west of Lake Superior, and large numbers of furs were funnelled through Wisconsin over the Fox-Wisconsin waterway. Control over this route stayed in British hands, and they continued to control the trade. The traders themselves joined in the war, raising warriors and fighting when they were needed. Fox and Sauk Indians, for example, were recruited to fight in campaigns as far east as New York (Thwaites 1888). Other Indians tried to stay neutral in the conflict between the British and their American "children" and could not be relied on to support one side or the other. The Santee remained loyal to the British as long as their furs had to move over British-controlled water routes and were directly involved in the war. One of the larger military actions of the war in Wisconsin was a British-Santee raid down the Mississippi against St. Louis in 1780 (Thwaites 1906). This inconclusive campaign included some British and French military men, but it was mainly composed of Indians and traders with leadership roles in the hands of the fur traders, not military officers.

Trade during the American Revolution continued to be dominated by the British, but many Indians used the presence of Spanish and French alternatives to put pressure on them. The British could never be sure that Indians were not taking their furs elsewhere, and their need for Indian allies in warfare or at least having Indians stay neutral gave the diplomatic advantage to Indians. Balancing their own needs against British concerns let Indians continue the strategy they had found so useful in their years of dealing with Europeans.

American Trade Period

Peace after the Revolutionary War should have ended British trade in Wisconsin, but the British remained. The British fur trade as a business depended on the Northwest Territory; and partly in response to pressure brought by commercial interests, Americans and British worked out a compromise known as the Jay Treaty (A. Smith 1973). By means of this treaty, British traders were allowed to continue to trade, holding on to trade routes and trade sources they had inherited from the French.

The major source for furs became lands west of the Mississippi, and the whole scope of the trade changed as it became a more modern business. Its form underwent a significant change as commercial trading companies came to dominate the trade. These organizations--the North West Company, the Mackinac Company, the XY Company-- operated sometimes in competition, then in combination for the trade of the Northwest (Oerichbauer 1982). Smaller independent traders continued to carry on in the old way, getting their supplies from Mackinac once a year and then returning to Indian territory, but their share of the business dwindled.

During 1802 and 1803, employees of the North West Company and the XY Company built adjacent wintering posts on the Yellow River in Burnett County (Oerichbauer 1982). Archaeological excavation of the sites where these posts once stood has produced a vivid picture of how the traders lived and what kind of structures they built in Wisconsin. Like Ft. Beauharnois, the North West Company's outpost was fortified. It had a stockaded enclosure, 40 by 45 feet, protected by defensive bastions on two opposite corners; and it must have looked like a small fort, stoutly defended. Inside the enclosure were three buildings, two of which were rectangular "cabins," with planks for floors and stone or clay fireplaces. Window glass, fragments of china and glass bottles, and a stoneware snuff or tobacco jar indicate at least some refinement in life for the traders. They were now shopkeepers rather than individual adventurers in the wilderness. The nearby XY post was similar to the cabins in the North West Company stockade, but it was undefended. Thanks to threats of attack by the Santee, the XY traders moved themselves into the North West Company enclosure and sheltered there with their competitors. The commercialization of the trade was complete: the North West Company built no chapels and had no quarters for soldiers; its wintering post was no longer an outpost of empire, at least not in a political sense.

Until the War of 1812, Indians continued their policy of playing one government off against another. By the end of that war, however, the British moved out of Wisconsin for good; and Indians were left with only one non-Indian group to deal with. It would become harder and harder for them to have an important impact on government policy through the kind of diplomacy they had practiced earlier.

One of the best descriptions of the fur trade from the point of view of the Indians during the American Period is the narrative of John Tanner (1830). In his time, the fur trade in the Northwest was not yet a monopoly of the great fur companies, and it was very competitive. Tanner and his Indian family moved into country beyond Lake Superior, where they had no rights to hunt but neither did any of the many other eastern Indians who were also there. The trade was open in the sense that people moved at will to where they expected beaver and at first found few other Indians to object to their coming. Hunting furs for the market was what drew people into an area where there was not enough game to support even a thin and scattered population. The fur hunters and their families underwent great hardship, frequently suffering from near starvation. As the Indians went farther west, they reached lands where other Indians blocked their way and resented their coming. Quarrels over rights to game were common, and because no authority of chiefs or elders was recognized, violence was often the means of settling disputes.

Tanner learned to be an excellent hunter and trapper; and as he became expert, his position in his Ottawa-Ojibwa family improved. His first beaver hunt was with a mixed Ottawa-Ojibwa-Cree group that moved up the Red River where beaver were then plentiful. It took this group three months to clean out all game so that no one could live there any more by hunting alone. As time passed, Tanner noted that he was able to kill 100 beaver per month (1830: 40), and his catch improved until he managed 42 beaver in ten days. His take of other animals--muskrat, bear, bison--was also impressive; and, of course, he hunted moose, caribou, deer, rabbits, and any other game he could find to feed his family. At first this involved only his adoptive mother and her relations, but later he had a wife, many children, and relatives on both sides. Tanner followed the usual Indian practice of sharing food with others in need when he had it, and his most bitter comments were for those who disregarded this life-preserving custom.

What became of the furs brought out by Tanner and others is typical of the fiercely competitive nature of the trade at that time. Again and again, the furs gathered with so much industry and effort went almost immediately into rum, often diluted, but still the source of drunkenness and drink-induced violence. Even Tanner's mother, a careful and canny woman, was caught up in the desire for rum and traded all her furs for kegs of it. The rum trade was less attractive for Tanner than for most Indians, but he was subjected to other pressures. The local North West Company trader tried to steal his furs, and Tanner was forced into a prolonged struggle to hang on to what he had hunted. Even Indians stole from each other. The competitive conditions of the fur trade caused changes in behavior: "Indians who live remote from whites have not learned to value their peltries so highly that they will be guilty of stealing them from each other" (Tanner 1830: 46). There were few checks or regulations to protect the rights of Indian suppliers.

The fur trade in Wisconsin was not all one thing. It changed through time as it moved from the hands of the French to the British and finally to Americans. As a business it evolved from a marginal adjunct to French foreign policy to a vastly expanded, highly competitive industry. Throughout, Indians were the main suppliers of furs, and their lives changed as the fur market fluctuated and its goals shifted. Its impact on Indian society was far-reaching and profound, both the source of often exuberant changes in everyday life and the root of warfare, re-settlement, and personal crisis.

CHAPTER 9
Land Dispossessions in the Nineteenth Century

The years of the fur trade were years of great social change, but Indian culture survived them and in some ways flourished (Kay 1984). Indian societies were able to survive because people continued to live by hunting, fishing, gathering, and gardening; they were still able to depend on their own efforts to obtain food. The fur trade notwithstanding, Indians also managed a politically independent life, a life where their own goals influenced everyday decisions, and they were not under someone else's direct control. Through the years, they had become skilled at playing off one European group against another and used their expertise to their own advantage. As long as they had free access to land and could move within that land for basic subsistence, they were able to live as Indians even though familiar patterns of life were changing.

The first half of the nineteenth century, however, was different. Non-Indian settlement of Wisconsin intensified; and the old British-French-American rivalry was finally gone. New definitions and conceptions of the land and its resources replaced those of the Indian inhabitants and the old European powers. American settlers coming to Wisconsin had strikingly different goals from the French and British who had preceded them, and their perceptions of what they were doing were equally different. Americans came to settle the land, farm it, mine it, reduce its forests to lumber, and extend their own visions of order and plenty into what they thought was a trackless--or nearly trackless--wilderness. Their ideas about land use and the power they possessed to enforce those ideas meant that other, competing opinions were bound to be regarded as inefficient or out-of-date or both. Americans did not come to Wisconsin to trade with Indians for the products of the land; what they wanted was the land itself.

American settlement was different from French or British occupations in many ways. For one thing, the number of settlers increased dramatically. For generations, Wisconsin Indians had become familiar with small, more or less permanent groups of French settlers at places such as Prairie du Chien, Chequamegon, or Green Bay. These little French settlements with their claims laid out fronting the river or lake in long strips were smaller than many Indian villages. The people who lived in them, often traders with Indian wives, were not numerous. British settlers came in larger groups and built more impressive centers, but they, too, were not representative of the size or make-up of the European populations then settling the American continent along the East Coast. In contrast to the relatively few British or French settlers, the Americans came in great numbers and brought along their families, following a westward movement that never seemed satisfied with the land it had already consumed. By 1830, three thousand Americans unconnected with the military were in Wisconsin, but only six years later, the population had quadrupled (A. Smith 1973) with no end in sight. At this point, Indians began to be outnumbered by American settlers, most of whom were in the southern, Carolinian Zone and in the eastern part of the Transition Zone.

The settlers' use of land was different, too. Their principal activity was, of course, farming; and their choice of land was bound to come into conflict with the preferences Indians had for the same land. Sharing the land, with settlers and Indians living in adjacent communities, would never work. Settlers and Indians had radically different approaches to the land and its use. Indian farming was gardening, small scale crop raising by American standards, and it was always accompanied by hunting and gathering. American farming was full plow agriculture, not likely to tolerate large tracts of perfectly usable land left untouched because of the needs for game cover or berry picking.

The Americans knew that the Indians had to go, and any disagreements were over how it was to be managed, not whether or not it was to take place. Since the United States was now a responsible sovereign power, Indian lands could not be simply snatched away and Indian claims extinguished without some legal grounds. The first step in eventual dispossession was deciding who had claims to what lands. The extent of land claims was in the public record as part of the Prairie du Chien Treaty of 1825 (Kappler 1973). The main aim of the treaty was to settle the Santee-Chippewa wars and for that matter all the disputes between the Santee and anyone else in the region. As part of the final treaty, though, boundaries were drawn for all the tribes that attended and for some, such as the

Menomini, who were not sure at the time where their boundaries might be.

The lands claimed by Indians in the Treaty of 1825 were not the lands they occupied at the beginning of the Historic Period (see Chapter 3). They were the result of well over a century of jockeying for possession and pushing-coming-to-shove on the part of both original peoples and all the seventeenth and eighteenth century refugees. Land claims on the part of any particular tribe were essentially what that group thought it could get away with at the time. The actual boundaries drawn by the 1825 Treaty were never really regarded by Wisconsin Indians as meaning much when it came to hunting or living space, but the boundary lines gave Americans an idea of where to begin when the need arose for obtaining title to Indian lands.

The years following the Treaty of Prairie du Chien were a time of great dislocation and trouble for Wisconsin Indians as Americans moved in and occupied the land. The American government, responding to public feelings of the time, was in favor of an Indian Territory somewhere beyond the Mississippi River. This Indian land would be available only to Indians and not open to use by others. American settlers generally agreed that Indians should be removed beyond the Mississippi into Indian Territory and the lands east of the river freed for settlement, and the pressures put upon Indians were enormous. By 1834, much of southeastern Wisconsin had been ceded to the government, and it was put up for sale as "public land." Treaty after treaty followed, as Indians gave up legal title to the land; by the middle of the nineteenth century, Indians no longer had any claim to land in Wisconsin (A. Smith 1973). American lead mines, sawmills, farms, and communities were replacing the Indian world.

The reactions of Indians during this time were a combination of alarm, fear, anger, and frustration. The best of the farming lands were now legally gone from Indian control, and the horticultural way of life itself was threatened as a result. Another resource, the lead found in quantity in southwestern Wisconsin, was opened to American mining; and a valuable source of income was taken away. Indians knew the value of the lead-mining area; they had been mining and smelting lead for a long time (see Chapter 5). By 1811, many Indians around Prairie du Chien had given up hunting for the fur trade in favor of becoming lead miners; they were recorded as having produced 400,000 pounds of lead in one season, testifying as to how seriously they were pursuing this occupation (Oerichbauer 1976). In the deliberations at Prairie du Chien before signing the Treaty, many of them went out of their way to specify rights to lands where the lead mines were located. Now lead mining leases were in the hands of others, and Indians were forced out, often under circumstances beyond the bounds of legal or ethical behavior on the part of lead miners.

American control over Wisconsin was aided by the presence of several forts, from which the army could move to protect settlers or miners in need. Ft. Howard at Green Bay, Ft. Winnebago at the Fox-Wisconsin portage, and Ft. Crawford at Prairie du Chien formed a line across the state of great strategic importance. The forts were not always supplied or manned up to the perceived needs of the military on the frontier, but they were impressive features, physical reminders of the power of the new government.

American settlement was accompanied by road construction, making transportation quicker and physical control of the territory easier for the government. The rivers that had been the main means by which people moved across the state were replaced by roads cut through the forests or laid over the prairies. Horses became a common means of transportation, and Indians as well as Americans now regularly used horses rather than canoes or dugouts. The switch-over was so marked that by the first decades of the nineteenth century, Wisconsin Indians are mentioned more and more in written accounts as troops of horsemen and much less as canoe travelers (see, for example, the Winnebago at Ft. Winnebago in Kinzie 1976). The Old Military Road connecting the forts at Prairie du Chien and Portage with Ft. Howard in Green Bay was built between 1832 and 1837 (Durbin and Durbin 1984). This road was almost a complete replacement for the historic Fox-Wisconsin waterway, crossing the state from Green Bay to the Mississippi.

What Indians received for lands in Wisconsin was payment in cash or in goods, spread over a number of years. The Winnebago in eastern Wisconsin, for example, received $15,000 annually, "a considerable amount of presents," and bread and pork to be given out at various times during the year (Kinzie 1975). The Potawatomi, in a treaty negotiated in Michigan, received funds for land clearing and fencing, hiring farm laborers, buying animals and farm tools, and providing Indians with tobacco, iron, and steel (Clifton 1977). The payments were distributed at special places where Indians had to come to receive them. At payment time, Prairie du Chien attracted thousands of Indians in gatherings that rivaled the great trade fairs of earlier times (Oerichbauer 1976). Like the trade gatherings, the time for annuity payments came to be periods of excess, often involving drunkenness and disorder; and Indians dispersed or consumed much of what they had received in a very short time. They were often helped along by unscrupulous people who managed a share of the annuity payments or other property in spite of not being legally entitled to any of it.

What is clear is that money or goods given out in such a prodigal way over a number of years could not meet the new and disastrous problem of the melting away of lands needed for raising crops or hunting. What Indians were to do when the annuity payments stopped and the land was in the hands of others was a serious question for thoughtful Indians and Americans alike. Indians may not have entirely grasped what ceding land meant, and Black Hawk's plain statement that "my reason tells me that *land cannot be sold*" (D. Jackson 1964: 101) sums up what many Indians felt. Indians no longer had legal title to land in Wisconsin, but they could not manage to live without a place to plant their crops and hunt game. The Indian Territory beyond the Mississippi was no solution; the land there was different, the climate was not the same, the resources were not what they had been used to, and the land was filled with alien people. Indians could not be expected to follow their old ways of life in what was a brand new environment, among other Indians who regarded them as invaders.

The responses of Wisconsin Indians to events during the first half of the nineteenth century were varied. At first, the fact that they had become intruders on the land was not immediately clear to them. Removal did not begin with the signing of treaties, and often it was years before Indians appreciated that they were expected to vanish as the land was sold to others. Settlers moving in and clearing farms often regarded Indians as nuisances, especially when the land Indians used for villages and cropland was ideal for modern agriculture. Villages were sometimes sold from under the Indians, and they were told to "go away" (D. Jackson 1964), preferably where they would not interfere with the cultivation and taming of the land by the new farmers. Indians often attempted to retain a hold on some parts of their land by cultivating gardens in unused corners or by continuing to hunt over old lands. These practices led to problems with settlers whose fences, cleared land, and cultivated fields interfered with the movements and activities of the Indians. Indians who became "surrounded and hemmed in by the white settlers" (Kinzie 1975: 361) found themselves at odds with their new neighbors and not able to fit into the new landscape.

Indians were not tied to old ways or so bound to "tradition" that they would not try new techniques and adapt to new conditions if they could: their whole history was one of adjusting to new things. They had amply demonstrated their flexibility in trying new subsistence techniques during the Historic Period itself: the Menomini, the "Wild Rice" people, became farmers, growing corn and other crops as they came to live along the banks of the Lower Fox River; the Santee, moving south from the headwaters of the Mississippi grew corn, beans, and squash as they entered warmer areas; Indians supplied food on a large scale to others as they became surplus-producing farmers; people took up commercial maple sugar production wherever they could. There is a long list of what people attempted, given resources and markets in which to sell what they had produced. The problems of dislocation in the early nineteenth century, however, were too great even for the flexible, adaptable Indian societies to handle. These problems were often severe enough to cause local disasters as the food supply became uncertain. Increased warfare between tribes meant that some people could not safely plant gardens and thus had no corn at all (Kinzie 1976); famine at the end of winter meant starvation on a large scale as whole communities were reduced to eating the bark of trees, and many died as a result.

American farmers, all of them immigrants, cannot be expected to have understood the tragedy of Indian displacement. They were displaced themselves, struggling for a new life; and Indian affairs seldom seemed anything more than one more problem to be surmounted. John Muir's father, living on a farm grubbed out of central Wisconsin after years of back-breaking labor, thought uncomfortably about Indian land losses, but he was able to reason them away. He spoke for many when he said that "surely it could have never been the intention of God to allow Indians to rove and hunt over so fertile a country . . . while . . . farmers could put it to so much better use" (Muir 1965: 174). Indians coming through his land were seen as probable thieves, as ready to kill domestic animals as wild ones, and suspected of mischief whenever they appeared. And as their land base diminished and their access to hunting lands was curtailed, Indians turned to raiding homesteads, killing stock, and stealing as their other options vanished.

Given the loss of land, it is not difficult to understand why the first part of the nineteenth century involved an increase in armed conflict between Indians and Americans. Indian uprisings and fear of uprisings were uppermost in settlers' minds; raids occurred regularly. Each of the Indian wars had the effect of lessening Indian political leverage and putting them in a worse position, no matter what initial military successes might have come their way. The Red Bird affair of 1827 is a case in point. Now celebrated in story, poetry, and even statuary, Red Bird was a Winnebago caught up in the violence as the lead mines were being taken over by American miners: lead and competition for access to the lead mining regions were the root causes of the trouble. After a series of outrages against individual Indians, Red Bird and his companions were chosen to begin vengeance raiding against their enemies, the usual Indian method of responding to aggression from others. They set upon the proverbial innocent bystander, a French settler and his family, people who had nothing to do with the lead mines or the violence directed at the Winnebago. Red Bird reasoned that an attack on one settler, no matter which one, was an attack on the whole enemy population and the proper way of addressing the problem of Indian grievances in the lead mining districts. In the conflict that followed, the Winnebago had to give up Red Bird to American justice in the face of a large American army able to back up its demands with force. In this interchange, Winnebago political authority was diminished, and Winnebago maneuvering room in the political arena received a significant check. Indeed, the Red Bird affair led directly to a major loss of other land in addition to losing the lead mining rights the Winnebago thought they had (Lurie 1978).

The Black Hawk War in 1832 is another of the conflicts whose origins are owed to the not-so-simple problem of what the Indians were to do when they were deprived of land (D. Jackson 1964). The Sauk leader Black Hawk, in a complex series of movements designed to regain land he thought was illegally taken from his band, attempted to return to the Rock River area in Illinois from exile in Iowa. In the following hue and cry, the militia, the regular army, and a steamboat all combined to crush this Indian "uprising," and in the process to inflict heavy casualties on the luckless men, women, and children of Black Hawk's band as they fled back toward Iowa (Callender 1978a). The epic pursuit of Black Hawk and his people took place across southern Wisconsin, ending in the Battle of Bad Axe near the Mississippi River. While it lasted, the Black Hawk War caused near hysteria among many American settlers of Wisconsin (see Kinzie 1975), and after it was over, it became a lever for prying even more land cessions from the Sauk.

Other reactions to the chaos of the early nineteenth century on the part of Indians included attempts at accommodation, following a policy of peaceful resistance and peaceful resolution of problems. Most of the steps in this kind of action involved postponing the inevitable land losses and trying to get as much as possible from treaties. Black Hawk himself thought that this posture was wrong (D. Jackson 1964) and bound to fail. The presence of people who wanted accommodation as well as those who recommended more aggressive responses caused deep divisions in Indian communities. Factions on either side were to experience the same ultimate defeat in the presence of armies beyond their strength or negotiators beyond their skills; but because people were not united in facing the assault on Indian lands, their problems were made all the worse.

The crises of the period of land dispossession were a fertile ground for the spread of religious movements that tried to support individuals during the series of catastrophes that were overtaking Indians on all sides. Black Hawk, for example, considered himself supernaturally inspired and felt that he was carrying on in the footsteps of Tecumseh. The Drum or Dream Dance and the Peyote Religion, both of which took shape in the latter part of the nineteenth century, were rooted in the troubles of the period of land dispossession. People who had moved from an independent life to become hangers-on in someone else's success story were ready for religious teachings that offered them help. Even the older Midewiwin or Medicine Society became a means of self-identification and a promise of renewal for Indians whose problems continued to mount. Religion also offered a means for some individuals to achieve higher status and even wealth when other routes to the same ends were curtailed or closed.

Events of the Nineteenth Century:
Specific Groups

The dismal course of land dispossession was the same for all Wisconsin Indians in that they lost title to what they thought they had in the way of living space. For each group, though, the way in which it occurred was different as their various histories were themselves different.

Winnebago

At Prairie du Chien in 1825, the Winnebago claimed a territory that included most of southern Wisconsin. In the formal description in the Treaty of 1825, Winnebago land lay within an area bounded on the southeast by the Rock River, on the west by the Mississippi, and on the north by the line of the Fox-Wisconsin waterway, up to and including all of Lake Winnebago and parts of the Lower Fox as high as what is now Kaukauna (Kappler 1973). This vast territory included much of Wisconsin's most desirable farmland, the lead mines, and the main water routes through the region. If extensive American settlement were to take place, competing Indian land claims had to be done away with.

American settlement did not wait for the niceties of diplomacy, and the land claimed by the Winnebago soon contained enough American settlers, miners, and others to bring pressure for the land to become a part of the United States and opened for public sale. In 1829 and again in 1832, major land cessions were made (Lurie 1978), and the Winnebago, as part of the payment, were offered a reserve west of the Mississippi, unluckily in a place claimed by other Indians. Further land cessions followed. In 1837, a treaty was extorted from a group of Winnebago leaders, who were brought to Washington and kept there until they--under protest--signed a document whose provisions had not been correctly translated for them. Under this treaty, all the Winnebago were expected to leave Wisconsin by the spring of the following year. Thanks to this treaty, the Winnebago were to lose all remaining rights to land in Wisconsin.

The provisions of the 1837 treaty led to a split between those who thought it best to obey the orders to move and those who wanted to defy the government. The former group accepted a reservation in Minnesota and lived there for many years, following American farming patterns and looking more and more like any other rural people in Minnesota. However, simply because they were Indians, they were unceremoniously evicted from their reserve during the Santee uprising of 1862 (Lurie 1978). After great hardship and the loss of all they had gained in Minnesota, these treaty-abiding Winnebago were settled on part of the Omaha reservation in Nebraska. Conditions on this reservation were very bad; and toward the end of the nineteenth century, the Nebraska Winnebago faced greater problems and more difficult times than anyone might have imagined, considering what their lives were like only a hundred years before. The Winnebago who refused to leave Wisconsin were fugitives for a long time. They lived wherever they could, planting small fields and hunting; and when they were caught by the authorities and shipped to Nebraska, they would return to take up as inconspicuous a life as possible on the edges of the rural American world. Eventually, they were allowed to stay and take up farmsteads in the land where their ancestors had once been the principal Indian people (Lurie 1971).

Memomini

At the beginning of the nineteenth century, Menomini claims in Wisconsin stretched from Green Bay and Lake Michigan on the east to at least the Black River in the west and the Milwaukee River in the south (Kappler 1973). By 1821, thanks to land dealings back in New York (Hoffman 1896), the Menomini were pressured to share their lands with Oneida, Stockbridge Indians, and others, who could then be evicted from New York. In a treaty accepted by the Menomini in 1821, they turned over their legal claims to land in Wisconsin to the New York Indians through a scheme of "sharing" title; the smaller group of Menominis would be out-maneuvered in deliberations by the more numerous and experienced New York Indians who were to share their land. On thinking things over, the Menomini rejected this treaty on the grounds that many of their most important men had not been present to consider it. What had or had not been given to the New York Indians was confused enough that by the time of the Treaty of Prairie du Chien in 1825 the Menominis were referred to as "not being sufficiently acquainted with their proper boundaries" to allow firm lines to be drawn (Kappler 1973: 252).

In 1827, the Treaty of Butte des Morts attempted again to sort out what the Menominis wished to cede to the New York Indians. It seems clear that the Menomini were very apprehensive about sharing rights in the land with the Oneida. In some of the discussions of the time, leading Menominis expressed the feeling that the New York Indians were to be only tenants, not in any way owners of the land (Hoffman 1896). Treaty after treaty was drawn up in this matter of the cessions of land to the New York Indians, and finally the Menomini agreed to set apart land as homes for the various Indians of New York.

The matter of land for the New York Indians was no sooner settled than the newly formed state of Wisconsin began to pressure the Menomini to sell their remaining lands in Wisconsin. By the end of 1849, the Menomini had been persuaded to give up the land in Wisconsin for a sum of money and a large grant west of the Mississippi River on land that had been taken from the Chippewa through a separate treaty. Their unwillingness to move to this refuge farther west was the reason that they were eventually given a permanent reservation "lying upon the Wolf River in the state of Wisconsin" (Hoffman 1896: 31). The wonder is not so much that the Menomini lost their land in Wisconsin but that they managed to hold on to even a part of it. Perhaps at the time the Menomini Reservation was officially set up, the land was considered of little value and the lumbering interests had enough to keep them busy without coveting such a relatively small place.

Santee Dakota

The Santee were the main reason behind the gathering at Prairie du Chien for the Treaty of 1825. That conference, through the deliberations of leaders from all the interested tribes, was supposed to put firm boundaries between the Santee and the Chippewa, ending the conflict between them. The wars between the Santee and the Chippewa were based on competition for resources in the Transition Zone (Hickerson 1962) and were not likely to be settled by a committee, even one with sincere hopes for peace (see Chapter 3).

The lines that were drawn in 1825 were just a pause in the Chippewa-Santee wars, but they are important for understanding the shifting claims and counter-claims of both groups since the seventeenth century. The Santee had been moving southward and westward, and by the time of the Treaty of Prairie du Chien, they were sometimes as far south as what is now the Iowa border country. Their main settlements remained on the Minnesota River. In the treaty, they still had claim to lands in Wisconsin. These lands included a section east of the Mississippi River from a point opposite the Iowa River and then north to the Black River and to the falls on the Chippewa (Kappler 1973). Their borders faced off against Chippewa lands and put both groups eyeball-to-eyeball in the deer-rich Transition Zone. It was not an arrangement that could last.

In addition to troubles with the Chippewa and others, the Santee themselves were facing increased pressure on their lands in Minnesota Territory. Settlers hoped to move into the area, and official government policies reflected these hopes, aiming to remove the Santee from the rich agricultural lands of southern Minnesota as soon as it could be arranged. In 1837 a Santee delegation in Washington was pressured into signing a treaty that gave up all Santee lands east of the Mississippi River (Meyer 1980). In 1851, another treaty was signed that sold remaining Santee lands and reduced their holdings to a narrow strip along the Upper Minnesota River (Carley 1976).

Ottawa

The Ottawa came into Wisconsin with the Huron and Petun in the sixteenth century, and from then on, some of them used hunting lands and lived in mixed villages within its borders. By the early part of the nineteenth century, as many as 500 Ottawa Indians were included in a census as residents, mainly around the mouth of the Milwaukee River where they lived in villages with Potawatomis and Chippewas (Feest and Feest 1978). In the Treaty of Prairie du Chien, southeastern Wisconsin between the Rock River and Lake Michigan, along with a large piece of northern Illinois, was described as held in common by Chippewas, Potawatomis, and Ottawas (Kappler 1973). After 1825, a series of treaties, ending with the Treaty of Chicago in 1833, ceded all these lands in exchange for a reservation on the Missouri River in what is now Kansas. After the Treaty of Chicago, Ottawas were no longer residents of Wisconsin.

Potawatomi

In 1825, the Potawatomi were written into the Treaty of Prairie du Chien as having a legal claim, along with the Ottawa and the Chippewa, to the southeast corner of Wisconsin. This huge tract was only a part of the land they had used and occupied in Wisconsin in the nineteenth century (Clifton 1977) and considerably less than they thought they had a right to. Potawatomi villages could be found well north of the Milwaukee River along the shore of Lake Michigan, and Potawatomi land claims overlapped with those of the Menomini. The Treaty of Prairie du Chien ignored the northern villages, leading to a feeling on the part of the Potawatomi that lands legitimately their own had become part of Menomini territory. The claim of the Menomini to the eastern part of Wisconsin along the lake shore was written into another treaty (in 1831), giving the Potawatomi reason to be suspicious when treaty-making time approached again.

The Treaty of Chicago in 1833 was the document that sold the remaining Potawatomi lands in Wisconsin to the United States. It was an agreement made in the midst of confusion as Indians, officials, settlers, and others gathered in great numbers. Thousands of Indians had come to Chicago to attend the treaty-making session, and many settlers, anticipating the opening of the rich farmland of Illinois and Wisconsin, had joined them. In an almost carnival atmosphere, the Indians and commissioners produced a treaty reached through hard bargaining and long, tiresome disputes over details. The details were the hard part; the major thrust of the treaty was simply to gain title to Potawatomi land and to get them out of the way as fast as possible.

In exchange for the land, the Treaty of Chicago gave the Wisconsin Potawatomi a stretch of territory west of the Mississippi river, five million acres, plus a large number of other compensations--goods, money, payment of debts. The land west of the Mississippi originally promised in the treaty was already spoken for and those five million acres never became a Potawatomi homeland in Indian Territory. Other lands were substituted, and problems with the new lands in the west were substantial. The problems were so great that many Potawatomi did not obey the provisions of the treaty to move themselves beyond the Mississippi for good. They went instead to Canada, Michigan, or back to Wisconsin. Many of them were rounded up and shipped to Kansas, often by commercial firms specializing in Indian removal (Trennert 1979).

The Potawatomi who stayed in Wisconsin lived among other Indians or on their own, not as villages but as scattered families. They moved north as the southern and eastern parts of the state became more settled, and they came to be identified with the northern forests. One of the names given to them in the nineteenth century, "Strolling

Potawatomi," provides a vivid word picture of the unsettled condition of this way of life. The population was increased substantially when other Potawatomis came back into Wisconsin after about fifty years in the west and settled near Wisconsin Rapids. By the twentieth century, small reservations at Stone Lake and Wabeno were created for the Forest Potawatomi from homestead land grants (Clifton 1977). These Potawatomi and the Skunk Hill Band from Wisconsin Rapids are the major groups of Potawatomi still in Wisconsin.

Sauk and Fox

By the nineteenth century, the Sauk and Fox were treated as a single group, a "united tribe," and their lands described as held in common by both. The territory they had in Wisconsin included a tract running south from the Wisconsin River, southeast into Illinois. In the Treaty of 1804, their rights to this land were transferred to the United States, along with other, more extensive lands in Illinois. Afterwards they insisted that they had not fully understood what the treaty meant and had never intended to sell their land. Apparently they thought the Treaty of 1804 confirmed their title to the land through formal recognition by the government of the United States (Wallace 1982).

One clause in the treaty allowed the Sauk and Fox to continue to use the ceded land until it was sold by the government, and it was not immediately opened up to settlers. The Sauk and Fox continued to live there, but as part of a growing population of Indians along the Mississippi on both sides, they increasingly found themselves competing with others for hunting lands. They came to blows with the Santee, who were moving south. The Treaty of Prairie du Chien in 1825 referred to the Sauk and Fox as directly involved in the endless wars with the Santee; and one of the main provisions of the treaty was to settle matters between the Santee and the Sauk and Fox as well as between the Santee and the Chippewa. One of the first clauses of the Treaty of 1825 was aimed at ending all Sauk and Fox claims to the already ceded land on the east side of the Mississippi and giving those lands to the Santee (Kappler 1973).

By 1825, an added complication was the fact that the frontier had moved farther west. Settlers, miners, and others entered the ceded lands still occupied by the Sauk and Fox. The Indians came under increasing pressure to leave, abandoning those lands for other lands beyond the Mississippi. It was after the withdrawal of the Indians into Iowa that Black Hawk, considering the provisions of the Treaty of 1804 and other treaties illegal, started the chain of events leading to the Black Hawk War in 1832. Most of the Sauk and all of the Fox remained neutral during that war, but other land cessions were forced from them as a kind of reparation. Eventually, the Sauk came to live in Kansas and later, Oklahoma; many of the Fox remained in Iowa, on land they bought themselves as a place of refuge (Callender 1978).

Chippewa

The line between the Santee and the Chippewa in the Treaty of Prairie du Chien was anchored in Wisconsin on the Chippewa River and ran west across the Red Cedar River and finally across the St. Croix into what is now Minnesota (Hickerson 1970). The lands north of that line were to be occupied by the Chippewa in terms of a "firm and perpetual peace" with the Santee (Kappler 1973: 250). The reasons for war between the Chippewa and the Santee involved such tangibles as hunting and trapping territory, wild rice beds, and access to the all-important resources of the Transition Zone; their long-standing competition was not likely to be settled through any treaty. Raids, counter-raids and full scale warfare did not end until 1858, but most of it took place in Minnesota, not in Wisconsin.

The Wisconsin lands were initially not of much interest to settlers, but official interest in Chippewa affairs began even before the Treaty of Prairie du Chien. A War Department agency was put at Sault Ste. Marie in 1822, perhaps in the hope of having some influence on frontier wars among the Indians. Ten years later, another agency was put at La Pointe with an Indian school attached to it. Interest in Chippewa lands centered on mineral rights, and in 1826, the Chippewa sold the mineral rights for annuity payments that lasted over a number of years. The way was now clear for treaties to arrange the sale of the land as well. Pressures to obtain title to the land and push the Chippewa west into Indian Territory built rapidly when large copper deposits were found along the south shore of Lake Superior (Vecsey 1983).

Between 1833 and 1854, treaties were signed that surrendered most of the land to the United States. The south shore of Lake Superior was ceded in 1842 and other lands followed. The Chippewa in Wisconsin steadily lost title to land, but they kept a few small tracts. Treaties, such as the Treaty of La Pointe in 1854, created reservations, in this case at Lac Court Oreilles, Bad River, and Red Cliff. Other reservations were established later, giving the Wisconsin Chippewa a checkerboard of many small reservations scattered over the northern area.

Afterward

The land dispossessions of the early nineteenth century did not mean the end of Indian culture (Hodge 1975). Indian people and their historic traditions moved from there into the difficult and hazardous reservation period. Too small to allow older subsistence techniques to be followed and too isolated to let Indians freely seek outside employment and education, the reservations sometimes became "slums in the wilderness." They were nevertheless Indian places, refuges from a world that was neither safe nor accepting of Indian difference. At the end of the nineteenth century, even these refuges were threatened as attempts were made to destroy the reservations through allotment. Wisconsin Indians came into the twentieth century with nowhere to go but up. The Indian Re-organization Act of 1934 gave them some of the tools they needed, and in time, education and home-grown expertise have followed. The complexities of the modern period and Indian-government relations have put greater demands on Indians for active and informed responses to new adaptations, and the way has not been easy (Lurie 1982). It is clear, however, that Wisconsin Indians are taking charge of their own affairs again.

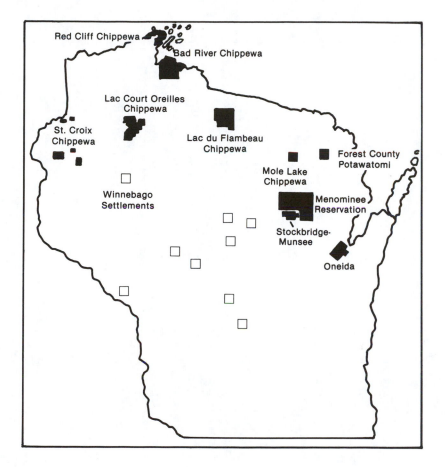

Red Cliff Chippewa

Bad River Chippewa

Lac Court Oreilles
Chippewa

St. Croix
Chippewa

Lac du Flambeau
Chippewa

Forest County
Potawatomi

Winnebago
Settlements

Mole Lake
Chippewa

Menominee
Reservation

Stockbridge-
Munsee

Oneida

Locations of modern Indian reservations (courtesy of Nancy O. Lurie and The
State Historical Society of Wisconsin)

Works Cited

Adams, Arthur T. (ed.)
1961 The Explorations of Pierre Esprit Radisson. Minneapolis: Ross and Haines, Inc.

Adney, Edwin Tappen and Howard I. Chapelle
1964 The Bark Canoes and Skin Boats of North America. Washington: Smithsonian Institution.

Barnouw, Victor
1954 Reminiscences of a Chippewa Mide Priest. Wisconsin Archaeologist vol. 35, no. 4, n.s. pp. 83-112.

1960 A Chippewa Mide Priest's Description of the Medicine Dance. Wisconsin Archaeologist vol. 41, no. 4, n.s. pp. 77-97.

Barrett, S.A.
1911 The Dream Dance of the Chippewa and Menominee Indians of Northern Wisconsin. Bulletin of the Public Museum of the City of Milwaukee vol. 1, no. 4, pp. 252-369.

1933 Ancient Aztalan. Bulletin of the Public Museum of the City of Milwaukee vol. 13

Barrett, S.A. and Alanson Skinner
1932 Certain Mounds and Village Sites of Shawano and Oconto Counties, Wisconsin. Bulletin of the Public Museum of the City of Milwaukee vol. 10, no. 5, pp. 401-552.

Birk, Douglas A. and Judy Poseley
1978 The French at Lake Pepin: An Archaeological Survey for Ft. Beauharnois, Goodhue County, Minnesota. St. Paul: State Historical Society of Minnesota.

Blair, E.H.
1911   The Indian Tribes of the Upper Mississippi Valley and Region of the Great Lakes. 2 vols. Cleveland: Arthur H. Clark Co.

Blakeslee, Donald J.
1981   The Origin and Spread of the Calumet Ceremony. American Antiquity vol. 46, no. 4, pp. 759-768.

Brose, David S.
1978   Late Prehistory of the Upper Great Lakes Area. Handbook of North American Indians vol. 15, ed. by Bruce G. Trigger. Washington: Smithsonian Institution.

Callender, Charles
1978a   Sauk. Handbook of North American Indians vol. 15, ed. by Bruce G. Trigger. Washington: Smithsonian Institution.

1978b   Fox. Handbook of North American Indians vol. 15, ed. by Bruce G. Trigger. Washington: Smithsonian Institution.

1978c   Miami. Handbook of North American Indians vol. 15, ed. by Bruce G. Trigger. Washington: Smithsonian Institution.

Callender, Charles and Lee M. Kochems
1983   The North American Berdache. Current Anthropology vol. 24, no. 4, pp. 443-470.

Carley, Kenneth
1979   The Sioux Uprising of 1862. St. Paul: Minnesota Historical Society.

Chafe, Wallace L.
1973   Siouan, Iroquoian, and Caddoan. Current Trends in Linguistics, ed. by Thomas A. Sebeok. Vol. 10 of Linguistics in North America, pp. 1164-1204. The Hague: Mouton.

Cleland, Charles E.
1966   The Prehistoric Animal Ecology and Ethnozoology of the Upper Great Lakes Region. Anthropological Papers, Museum of Anthropology, University of Michigan no. 29. Ann Arbor.

1982   The Inland Shores Fishery of the Northern Great Lakes: Its Development and Importance in Prehistory. American Antiquity vol. 47, no. 4, pp. 761-784.

Clifton, James A.
1977   The Prairie People. Lawrence: The Regents Press of Kansas.

Coe, Ralph T.
1977   Sacred Circles. London: Arts Council of Great Britain.

Cooper, L.R.
1933   The Red Cedar River Variant of the Wisconsin Hopewell Culture. Bulletin of the Public Museum of the City of Milwaukee vol. 16, no. 2, pp. 47-108.

Curtis, J.T.
1959   The Vegetation of Wisconsin. Madison: University of Wisconsin Press.

Dallman, John
1968   Mastodons in Wisconsin. Wisconsin Academy of Sciences, Arts, and Letters Review vol. 15, no. 2, pp. 9-13.

Day, Gordon M.
1953   The Indian as an Ecological Factor in the Northeastern Forest. Ecology vol. 34, no. 2, pp. 329-346.

Densmore, Frances
1910   Chippewa Music - I. Bureau of American Ethnology Bulletin 45, Smithsonian Institution.

1913   Chippewa Music - II. Bureau of American Ethnology Bulletin 53, Smithsonian Institution.

1979   Chippewa Customs (reprint edition). St. Paul: Minnesota Historical Society. Originally published in 1929 as Bulletin 86, Bureau of American Ethnology, Smithsonian Institution.

Dice, Lee R.
1943   The Biotic Provinces of North America. Ann Arbor: The University of Michigan Press.

Dobyns, Henry F.
1983   Their Number Became Thinned. Knoxville: University of Tennessee Press.

Draper, Lyman C.
1888   Early French Forts in Western Wisconsin. Collections of the State Historical Society of Wisconsin vol. 10, pp. 321-372.

Driver, Harold E. and William C. Massey
1957   Comparative Studies of North American Indians. Transactions of the American Philosophical Society n.s., vol. 47, pt. 2. Philadelphia: American Philosophical Society.

Durbin, Richard D. and Elizabeth Durbin
1984   Wisconsin's Old Military Road: Its Genesis and Construction. Wisconsin Magazine of History vol. 68, no. 1, pp. 3-42.

Feest, Christian
1980   Native Arts of North America. New York: Oxford University Press.

Feest, Johanna E. and Christian Feest
1978   Ottawa. Handbook of North American Indians vol. 15, ed. by Bruce G. Trigger. Washington: Smithsonian Institution.

Fitting, James E.
1970   The Archaeology of Michigan. Garden City, New York: Natural History Press.

1976   Archaeological Excavations at the Marquette Mission Site, St. Ignace, Michigan, in 1972. Michigan Archaeologist vol. 22, nos. 2 and 3, pp. 103-282.

1978   Regional Cultural Development 300 B.C. to A.D. 100. Handbook of North American Indians vol. 15, ed. by Bruce G. Trigger. Washington: Smithsonian Institution.

Fitting, James E. and Charles E. Cleland
1969   Late Prehistoric Settlement Patterns in the Upper Great Lakes. Ethnohistory vol. 16, no. 4, pp. 289-302.

Flint Institute for the Arts
1973   Art of the Great Lakes Indians. Flint, Michigan.

Ford, Richard I. and David S. Brose
1975   Prehistoric Wild Rice from the Donn Farm Site, Leelanau County, Michigan. Wisconsin Archaeologist vol. 56, no. 1, n.s., pp. 9-15.

Fowler, Melvin L.
1978   Cahokia and the American Bottom: Settlement Archaeology. Mississippian Settlement Patterns, ed. by Bruce D. Smith. New York: Academic Press.

Fredrickson, Jaye
1980   The Covenant Chain, Indian Ceremonial and Trade Silver. Ottawa: National Museums of Canada.

Gates, Charles M. (ed.)
1965   Five Fur Traders of the Northwest. St. Paul: Minnesota Historical Society.

Gibbon, Guy
1972   The Walker-Hooper Site, a Grand River Phase Oneota Site in Green Lake County. Wisconsin Archaeologist vol. 53, no. 4, n.s., pp. 149-290.

Gilman, Carolyn
1982   Where Two Worlds Meet, the Great Lakes
               Fur Trade. St. Paul: Minnesota Historical
               Society.

Goddard, Ives
1978a   Central Algonquian Languages.
               Handbook of North American Indians
               vol. 15, ed. by Bruce G. Trigger.
               Washington: Smithsonian Institution.

1978b   Mascouten. Handbook of North American
               Indians vol. 15, ed. by Bruce G. Trigger.
               Washington: Smithsonian Institution.

Graham, Russell, C. Vance Haynes, Donald Lee Johnson,
and Marvin Kay
1981   Kimmswick: A Clovis Mastodon
               Association in Eastern Missouri. Science
               vol. 213, no. 4, pp. 1115-1116.

Grand Rapids Public Museum
1977   Beads: Their Use by Upper Great Lakes
               Indians. Published by the Museum and
               the Cranbrook Academy of Art/Museum.

Green, William, James B. Stoltman, and Alice B. Kehoe
1986   Introduction to Wisconsin Archaeology.
               Wisconsin Archaeologist vol. 67, no. 3 &
               4.

Griffin, James B.
1978   The Midlands and Northeastern United
               States. Ancient Native Americans, ed. by
               Jesse D. Jennings, pp. 221-280. San
               Francisco: W. H. Freeman and Co.

Hall, Robert L.
1962   The Archaeology of Carcajou Point.
               Madison: University of Wisconsin Press.

1982   A Second Look at Gunstock Warclubs.
               The Wisconsin Archaeologist vol. 63, no.
               3, n.s., pp. 246-253.

Heidenreich, Conrad
1971   Huronia. Ontario: McClelland and
               Stewart Limited

Hennepin, Louis
1966   A Description of Louisiana. Reprinted (orig. pub. in 1880). Ann Arbor: University Microfilms.

Hickerson, Harold
1960   Algonkian Feast of the Dead. American Anthropologist vol. 62, no. 1, pp. 81-107.

1962   The Southwestern Chippewa: An Ethnohistorical Study. American Anthropological Association Memoir 92.

1963   The Sociohistorical Significance of Two Chippewa Ceremonials. American Anthropologist vol. 65, no. 1, pp. 67-85.

1970   The Chippewa and Their Neighbors: A Study in Ethnohistory. New York: Holt, Rinehart and Winston.

Hilger, Inez
1951   Menomini Child Life. Society of Americanists vol. 40, pp. 167-171.

Hodge, William H.
1975   The Indians of Wisconsin. The 1975 Wisconsin Bluebook, pp. 96-192.

Hoffman, Walter J.
1891   The Midewiwin or "Grand Medicine Society" of the Ojibwa. Bureau of American Ethnology Annual Report 7, pp. 149-300. Washington: Government Printing Office.

1896   The Menomini Indians. Bureau of American Ethnology Annual Report 14. Washington: Government Printing Office.

Hole, Francis
1976   The Soils of Wisconsin. Madison: University of Wisconsin Press.

Hough, Jack
1963   The Prehistoric Great Lakes of North America. American Scientist vol. 51, no. 1, pp. 84-109.

Hunt, George T.
1960 Wars of the Iroquois. Madison: University of Wisconsin Press.

Hurley, William M.
1975 An Analysis of Effigy Mound Complexes in Wisconsin. Anthropological Papers, Museum of Anthropology, University of Michigan no. 59. Ann Arbor.

1979 Prehistoric Cordage. Washington: Taraxacum Press.

Innis, Harold A.
1973 The Fur Trade in Canada (rev. ed.). Toronto: University of Toronto Press.

Jackson, Donald (ed.)
1964 Black Hawk: An Autobiography. Urbana: University of Illinois Press.

1966 The Journals of Zebulon Montgomery Pike. Normal: University of Oklahoma Press.

Jackson, H.H.T.
1961 The Mammals of Wisconsin. Madison: University of Wisconsin Press.

Jenks, Albert E.
1900 The Wild Rice Gatherers of the Upper Lakes. Bureau of American Ethnology Annual Report 19, Washington: Government Printing Office.

Johnson, Elden
1969 Preliminary Notes on the Prehistoric Use of Wild Rice. Minnesota Archaeologist vol. 30, no. 2, pp. 31-43.

1985 The Seventeenth Century Mdewakanton Dakota Subsistence Mode. Archaeology, Ecology, and Ethnohistory of the Prairie-Forest Border Zone of Minnesota and Manitoba, ed. by Janet Spector and Elden Johnson. Lincoln, Nebraska: J. and L. Reprint Co.

Kappler, Charles J. (ed.)
1973   Indian Treaties 1778-1883. New York: Interland Publishing.

Kay, Jeanne
1979   Indian Responses to a Mining Frontier. The Frontier, Comparative Studies: vol. 2, pp. 193-203, ed. by William Savage and Jerome Steffer.

1984   The Fur Trade and Native American Population Growth. Ethnohistory vol. 31, no. 4, pp. 265-287.

Keesing, Felix M.
1939   The Menomini Indians of Wisconsin: A Study of Three Centuries of Cultural Contact and Change. Memoirs of the American Philosophical Society vol. 10.

Kehoe, Alice B.
1981   North American Indians. Englewood Cliffs, New Jersey: Prentice-Hall.

Kellogg, Louise Phelps
1925   The French Regime in Wisconsin and the Northwest. Madison: State Historical Society of Wisconsin.

1935   The British Regime in Wisconsin and the Northwest. Madison: State Historical Society of Wisconsin.

Kinietz, W. Vernon
1940   The Indians of the Western Great Lakes 1615-1760. Occasional Contributions of the Museum of Anthropology of the University of Michigan no. 10. Ann Arbor: University of Michigan Press.

Kinzie, Juliette (Mrs. John)
1975   Wau-bun. Portage, Wisconsin: The National Society of Colonial Dames in Wisconsin.

Kroeber, A. L.
1953   Cultural and Natural Areas of Native North America. Berkeley: University of California Press.

Landes, Ruth
1968a   Ojibwa Religion and the Midewiwin. Madison: University of Wisconsin Press.

1968b   The Mystic Lake Sioux: Sociology of the Mdewakanton-Santee. Madison: University of Wisconsin Press.

1969   Ojibwa Sociology. New York: AMS Press (orig. published in 1937 by Columbia University Press).

Lapham, I.A.
1855   The Antiquities of Wisconsin. Smithsonian Contributions to Knowledge vol. 7, memoir IV. Washington: Smithsonian Institution.

Latorre, Felipe A. and Dolores L. Latorre
1976   The Mexican Kickapoo Indians. Austin: University of Texas Press.

Lugthart, Douglas
1968   The Burnt Bluff Rock Paintings. The Prehistory of the Burnt Bluff Area, Anthropological Papers, Museum of Anthropology University of Michigan no. 34, ed. by James E. Fitting. Ann Arbor.

Lurie, Nancy
1953   Winnebago Berdache. American Anthropologist vol. 55, pp. 708-712.

1960   Winnebago Protohistory. Culture in History, ed. by Stanley Diamond. New York: Columbia University Press.

1971   Mountain Wolf Woman. Ann Arbor: University of Michigan Press.

1978   Winnebago. Handbook of North American Indians vol. 15, ed. by Bruce G. Trigger. Washington: Smithsonian Institution.

1982   Wisconsin Indians. Madison: The State Historical Society of Wisconsin.

Mahan, Bruce E.
1926   Old Fort Crawford and the Frontier. Iowa City: State Historical Society of Iowa.

Marriott, Alice
1959   Ribbon Applique Work of North American Indians, pt. 1. Bulletin of the Oklahoma Anthropological Society vol. 6, pp. 49-59.

Marsh, Cutting
1900   Report to the Scottish Society, 1831. Wisconsin Historical Collections vol. 15.

Martin, Lawrence
1932   The Physical Geography of Wisconsin. Bulletin of the Wisconsin Geological and Natural History Survey no. 36.

Martin, Paul S.
1967   Prehistoric Overkill. Pleistocene Extinctions, ed. by P. S. Martin and H. E. Wright. New Haven: Yale University Press.

Mason, Carol I.
1981   Excavations on the Little Eau Pleine: Site 6. Wisconsin Archaeologist vol. 62, no. 1, n.s., pp. 84-111.

1985   Prehistoric Maple Sugaring Sites? Midcontinental Journal of Archaeology vol. 10, no. 1, pp. 149-152.

Mason, Carol I. and Ronald J. Mason
1967   A Catalogue of Old Copper Artifacts in the Neville Public Museum, Green Bay, Wisconsin. Wisconsin Archaeologist vol. 48, no. 2, n.s., pp. 81-128.

Mason, Ronald J.
1963   Two Late Paleo-Indian Complexes in Wisconsin. Wisconsin Archaeologist vol. 44, no. 4, n.s. pp. 199-211.

1970   Hopewell, Middle Woodland, and the Laurel Culture: A Problem in Archaeological Classification. American Anthropologist vol. 72, no. 4, pp. 802-815.

1974   Huron Island and the Island of the Poutouatamis. Aspects of Upper Great Lakes Anthropology, Papers in Honor of Lloyd A. Wilford, ed. by Elden Johnson. St. Paul: Minnesota Historical Society.

1981   Great Lakes Archaeology. New York: Academic Press.

1986   Rock Island, Historical Indian Archaeology in the Northern Lake Michigan Basin. MCJA Special Paper no. 6. Kent State University Press.

Mason, Ronald J. and Carol Irwin
1960   An Eden-Scottsbluff Burial in Northeastern Wisconsin. American Antiquity vol. 26, no. 1, pp. 43-57.

Maxwell, Moreau S. and Lewis R. Binford
1961   Excavations at Fort Michilimackinac, Mackinac City, Michigan, 1959 Season. Michigan State University Museum, Cultural Series vol. 1, no. 1. East Lansing.

McKern, Will C.
1945   Preliminary Report of the Upper Mississippian Phase in Wisconsin. Bulletin of the Public Museum of the City of Milwaukee vol. 16, no. 3, pp. 109-285.

1963   The Clam River Focus. Milwaukee Public Museum Publications in Anthropology no. 9.

Meyer, Roy W.
1980   History of the Santee Sioux (orig.
                published in 1967). Lincoln: University of
                Nebraska Press.

Moffat, Charles R.
1979   Some Observations on the Distribution
                and Significance of the Garden Beds in
                Wisconsin. Wisconsin Archaeologist vol.
                60, no. 3, n.s., pp. 222-248.

Mott, Mildred
1938   The Relation of Historic Indian Tribes to
                Archaeological Manifestations in Iowa.
                Journal of History and Politics vol. 36,
                no. 3, pp. 227-314.

Muir, John
1965   My Boyhood and Youth. Madison:
                University of Wisconsin Press.

Norton, Thomas E.
1974   The Fur Trade in Colonial New York
                1686-1776. Madison: University of
                Wisconsin Press.

Ogden, J. Gordon III
1977   The   Later   Quaternary
                Paleoenvironmental Record of
                Northeastern North America. Annals of
                the New York Academy of Sciences vol.
                288, pp. 16-34.

Oerichbauer, Edgar S.
1976   Prairie du Chien: A Historical Study.
                Madison: State Historical Society of
                Wisconsin.

1982   Archaeological Excavations at the Site of
                a North West and XY Company
                Wintering Post (47-Bt-26): A Progress
                Report. Wisconsin Archaeologist vol. 63,
                no. 3, n.s., pp. 153-236.

Orchard, William C.
1971   The Technique of Porcupine-Quill
                Decoration Among the North American

Indians (2nd ed.). Contributions of the Museum of the American Indian, Heye Foundation vol. IV. New York.

1975   Beads and Beadwork of the American Indians. Contributions of the Museum of the American Indian, Heye Foundation vol. XI. New York.

Overstreet, David F.
1978   Oneota Settlement Patterns in Northeastern Wisconsin: Some Considerations of Time and Space. Mississippian Settlement Patterns, ed. by Bruce C. Smith. New York: Academic Press.

Palmer, Harris and Robert Camardo
1982   Gunstock Warclub Blades. Wisconsin Archaeologist vol. 63, no. 1, n.s., pp. 47-64.

Palmer, Harris A. and James B. Stoltman
1976   The Boaz Mastodon: A Possible Association of Man and Mastodon in Wisconsin. Midcontinental Journal of Archaeology vol. 1, no. 2, pp. 163-177.

Parker, John (ed.)
1976   The Journals of Jonathan Carver and Related Documents. St. Paul: Minnesota Historical Society.

Pendergast, James F.
1974   The Sugarbush Site: A Possible Iroquoian Maple-sugar Camp. Ontario Archaeology Publication no. 33.

1982   The Origin of Maple Sugar. Syllogeus no. 36. Ottawa: National Museums of Canada

Peske, G. Richard
1966   Oneota Settlement Patterns and Agricultural Patterns in Winnebago County. Wisconsin Archaeologist vol. 47, no. 4, n.s., pp. 188-195.

Porter, James W.
1961   Hixton Silicified Sandstone: A Unique
              Lithic Material Used by Prehistoric
              Cultures. Wisconsin Archaeologist vol. 42,
              no. 2, n.s., pp. 78-85.

Prufer, Olaf H.
1964   The Hopewell Cult. Scientific American
              vol. 211, no. 6, pp. 90-102.

Quaife, Milo M. (ed.)
1921   Alexander Henry's Travels and
              Adventures. Chicago: Lakeside Press.

1922   John Long's Voyages and Travels.
              Chicago: Lakeside Press.

Quimby, George I.
1963   Indian Life in the Upper Great Lakes.
              Chicago: University of Chicago Press.

1966   Indian Culture and European Trade
              Goods. Madison: University of Wisconsin
              Press.

Radin, Paul
1923   The Winnebago Tribe. Bureau of
              American Ethnology Annual Report 37.
              Washington: Government Printing Office.

1945   The Road of Life and Death. New York:
              Pantheon Books.

1963   Autobiography of a Winnebago Indian
              (orig. pub. in 1920). New York: Dover
              Publications.

1973   The Trickster (1956 reprint edition). New
              York: Schocken Books.

Riley, Thomas J. and Glen Freimuth
1979   Field Systems and Frost Drainage in the
              Prehistoric Agriculture of the Upper
              Great Lakes. American Antiquity vol. 44,
              no. 2, pp. 271-284.

Ritzenthaler, Robert E.
1957   The Old Copper Culture of Wisconsin.
                Wisconsin Archaeologist vol. 38, no. 4,
                n.s., whole vol.

1972   The Pope Site. Wisconsin Archaeologist
                vol. 53, no. 1, n.s., pp. 15-19.

Ritzenthaler, Robert E. and Pat Ritzenthaler
1970   The Woodland Indians of the Western
                Great Lakes. Garden City: Natural
                History Press.

Rohrl, Vivian
1968   The Drum Societies in a Southwestern
                Chippewa Community. Wisconsin
                Archaeologist vol. 49, no. 3, n.s., pp. 131-
                137.

Rowe, Chandler
1956   The Effigy Mound Culture of Wisconsin.
                Milwaukee Public Museum Publications
                in Anthropology no. 3.

Sahlins, Marshall D.
1972   Stone Age Economics. New York: Aldine.

Salzer, Robert
1969   An Introduction to the Archaeology of
                Northern Wisconsin. Ann Arbor:
                University Microfilms.

1972   Bear-walking, A Shamanistic Phenomenon
                Among the Potawatomi Indians of
                Wisconsin. Wisconsin Archaeologist vol.
                53, no. 3, n.s., pp. 110-146.

1974   The Wisconsin North Lakes Project: A
                Preliminary Report. Aspects of Upper
                Great Lakes Anthropology, Papers in
                Honor of Lloyd A. Wilford, ed. by Elden
                Johnson. St. Paul: Minnesota Historical
                Society.

1987   A Wisconsin Rock Art Site. Wisconsin
                Academy Review, Wisconsin Academy of
                Sciences, Arts, and Letters vol. 33, no. 2,
                pp. 67-72.

Schneider, Richard C.
 1974 Crafts of the North American Indians. New York: Van Nostrand Reinhold

Shay, C. Thomas
 1971 The Itasca Bison Kill Site: An Ecological Analysis. St. Paul: Minnesota Historical Society.

Shorger, A. W.
 1965 The Beaver in Early Wisconsin. Transactions of the Wisconsin Academy of Sciences, Arts, and Letters vol. 54, pp. 147-179.

Silverberg, James
 1957 The Kickapoo Indians: First 100 Years of White Contact in Wisconsin. Wisconsin Archaeologist vol. 38, no. 3, n.s., pp. 61-181.

Skinner, Alanson B.
 1921 Material Culture of the Menomini. Indian Notes and Monographs, Museum of the American Indian, Heye Foundation. New York: Museum of the American Indian.

 1924 The Mascouten or Prairie Potawatomi Indians. Bulletin of the Public Museum of the City of Milwaukee vol. 6.

 1926 Ethnology of the Ioway Indians. Bulletin of the Public Museum of the City of Milwaukee vol. 5.

Slotkin, James S.
 1956 The Peyote Religion. Glencoe: Free Press.

 1957 The Menomini Powwow. Milwaukee Public Museum Publications in Anthropology no. 4.

Smith, Alice E.
 1973 The History of Wisconsin, Vol. I. Madison: State Historical Society of Wisconsin.

Smith, James G.E.
1973   Leadership Among the Southwestern
            Ojibwa. National Museums of Canada
            Publications in Ethnology no. 7.

Speck, Frank G.
1982   The Double-Curve Motive in
            Northeastern Algonkian Art. Native
            North American Art History, ed. by Zena
            Pearlstone Mathews and Aldona Jonaitis.
            Palo Alto, California: Peek Publications.

Spector, Janet D.
1975   Crabapple Point (Je 93): An Historic
            Winnebago Indian Site in Jefferson
            County, Wisconsin. Wisconsin
            Archaeologist vol. 56, no. 4, n.s., pp. 270-
            345.

Spindler, George and Louise Spindler
1971   (reissued 1984) Dreamers With Power:
            The Menominee. Prospect Heights, Ill.:
            Waveland Press, Inc.

Stoltman, James B.
1978   Temporal Models in Prehistory: An
            Example From Eastern North America.
            Current Anthropology vol. 19, no. 4, pp.
            703-746.

Stoltman, James B. and Karen Workman
1969   A Preliminary Study of Wisconsin Fluted
            Points. Wisconsin Archaeologist vol. 50,
            no. 4, n.s., pp. 189-214.

Tanner, John
1830   A Narrative of the Captivity and
            Adventures of John Tanner. New York:
            G. and C. and H. Carvill.

Thwaites, Ruben G.
1888   Collections of the State Historical Society
            of Wisconsin vol. 11. Madison.
1896-1901   The Jesuit Relations and Allied
            Documents. 73 vols. Cleveland: Burrows
            Brothers.

1902   The French Regime in Wisconsin, Vol. I. Collections of the State Historical Society of Wisconsin vol. 16.

1906   The French Regime in Wisconsin, Vol. II. Collections of the State Historical Society of Wisconsin vol. 17.

Trennert, Robert A.
1979   The Business of Indian Removal: Deporting the Potawatomi from Wisconsin, 1851. Wisconsin Magazine of History vol. 63, no. 1, pp. 36-50.

Trigger, Bruce G.
1976   The Children of Aataensic, A History of the Huron People to 1660. 2 vols. Montreal: McGill University Press.

Turnbaugh, William A.
1979   Calumet Ceremonialism as a Nativistic Response. American Antiquity vol. 44, no. 4, pp. 685-691.

Vecsey, Christopher
1983   Traditional Ojibwa Religion and Its Historical Changes. Philadelphia: American Philosophical Society.

Vennum, Thomas, Jr.
1973   Constructing the Ojibwa Dance Drum. Wisconsin Archaeologist vol. 54, no. 4, n.s., pp. 162-174.

1982   The Ojibwa Dance Drum. Smithsonian Folklore Studies no. 2. Washington: Smithsonian Institution Press.

Wallace, Anthony F.C.
1970   The Death and Rebirth of the Seneca. New York: Alfred A. Knopf.

1982   Prelude to Disaster: The Course of Indian-White Relations Which Led to the Black Hawk War of 1832 (orig. pub. in 1970). Wisconsin Magazine of History vol. 65, no. 4, pp. 247-288.

Warren, William W.
1984   History of the Ojibwa People (orig. pub.
              in 1885). St. Paul: Minnesota Historical
              Society.

Wedel, Mildred Mott
1974   Le Sueur and the Dakota Sioux. Aspects
              of Upper Great Lakes Anthropology:
              Papers in Honor of Lloyd A. Wilford, ed.
              by Elden Johnson. St. Paul: Minnesota
              Historical Society.

West, Robert M. and John E. Dallman
1980   Late Pleistocene and Early Holocene
              Vertebrate Fossil Record of Wisconsin.
              Geoscience Wisconsin vol. 4, pp. 25-45.

Wheeler, Robert C., Walter A. Kenyon, Alan R. Woolworth,
and Douglas Birk
1975   Voices from the Rapids, an Underwater
              Search for Fur Trade Artifacts. 1980-
              1973. St. Paul: Minnesota Historical
              Society.

Whiteford, A.
1977a   Fiber Bags of the Great Lakes Indians.
              American Indian Art Magazine vol. 2, no.
              2, pp. 52-64, 85.

1977b   Fiber Bags of the Great Lakes Indians II.
              American Indian Art Magazine vol. 3, no.
              1, pp. 40-47, 90.

Wilson, Lee Ann
1982   Bird and Feline Motifs on Great Lakes
              Pouches. Native North American Art
              History, ed. by Zena Pearlstone Mathews
              and Aldona Jonaitis. Palo Alto,
              California: Peek Publications.

Wittry, Warren L.
1959   The Raddatz Rockshelter, SK5,
              Wisconsin. Wisconsin Archaeologist vol.
              44, no. 1, n.s., pp. 1-57.

1963   The Bell Site, Wn 9, An Early Historic
              Fox Village. Wisconsin Archaeologist vol.
              44, no. 1, n.s., pp. 1-57.

1969   America's Woodhenge. Explorations into Cahokia Archaeology, ed. by Melvin Fowler. Bulletin 7 of the Illinois Archaeological Survey.

Wright, Gary
1967   Some Aspects of Early and Mid-seventeenth Century Exchange Networks in the Western Great Lakes. Michigan Archaeologist vol. 13, no. 4, pp. 181-197.

Wright, H. E. (ed.)
1983   Late-Quaternary Environments of the United States. Vol. 2. Minneapolis: University of Minnesota Press.

Wright, H.E., and David G. Frey (eds.)
1965   The Quaternary of the United States. Princeton: Princeton University Press.

Yarnell, Richard A.
1964   Aboriginal Relationships Between Culture and Plant Life in the Upper Great Lakes Region. Anthropological Papers, Museum of Anthropology, University of Michigan no. 23. Ann Arbor.

1976   Early Plant Husbandry in Eastern North America. Cultural Change and Continuity, Essays in Honor of James B. Griffin, ed. by Charles E. Cleland. New York: Academic Press.

INDEX